# TEST

"A masterful story by ( an absorbing tale the p written with fascinatil important a book as *Rachel Carson's The Sea Around Us.*"—**Clive Cussler**

✦✦

"...*an exciting and introspective journey toward oneness with the sea. From California, the Sea of Cortez, Fiji, Bahamas, and ultimately to the isolated Revillagigedos Islands, readers are treated to spine-tingling shark encounters, manta flights of fancy, and undersea hunting struggles contrasting with moments of deep intimacy with the ocean. Carlos is an underwater guru!*"—**Dale Sheckler, Publisher, *California Diving News***

✦✦

"*Traveling with Carlos Eyles to the once prolific Sea of Cortez is a journey with a sage in possession of a unique grasp of the ocean wilderness. Carlos journeys some 250 miles south from the tip of the Baja Peninsula to the primeval collection of volcanic islands known as the Revillagigedos. Here on the blue edge he...plunges into a sea overflowing with power and majesty.* The Blue Edge *invites the reader into Carlos' almost mystical interaction with the ocean's inhabitants. His encounters are extraordinary...his insights come from the heart...he takes us to the very soul of the natural world.*"—**David Smith from the Foreword of *The Blue Edge***

✦✦

"*Eyles writes about a wilderness—the wilderness within each of us—as it is reflected back through the environment. He takes us beyond the safe confines of the unknown, like the free diver, unencumbered, vulnerable, operating in an alien environment with uncommon ease.*"—**Michael Menduno from the Foreword of *Secret Seas***

# The Blue Edge

Carlos Eyles

AQUA QUEST PUBLICATIONS, INC. ■ NEW YORK

Library of Congress Cataloging-in-Publication Data

Eyles, Carlos.
    The blue edge / by Carlos Eyles.
        p. cm.
    ISBN 1-881652-27-0 (alk. paper)
    1. Skin diving--Mexico--California, Gulf of. 2.
Eyles, Carlos. 3. Skin divers--United States--
Biography. I. Title.

GV838.673.M6 E95 2000
797.2'3--dc21

                                00-044203

All photographs, including the cover, are by the author unless otherwise
stated.

Cover design by Justin Valdes.

Printed in the United States of America

10 9 8 7 6 5 4 3 2 1

# DEDICATION

For David Smith
who encouraged and inspired
For Margaret,
my wife, who endured the inspiration

# ACKNOWLEDGEMENTS

I am especially grateful for the help, guidance, and good company of those creatures of the sea who have played significant roles in this underwater journey of mine. Some gave their lives, others their wisdom, all gave graciously and with nobility. To those people mentioned in the book, I also give my heart-felt thanks, for without them this book would never have come into being. For their diligence and time put forth in the service of this work, particularly that of research, I am grateful to Sam Miller, Mike McGettigan, Tessa Roper, Chuck Rawlinson, Jack and Monica Hunter, Dr. Erich Ritter, Dr. Paul Bauer, and Steven L. Maddex. I should also like to extend my thanks to Peter Mounier for his assistance with photographs, and to Kevin Keys for his work with the charts. Lastly, to Michael Menduno and his editorial insights for which I am deeply grateful.

# FOREWORD

Traveling with Carlos Eyles to the once prolific Sea of Cortez is to journey with a sage in possession of a unique grasp of the ocean wilderness. He sees this place with two sets of eyes: those with which he first beheld its mystical waters in the late 1960's and throughout the 1970's, and those with which he has observed its sad fate at the end of the twentieth century.

Thirty years ago, a young Eyles set off to the Sea of Cortez as a big game spearfisherman. What he found was a place so replete with life that the water and air could hardly contain it. Giant grouper, sharks, pelagics, whales, dolphins, sea lions and birds seemed to be breathing the Gulf into a life as vibrant as it was dangerous. Carlos and his fellow hunters were pushing open the door to the Underwater Age. It was a time when the development of underwater hunting and diving gear began to converge, attracting a special breed of men who were the first to hunt and explore on a breath-hold dive the still unsullied waters of the undersea world.

How fleeting that Age would be, they had no inkling, for now, thirty later it has all but vanished.

In search of one last portal to that magical past, Carlos journeys some two hundred fifty nautical miles south of the tip of the Baja Peninsula to the primeval collection of volcanic islands known as the Revillagigedos. Here, in the blue edge, he discovers it is still possible to travel back in time and plunge into a sea overflowing with power and majesty. *The Blue Edge* invites the reader into Carlos's almost mystical interaction with the ocean's inhabitants, most notably large open water sharks and giant pacific manta rays.

The sharks, we learn, are the last of our culture's mythical creatures, and they play a significant role in Carlos's long journey. His encounters during the vulnerable state of a breath-hold dive are, in a word, extraordinary. Now an underwater photographer, Carlos brings a perspective of the sea like none other, for he has been touched by the ocean— touched in the way Native Americans were touched by the land. His insights come from the heart, and by way of an intuitive compass, he takes us to the very soul of the natural world.

In the grand tradition of Joseph Campbell's heroes, Carlos has returned from his life-long journey into the sea with a message of startling insight fraught with danger, that reveals a profound wisdom such journeys bring. *The Blue Edge* is a rare opportunity for an awakening, for buried within and between the words, Carlos takes us into the unnamed mysteries of the sea where lie the hidden markers of our own souls, our deepest fears and our greatest longings. It is a voyage of the heart that inspires and enlivens, a deeply mystical plunge into the magic of our common Mother, the Water Planet.

David Michael Smith
Portland, Oregon
September 2000

# INTRODUCTION

My first shark encounter occurred in the summer
of 1955 when I was fourteen years old. Having never
seen a shark in the water prior to that time, I knew
them only through myth. A friend and I were on
his red paddleboard tooling around the shoreline
of Doheney Beach, on our way to do some spearfishing. We had our pole spears, mask, fins and snorkels laid carefully on the board that was twelve feet
in length, plenty of room for two boys. I looked down
into the shallow water and swimming directly beneath us were three sharks all over five feet in
length, the largest animals I had ever seen in the
water. It was the last thing I expected or wanted to
see, and we did what any boy would do upon seeing
sharks in 1955; we panicked. Attempting to paddle
quickly away on the tipsy board, we turned it over,
dumping our gear and us into the water directly
above the sharks. The terror in those moments
while clambering back up on the board was as real
as any I would experience in my life at sea. A decade later I learned that the leopard sharks we had
seen were harmless and no threat to man whatsoever. However, the shark was still very much ingrained in the mythology of our culture, and it
would take another forty years before it was demy-
thologized and came to be appreciated for its grace,
power and superb survival skills.

This book is a chronicle of that forty-year journey made by free divers like myself, who were willing to meet the sharks and all else we found in the
deep ocean on their terms, without the security of
scuba or much in the way of technological support
from our advanced culture. In a very real way the

final destination of that long journey was to San Benedicto Island in the Revillagigedo Archipelago, Mexico, where the last of the great shark populations reside in the Western Hemisphere.

In January of 1995 and again in February of 1996 I headed out of La Paz, in Baja California, Mexico, bound for the Revillagigedo Islands some two hundred and fifty miles southwest of Cabo San Lucas, the tip of the Baja Peninsula. For the purposes of this book, I have combined those two expeditions so they read as a single event.

In 1994 soon after the manta ray massacre, the Revillagigedo Islands were declared off limits to all boaters without a permit. Obtaining a permit was next to impossible and so we undertook both expeditions without one. If identified, it's quite possible the owner of the boat could be fined and his vessel confiscated. Therefore the name of the boat and its owner are fictitious in this account.

Additionally, over the course of the two expeditions we had two cooks, Peg Helm and Marlene Souligny. For reasons of continuity, I have chosen to consolidate them into one fictitious person having the name of Pam. All others mentioned in this book are real persons and their observations as reported to me as well as my own are as accurate as memory serves.

# PROLOGUE

In the summer of 1992, my wife, Margaret, came home with the news that a young man, who had read my book, *The Last of the Blue Water Hunters*, would like to meet with me. We set up a time and had lunch, and talked at length. He was new to blue water hunting, had a sailboat and was inspired to drop the world and do some serious diving. Did I have any suggestions? In truth I had been waiting for him, as he had been waiting for me. There was a place that I had wanted to dive for some time— San Benedicto Island in the Revillagigedo Archipelago. Was he interested in such a journey? Could his boat make such a journey, and then stay for a month? Yes, he said, it could, but not without a great deal of work and expense.

Over a year passed until I saw Jack again, though we had spoken on the phone several times. In truth, I had little faith that he could pull off such an undertaking, but he would call whenever he was in town and confirm the project was progressing as planned. When it began to seem feasible I wanted to know if Jack was the kind of man I perceived him to be. When he was about to move his boat from Avila Bay on the Central Coast of California to Dana Point I made myself available to crew, ostensibly to photograph blue whales that were rumored to be off of Santa Rosa Island, but I wanted to see how he conducted himself at sea before committing to a two-month voyage. There are many axioms with regards to boats and men but surely at the top of the list is. "People change at sea." Docile, sweet, and tolerant men become tyrants, and worse. The responsibility of the well being of the boat and its crew is enormous and bears down with great weight upon the shoulders of the individual in charge.

Once out of Avila Bay, in Open Ocean we sailed with a following sea in moderate swells of six feet. By mid-afternoon we rounded Point Conception, considered to be the most dangerous strip of water from Washington to Patagonia. Here great swells mount and strong currents conspire to push vessels towards shore, the point of jutting land that bends California southward and is the most westerly tip of the Continental United States. It was here that the greatest American peacetime naval disaster took place when seven ships ran aground in 1923.

As we neared the point, converging swells grew to fifteen feet and began to lift the boat high out of the water. Often, in the following sea, the entire aft end of the boat would be airborne. One such wave lifted the boat so high that air was sucked into the water intake that cooled the engine. Soon, unbeknownst to Jack, the water pump locked and was followed by an explosion of smoke and steam that engulfed the entire cabin. Jack immediately shut down the engine, placing us at the mercy of the winds for now we relied only on the sails alone in a difficult stretch of water. He displayed no sign of panic and went about the business of repairing the broken water pump. While he was squeezed into the engine compartment, I was at the helm sailing around Point Conception and Point Arguello. He ran into problem after problem, the impeller had frozen in the housing, and he simply tackled each new problem as it arose. All this with the boat plunging and lifting, sometimes swinging radically when caught in the fast moving swells. In such seas I lost control of the helm on more than one occasion with the boat rounding up and sliding sideways down the swell. But Jack never raised his voice or gave evidence of becoming anxious over the turn of events. This was the sort of fellow with whom I could spend two months at sea in Mexico. As it turned out the damage to the pump was irreparable, and the next day the wind died and it took us thirty-one hours to reach Santa Barbara, normally an eight-hour trip.

In the course of our slow journey to Santa Barbara, we firmed up our plans to meet in La Paz in November and from there begin our journey to San Benedicto Island.

Dome Peak
4000
Mechuda Mt.
San Ever...

La Paz Bay

Los Islotes
Isla Partida
Espiritu Santo I.

Sea of Cortez

Coyote Pt.

1481

San Lorenzo Channel

Ceralbo I.

L O W E R   C A L I F O R N I A

La Paz

R.Conejo
Freshwater

Freshwater
Limsio

Venturia R.

Muertos Bay

Tiquitati Ranch
Fresh water

Incantes Ranch
Fresh water

Salt water
Pond

Arenas de la Ventana

El Palmar

Ranch

Escudero Pt.

Ranch
Freshwater

BuenaVista
3478

El Picacho
6345

Sierra de
La Laguna

Las Casitas
6475

C. Pulmo

Santiago

Pacific Ocean

Todos Santo

5932

Los Frailos

La Savanita
1625

5941

Miraflores

7800

San Rafael

6725

Santa
Tenorria

Los Aquaptos
1225

1088

Jacinto

Sierra S Lazaro

S Filipe
3770

La Ballena
3621

Candelaria

N

Gp.FL.

Gorda Bank

Not To Scale

Cape San Lucas

xv

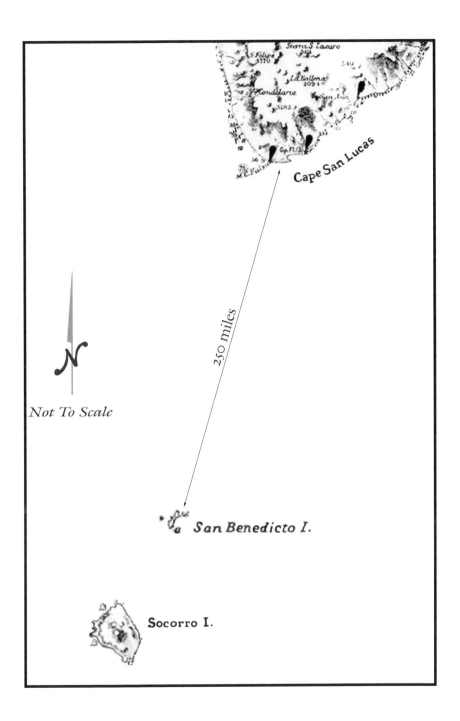

Cape San Lucas

250 miles

N

Not To Scale

San Benedicto I.

Socorro I.

# PART

# 1

## THE SEA OF CORTEZ

*The Way cannot be taught, it is only under-stood through the intuition.*—Zen Proverb

# DAY
# 1

F rom Los Angeles I fly into La Paz, known less as the capital of Baja California, Mexico, than as the central seaport in the Sea of Cortez. It is a two-and-a-half-hour flight, yet crosses decades to a time when the thoughts and deeds of man moved slower and with perhaps more care.

After a cursory pass by immigration authorities, I, along with everyone on the plane, enter a single room to collect our luggage so that we might stand in line to push a button affixed to what has all the appearances of a traffic light, which randomly comes up red or green. If green, one may pass through without inspection, if red, as mine does; one must open their bags to the authorities. I carry two aluminum suitcases holding cameras and lenses, a backpack jammed with two underwater strobes, a change of clothes, and toiletries. In this moment I am grateful for having the foresight six weeks ago to load my underwater camera gear, packed in two large ice chests, along with dive gear, on board the *Nirvana* before it left Avila Beach, on the Central California Coast.

Jack and Pam were to race the *Nirvana*, a Cal 34

sloop, down to Cabo San Lucas, the tip of Baja California, and then sail north to La Paz, where we are to meet here this evening at the airport.

The plan is to then make a day's sail to Los Isolates where we will visit the sea lion colony, and cruise and dive nearby islands for a week before heading south to Cabo San Lucas and our ultimate destination, San Benedicto Island in the remote archipelago of the Revillagigedo, located two hundred fifty nautical miles southwest of Cabo San Lucas.

After a half-hour wait and no sign of Jack or Pam, it occurs to me that anything could have happened and I would have no way of knowing. We have no alternate plan. The La Paz airport information booth, such as it is has no message for me. While I am second-guessing the entire operation, Pam, whom I had met six weeks previously as she and Jack prepared to embark from Avila Beach, arrives. She is indeed a fine sight, with wide green eyes and now a golden tan, as she directs me to the parking lot and a rusting VW Rabbit with a gringo at the wheel, cradling a quart bottle of beer between his legs. The car is stuffed with all matter of debris and Pam must wedge herself into the back seat while I, after placing the two camera cases between my legs on the floor and a backpack on my lap, sit in the front seat. Pam introduces me to the driver, Jerry, who is already quite drunk.

Down the lightless highway we weave as Pam explains what has happened. They had met with high winds and seas making their way up from Cabo San Lucas and could get no further then Bahia de Los Muertos, The Bay of the Dead. Jack stayed with the boat while Pam went ashore and commandeered

Jerry to make the hour-and-a-half drive North to La Paz to pick me up. Now ten minutes into the return trip Jerry must stop and pick up a case of beer. Pam also shops for supplies and in twenty minutes we are back on the dark, two-lane highway that in the spring of 1972 finally connected Cabo San Lucas with Tijuana nearly a thousand miles away. This is the very road that first brought hearty campers, and then RV's, later tourists, and finally hotels and more tourists, who eventually changed much of the face of Baja and to a significant degree, permanently altered the waters of the Sea of Cortez.

Jerry weaves his way southward, pulling on the bottle whenever the road straightens out. Once, I grab the wheel as he drifts over the center of the highway into oncoming traffic. He utters an "ooh" then laughs as he narrowly misses a wild burro standing in the middle of the road. Both Pam and I offer to drive, but Jerry refuses, explaining that he prefers to drink and drive. "That way if we crash, and we're bound to, I won't be tense. That's when people get hurt, when they're tense." Pam and I exchange looks.

Automobiles, people and civilization in general strike a certain, to use Jerry's word, "tension" in me. Not very long ago while in Los Angeles attending a script meeting that ran into the evening, several of us headed out on foot for a pizza in the heart of downtown Hollywood. The night people hung on street corners like ominous shadows, BMW's drifted by like prowling sharks, and I confided to a friend that I would be more comfortable swimming amongst a pod of killer whales than walking these streets at night. He appraised me in an odd, uncomprehending way while I attempted to explain that cities were beyond my grasp, and although I could sense danger in the ocean, I had no clue where or even how to look for or escape danger in a city. Cities breed uncertainty and fear in me and I spend as little time in them as possible, finding comfort in a small rural town on the Central Coast of California where the doors of my home and car remain unlocked.

An hour and two-quart bottles of beer later, we turn off the paved road and onto a well-groomed dirt road. We stay on this road for twenty minutes then twist off onto a road that is not a road at all but a riverbed. Once off the highway Pam and I are able to relax while the VW scales this rough terrain in fine fashion. Jerry stops frequently to pull on his beer for it is impossible to both drink and drive on this road, an alcoholic's nightmare.

This stream bed/road brings to mind the days when Baja was still new to the gringo. Forty years ago in the 1950's, the early spearfishermen found themselves endlessly bumping along at five miles an hour heading for some obscure spit of water that had never seen a diver. Later, into the mid-1960's as they became bolder and equipment could hold up to the big fish, they traveled these same worn roads to fish camps in the hope that a Mexican fisherman with a boat might take them out to an island that had never seen a diver. Up until the late 1970's, the Sea of Cortez was an unexplored wilderness where life and death played out in spectacular fashion. Each new expedition into the Gulf further broke me loose from my cultural chains and set me upon wild currents from which I emerged forever changed. Once in the water, I and others like me would descend into a sea more prolific than perhaps the world has ever known—the second most diverse marine body on the planet. We would spear the largest fish man had ever brought up from the depths on the North American Continent while on a breath-hold dive.

Heady stuff when one is 28 years old.

The stream bed/road ends in a cactus patch and our ride is finally, mercifully over. Knowing that Jerry will accept no money, Pam thoughtfully presents him with a bottle of vodka, the very item he needs, bringing him to near tears of gratitude. Within a half-hour I am on board the *Nirvana*, which rolls gently at anchor. Jack, smiling broadly, extends a hand saying, "We had a change in plans, but you're here; maybe the wind will settle enough for us to get on with it." Tall, with clean, striking Nordic features, long blonde hair pulled back into a pony tail, and pale blue eyes betraying a ready sense of humor, he is a sight to behold. Together, we sit and have a beer and speculate on the nature of the wind, and the possibilities of sailing out tomorrow. When the beers are finished I stow my gear. Pam and Jack go forward to their V berth and I settle into the couch of the main living quarters that will be my makeshift bed for the next two months. Though I cannot possibly envision what lies before me, I drift into the future, but the gentle rocking of the boat overcomes these fragmented speculations and soon I fall into fitful sleep.

# DAY
# 2

In the morning, awakened by the light, I stumble from my bunk and stagger out into the open cockpit. The light in the Gulf is unlike any I have seen elsewhere in the world. Here, in unique juxtaposition, a desert, with its clean, dry air, abuts a large body of water. This curious phenomenon was created by a great splitting of the earth twenty million years ago during the Oligocene epoch, about the same time the San Andreas Fault system came into place in California due to the North American Continent shifting from a westward to a northward movement. The land split gradually allowing the waters of the Pacific to seep in and, over time, make their way nearly eight hundred miles to the apex of its break where now the Colorado river leaks its remnants into arid salt flats left by twenty-foot tides near San Felipe, the most northern town on this body of water. The Sea of Cortez was thus born and continues to expand to this day.

The liquid light pours over rock and escarpment giving breadth and texture to the landscape; bleeding ocher cliffs, rendering the sand and sea bright as diamonds in detail so sharp as to deceive one into believing that what appears close is actually some distance away, and that which appears small may, in reality, be exceedingly large. The illusion here is grand and one is never quite sure what is being perceived either above or below the surface of the sea. The ethereal light falls across the land and sea like translucent silver, consuming all in its brilliance. Despite the calamities that have befallen the Gulf in these last years, the light remains unchanged.

A westerly wind blowing off the land brings soot—colored clouds that cast shadow and jigsawed light across land and sea. Bahia de Los Muertos is a large bay and the only substantial refuge for vessels traveling between Cabo San Lucas and La Paz. It has a sand bottom and a sand beach, with turquoise waters that are now vibrating to the thirty-knot wind. The water is clear and near the thirty-five-foot bottom a school of grunt have found shelter in the shadow of the boat. Beyond, minnow-sized bait spring from the surface like a fountain of dimes, chased by a single sierra mackerel. A dozen pelicans bobbing in the shallows near shore are the only sign of birds. Birds working from the sky indicate the presence of big fish in the water. The big fish in their feeding chase the small fish up from the depths where the birds attack them from the sky. Without big fish to herd the bait the birds must confine themselves to surface bait in the shallows of a shoreline. Sea birds in the sky are in direct proportion to big fish in the sea.

In the far northern corner of the bay lies a Mexican fish camp. To the south, along a twenty-foot-high bluff overlooking the sand beach, are the RV's, campers, and tents of Americans, some here for a week, some dug in for the duration. All are crowded together as if in terror of solitude.

Once, nearly twenty-five years ago, on a trip down to Animas Bay just south of Bahia de Los Angeles, Larry Brakovitch, my then-wife, Carol and I, found a nice little cove to ourselves. We had the fourteen-foot aluminum boat, *Low Now* and were planning to spend four days there. That first evening an RV pulled up not thirty feet from our campsite. No one emerged. Apparently they were content to enjoy the spacious skies of Baja by way of the window. At any rate, we were dismayed that they would crowd into our little cove on a coastline filled with coves, and park beside us. In the morning we got up, made breakfast and departed for a day of diving without the occupants of the RV ever opening their door. Upon our return that afternoon the RV was as we left it, a monolith of intrusion. Larry became angry and threatened violence. When we came ashore I took off my clothes. Larry, quickly catching on, did likewise, as did Carol. We strolled around naked for about five minutes before the RV engine fired up, and its unknown occupants backed quickly out of the cove never to be seen again. I came to discover that if one wished to camp in seclusion, as we often did in Baja, a little nudity went a long way.

In the early afternoon Jack and I take the eleven-foot inflatable skiff out for an afternoon dive. It is powered by a fifteen-horse outboard motor that runs smoothly enough and, after a couple of self-induced bounces, is able to get the skiff up on a plane. It seems to have two speeds, idle and flat out. Jack attempts to find some middle ground with the throttle, but to no avail. We blast toward the north-facing wall of the bay, he to look for fish to spear for dinner and I to begin the task of building up bottom time for the deep dives anticipated at San Benedicto. I take the Nikonos camera with a 20mm lens in the remote likelihood something interesting crosses my path.

We anchor up in twenty feet of water near a sand ledge with large boulders strewn about. The ledge angles down in ridge-like tiers to sixty feet and the true bottom of the bay. This is rather typical of the underwater terrain within the shoreline of the Baja peninsula. Not twenty years ago among the boulders in just about any sixty-foot bottom, big grouper could be found. These days it's unlikely that any can be found, but Jack goes off to investigate while I attempt to reacquaint myself with the waters of the Gulf.

When man submerged beneath the surface of an ocean for the first time without the benefit of guide or chart or any books of explanation, he entered a strange and unknown world through the door of the breath-hold. Breath-hold made the exploration possible, yet there was great reluctance to go forth. For that which lay beneath the surface was fraught with mythic tales of strange and horrific beasts. To cross into that country, where even pirates feared to tread and where the common man of the land would only dally near the shorelines in knee-deep water, was to flirt with one's deepest terrors. Beneath the surface lay a world the eyes could scarcely see, the fingers numbly feel, and the body unable to escape. It was a place that would hold him firm against itself and squeeze his breath away, while strange sensations nibbled at his torso, and creatures more powerful than could be imagined lay in wait to tear out his heart.

The early sailor knew only the surface of the sea, and with this limited knowledge was perhaps the bravest of all explorers, for he understood its exacting toll. The majority of sailors could not swim and were terrified of the water. To fall into the sea was almost certain death, if not from the foaming waters and cresting might of its waves, then from the sharks that followed the ships and ate their garbage. Still, the sailor went forth with a sharp eye for the edge of the world, and sturdy legs against the hard decks with only a strong back and a will bent on keeping his small boat afloat so that he might one day drift to other shores, never once desiring to venture beneath the surface.

Still, on calm days in balmy harbors the sailor must have wondered, as he looked over the side of his ship, what lay beyond the pale of the surface. Perhaps the underwater world was avoided because it so suggested a dark and foreboding jungle where demons lurked behind shadows and the shadow itself was a demon of untold cruelty.

On a single breath, taken and secured tightly in the chest, the first man descended, feeling almost immediate pressure inside his ears that announced oncoming pain. Pressure, as if the sea desired to compress the life force from his lungs, causing him to turn and rush for the surface, back to the world of light and air where his lungs expelled in a great noise and drew in oxygen causing its capillaries to blossom in gratitude. The man was down only seconds, yet soon discovered that in the breath-hold beneath the sea time is not measured by the clock, but by the experience. So he took another breath, and made another dive.

Initially, the dive to dark places in the sea was a terror-filled journey of ominous sounding clicks, chirps and moans unheard on land. In the dimming light, the constant movement disoriented as if a hard, relenting wind was bent on tricking the eye and deceiving the mind in the swirling dark water where one was unable to distinguish the real from the imagined, the demons of the mind from the demons of the sea.

The first dives in the first years were not in the water we see today. Today, the eyes are open in knowledge, and are able to see brightly colored fish dancing in spits of white sand dappled with flickering rays of diffused sunshine. In contrast, the first dives were dark even on the brightest days. The senses were closed down, strength diminished, and escape impossible. The first dives were like sinking into a quagmire where, beyond the terror, glimmered hidden beauty and, if one was willing to endure, one could, ever so briefly, feast his eyes on rare and strange sights. In the dimness there was beauty, and it was this that drew him down again and again. As if handfuls of light were brought to a nightmare and illuminated it into a dreamscape that dwarfed the imagination of every artist, writer and visionary that had ever laid pen to paper.

Unto this day the obscure light rearranges the mind, filling reef and kelp tree with strange and mystifying creatures. To dive into the ocean was and is a descent into the sphere of the unconscious, a probe into the corridors of our dark and hidden selves.

Entering this world would have been unthinkable without a weapon, not so much to protect the body as to quiet the mind. To justify the spear gun one had to hunt, and so within this alien realm, where no one had gone in such a vulnerable and naked way, man became a hunter.

It has been awhile since the first man entered the sea on a breath-hold; now I stand at the same threshold as I have stood a thousand times since I was a child, and looked down beyond the shimmering surface to liquid shapes and curious colors that will fire my imagination and ignite my sense of wonder.

In the winter the water in the Sea of Cortez, at sixty-five degrees, becomes uncomfortable if one is not wearing a wet suit. Made of neoprene rubber, the wet suit, in addition to keeping me warm, protects me from cuts and abrasions when rooting among rocks and ledges. "Into every empty corner," Henry Beston said, "into all forgotten things and nooks, nature struggles to pour life. Pouring life into the dead, and life into life itself." For the most part that life under the water is razor sharp in the form of barnacles, muscles, scallops, urchins, rock and reef. If it doesn't cut it will sting via a multitude of jellyfish species, as well as members of the sculpin family whose dorsal spines are poisonous, among them stonefish and scorpionfish. When diving around a reef I prefer to wear some kind of protection, and have become quite comfortable with a wet suit. A wet suit requires the diver to wear weights to compensate for the buoyancy neoprene rubber confers and, with twenty-four pounds, I am slightly overweighted, electing to let the weights do the work in my initial drop so as to conserve energy for the breath-hold. The payback comes on the free ascent where leg strength is required to push the weighted body up through the water to the surface. After inhaling and exhaling several deep breaths (hyperventilating—the oxygenating of the lungs, in effect to saturate the capillaries of the lung tissues with air which will sustain a breath-hold over a much longer period of time), then pulling in the last breath to full lung capacity, I turn as if into a hand stand, and drop head first beneath the surface, immediately squeezing my nose and forcing air up into the Eustachian tubes of my ears to equalize the outer water pressure, and continue to equalize as I drift down. Once submerged, two kicks glide an otherwise stilled body to a large boulder resting on the sand at twenty feet. Even with the high afternoon sun the feeling on the boulder is dark and visibility extends no more than twenty-five feet in all directions, like looking through a pair of reading glasses layered with dust.

The free-swimming creatures within visual contact have observed my short journey and as I lay unmoving and thus unthreatening on the boulder they begin to drift near. Five- to ten-pound cabrilla, fish hunters like their far larger cousin the grouper, cautiously venture to within fifteen feet, and warily gaze up from the sea floor. Hand-sized yellow and black butterflyfish dance inches above me and eventually surround me in benign curiosity. This behavior among the fish is due in part because I have made no noise or body movements in my descent to the boulder. This is in contrast to the scuba diver who, by producing bubbles and thus noise, would cause the fish to be nervous and wary, interpreting the disturbance to be, if not aggressive, then certainly disruptive to their serene state.

My breath-hold is poor; my lungs, unaccustomed to measured starvation, wail for relief by constricting the throat where the dead air gathers, pushing to be released and replaced. In less than a minute I lift from the boulder, startling the butterflyfish, which scatter like birds that have discovered a cat in their tree. Ascending to the surface, I labor in my kicks, my ears squeaking as pressure subsides, my chest expanding with the uncompressing air.

Having body surfed the Central coast waves for a month prior to leaving on this expedition, I believed my legs would be in reasonable shape, but rising from depth, even in water as shallow as twenty feet, puts more stress on the legs than the most strenuous of swims. Water is heavy, seawater heavier than fresh water. Water pressure at thirty-three feet is two atmospheres, or approximately twenty-eight pounds of pressure per square inch, which at depth is barely noticeable. What is noticeable are the pounds of water, tonnage really, that one must kick through on each ascent. At thirty feet it is over 1,900 pounds, nearly a ton of water per square foot. At sixty feet the pressure increases to 3,851 pounds per square foot, or nearly two tons of water. In addition, twenty-four pounds of lead weight around the waist is enough to discourage anyone out of shape. If one does not have the legs for the necessary return trip to the surface, as I do not, then most likely the uncertainty of the moment will fuel the final kicks to the top.

My breath-hold is almost non-existent, or so it feels. Probably forty seconds on this first dive. These days much is made on the length of the breath-hold in free diving. However, the breath-hold is only the first of many thresholds for the free diver to cross (though perhaps the most difficult) simply because the initial entrance into what is perceived to be an alien environment is fraught with doubt, fear and misconception. As it was with the sailor who made the first dive, breath-hold diving is, in fact, far less a physical undertaking as it is a psychological journey with mythological overtones.

Today's divers take into the water with them fears based on and perpetuated by stories on film and television. The movie *Jaws*, for example, effectively created a consensus among viewers that the threat of the shark to man was real and ever present. This view neatly entered the collective psyche of the audience, taking residence in their belief system. The new diver through projection and imagination later encounters this shark when first experiencing the ocean. It is the same shark that must be exorcised before one can venture into deeper water. In many ways we are no further along than the sailor of the 1500's.

Yet beyond the shark and the negative effects of television and film lies an ocean that is more accessible to mankind than ever before. For in documentary film today there is a balance of beauty and terror presented, and the ocean has become a friendlier more familiar place.

However, there are a great many more ocean barriers to work through before the sea becomes as friendly as depicted on the two-dimensional screen. The notion that we are not at the top of the food chain is unsettling for those who have known little else. This produces anxiety that is felt in the extreme when initially experiencing the deep ocean.

When the inability to either fight or flee, our basic survival instincts, is added to this mix these barriers of fear take on real significance. With all this bearing down very much like a great weight of water from above, it comes as no surprise that humans still feel vulnerable in the deep ocean. To venture into this defiant country one is asked to endure adversity from all fronts, an undertaking that requires diligence, time, courage, and an abiding passion to discover what can be found on the other side of that great blue door.

Jack is diving near two minutes at sixty feet, further emphasizing my ineptness. While resting on the surface, I watch him ascend. He shrugs his shoulders in mid-water indicating no spearable fish have been seen. For the next hour I dive from boulder to boulder, trying to regain my breath-hold. Generally in the first full day of diving one can double the length of their breath-hold. It's unlikely I have achieved that, clocking around a minute a dive. There is little to see here, save for the tropicals, a few cabrilla and the odd green snapper (pargo), all of which are under ten pounds. The fish life, though sparse, is enough to hold my attention, as the small tropicals dance and hover always appearing to be in a state of carefree joy. It is their freedom of mind and from gravity that I seek, so I lay content upon the boulders and allow the ocean to wash through me. The linear left hemisphere of my brain, given no tasks and knowing its place beneath the sea, relents to the right hemisphere, which has long known the way. Silence eventually envelopes my ever-busy mind, and the holding of the breath invokes a further stilling of the mind— the *prana* (Hindu for breath, and the focus point for many forms of meditation) held in check causes the heartbeat to reduce to thirty beats per minute. The body, ancient and all knowing, perhaps recognizing this familiar country from another millennium, slows, and slips gently, longingly into the solitude of the sea. A sense of connection prevails in these moments on the boulder, for the fish and I are of the same breath and heartbeat and atmosphere, and I am accepted both by the fish and in myself as a member of this community.

Jack had swum north an hour ago and is returning empty-handed. Saying nothing, we both turn and head for the skiff. Onboard he tells me he saw no big fish, nothing over ten pounds. This news surprises me, for even in what appears to be a fished-out area at a depth of sixty feet, a twenty-pound fish of some species ought to have been seen. However, this area is much traveled, too many people for too long; it should come as no surprise.

We had no such problems the first time I encountered the waters of the Gulf, as the Sea of Cortez came to be called by the spearfishermen who ventured here in the mid to late 1960's. In February of 1967 through a circuitous series of events, I found myself wedged into a small rented Cessna on my way to Cabo San Lucas to hunt *pez fuerte*. I was not the first choice of the two other divers on board, Sam Alcaraz and Leo Wooten, outlaws relative to my suit and tie status. In fact, I was their last desperate choice, for they could find no one else to cover a third of the cost of the plane and fuel. The pilot was a grease monkey kid of twenty-four who had not been flying for very long, and had never approached a flight of this magnitude.

We left the Torrance Airport west of Los Angeles in the early morning and after long delays at the border, landed in Cabo San Lucas near sunset on a dirt strip adjacent to the cannery (from what I understand is the only landmark that remains from that period). We unloaded our gear, walked a couple of hundred feet down to the beach, threw down our sleeping bags and set up camp. There was one hotel (I understand there are quite a few more now; I haven't been back since the trip in 1967) and a small village with a simple *mercado* (market).

At the time I was just getting interested in big game spearfishing, though I had never speared a game fish. My experience was exclusive to the Southern California coastline where, for the most part, I speared reef fish no bigger than twenty pounds. Nevertheless, I felt ready to make the jump into deeper waters, and that first morning we geared up and swam out in front of the cannery, not a hundred and fifty feet from shore. There, a deep underwater canyon ran almost to the edge of the beach, and big *pez fuerte* would work the pilings of the cannery for baitfish drawn to the spillage from the cannery. *Pez fuerte* means strong fish in Spanish. The Mexicans, never ones to mince words, knew what they had when they caught one. *Pez fuerte* are amberjacks and their bullet-shaped bodies and forked tails are built for power.

Sam and Leo spoke frequently of sharks—about how to get the fish out of the water fast before too much blood spilled, and how sometimes you had to give up the speared fish to an aggressive shark. Sam and Leo had me going with the sharks. If the water had not been so clear and inviting I might never have gone in, and if I had not been able to keep an eye on the fifty-foot bottom, I might not have stayed in. Almost immediately a fish swam beneath me and I dropped down on it more out of curiosity than anything. It was quite beautiful, the color of soft amber, with large, round eyes. It moved with a power and ease that was awesome in its grace. The fish turned and came toward me, affording an easy shot. Without really thinking I let the arrow fly. As it hit, the fish exploded away, a bolt of silver lightning. Line spun off the reel faster than I could swim to the surface. Upon reaching it, I was thoroughly out of breath and had no other thought but to bring in the fish before sharks appeared. The tension on the line in my hand, generated by the moving fish, was incredible. I had never known such power in the sea, never imagined such power. In the years to come I would spear many fish, and the event would ultimately distill down to this moment, both the fish and I vulnerable, both in a life and death struggle that was reduced to tension on the line. Such a plain thing. It had been this way not so long ago in the time before gunpowder, and five million years before that when all man had was the strength of his body and the skill to snare the game.

The line was everywhere, and this was dangerous, for I had forgotten that when a fish is pulled up and nears the surface often it will make another run, and if there is floating line it can hook on a weight, or an arm and the fish can drag the man down and drown him. But this fish was relatively small, thirty pounds, and was spent, and I placed a hand in its gills, looked around for sharks before swimming quickly to the beach.

It didn't seem possible that a man could swim out into a vast and mysterious ocean and while on

a breath-hold, spear a fish far more powerful than
he, and bring it to his hand. It defied a certain logic.
The following day I came across a *pez fuerte* that
may well have weighed a hundred pounds, maybe
more. I stared at it, without the slightest desire to
stalk it, much less spear it. The fish would have
been unstoppable, taking the shaft, the line, the gun
and me to the depths. It exuded a power that was
unsettling, its round eye, big as a coffee cup, was
fearless. It circled once then drifted off. Other men
would die spearing such fish.

Each of us speared a fish a day, both Leo's and
Sam's considerably larger than my own, and we
would trade the fish for three meals a day at Mama
Garza's place near the beach. Towards the end of
the week a boat owner took us out and around the
tip, Land's End, and in remarkably calm waters on
the Pacific side, we fished for marlin, having three
hookups at the same time, bringing one in then releasing it. Before returning to port we stopped and
anchored in a small cove to have lunch and dove
just to get wet. In the cove was a single reef, small,
the size of a Winnebago, that held more lobsters
than I had ever seen before or since. While three
divers free dove in forty feet of water I, using a
Super Eight underwater movie camera and housing, recorded the dive. There were more lobsters
than crevices to hold them and they walked around
on the sand and on top of the reef in broad day-
light. Their numbers were impossible to count, but
a conservative guess would put it near a thousand.
We collected fifty in fifteen minutes.

When, after a week of diving, and it was time to
depart Cabo San Lucas, Sam informed me that Leo
refused to leave. "I have a job, a career," I whined.

"What the hell is a career?" asked Sam in all sincerity. I pleaded, explaining I would lose my job. Sam shrugged as if to say, what's the problem here? He was trying to be kind and said, "You'll get another job. Me, I'd like to get back but Leo ain't going back for another week, maybe longer. He's going to jack around with the landing gear, so we don't have to pay extra."

"What!?"

"It's okay, man. He's done this before."

"A job is the most important thing a man can have," said my father repeatedly, both the quote and he a product of the Great Depression. Up until that moment my doubts regarding the accuracy of that statement had never been explored.

We stayed another week then flew out on a storm. The pilot became lost on the flight home and in the dark, over a rain-swept ceiling plunged through cloud cover and came over the ocean at five hundred feet. We flew east until sighting land then found a freeway we recognized and followed it to the Torrance Airport. Getting off the plane, I dropped to my knees on the wet concrete and kissed the ground.

In the early evening Pam fixes a pasta dish with all the trimmings. We eat in the cockpit and watch pelicans strafe the bait near shore in the last vestiges of cerulean light.

I volunteer to do the dishes for the remainder of the trip. Jack is delighted with this news, for the dishes had been his domain. Now neither he nor Pam need concern themselves. It is enough for Jack to be responsible for the boat and its occupants. His time will come soon enough.

# DAY
# 3

J ack is ready to depart for Cerralvo Island, but the wind continues to whistle through the stays at thirty knots. We shall remain in Bahia de Los Muertos another day. Which surprises me, for Jack does not shirk from wind or rough water. The *Nirvana* hit some devastating weather coming up from Cabo San Lucas and neither he nor Pam are eager to pound directly into oncoming wind and swell. Thankful for another day in the bay, I need to get into the water and establish some bottom time and put some zip into my legs.

We breakfast on strawberry pancakes prepared from scratch. Pam is a first-rate cook, unintimidated by the limitations of a rocking boat and a three-burner propane stove, turning out exquisite meals of breakfast, lunch and dinner. She and Jack go back a long way, however, there is an underlying tension between them that may well play out as the expedition progresses.

Taking our breakfast in the cockpit, we gaze out on the shoreline and the Americans' campers lined like locust along the edge of the bluff. Oddly, few take to the water. Apparently, they are content to sit in their air-conditioned homes on wheels and, I suppose, watch us. There was a time when the people of Bahia de Los Muertos handled their population problems much differently. In fact, it was how they acquired their name, Bay of the Dead. The story goes that one fine morning a large ship sailed into this protected cove displaying a flag that declared sickness on board. A deathly sickness, cholera perhaps. They needed supplies and water and wished to come ashore, but were not permitted. Nor did the villagers have an urgent desire to bring supplies out to the boat for fear of catching the illness and spreading it. Rather they set fire to the vessel and killed any of the crew who tried to escape into the sea. Word got around as often is the case in Mexico, and the bay was christened with a new name.

In the afternoon I swim off alone to find a shallow reef near the boat. The water is clear and tropical fish abound. As a young boy my first sighting of fish under the water was of small tropicals similar to the ones before me.

It was on the island of Oahu, Hawaii, and I was seven years old. I had just learned to swim the year before at a beach that was protected by short jetties that fingered out into the water several hundred feet from shore. From this same beach, Hawaiian divers would regularly swim up the jetties and out beyond their protection and return hours later with gunnysacks full of small tropical fish they had speared. One afternoon, inspired by their bravery, I swam out—actually I walked out to waist deep water—stuck my head in and opened my eyes. In that clear Pacific water I was able to see yellow fish with black stripes dancing about the rocks. It was as if I had come upon an invisible gateway and stumbled into a world that was unlike anything I had ever imagined. Thereafter, every outing to the beach would find me floating near the rocks watching the comings and goings of fish. Soon I was diving in the shallow water and holding on to the rocks that permitted me eye level observation of the fish.

One afternoon while playing by myself high on the beach, there came a commotion down on the shoreline. I ran down to find three Hawaiian divers, one with a pair of goggles, emerge from the low surf dragging a giant green sea turtle. They pulled it up on the beach and turned it over on its back. The turtle glistened with the sea and radiated an alien mystery. Crouching low to give it a good look, I touched its shell, examined its flippers that would suddenly start to flail and then stop. Its breath wheezed and its large reptilian eye blinked away the sand. Looking out across the surface of the glassy sea, I wondered what sort of creatures lived beyond the jetty, and in that moment of curiosity grew desire, and from desire a clear and perfect calling from the sea. Sitting beside the turtle my name was whispered in the shorebreak.

The Hawaiians picked up the turtle among back slaps and hoots of luau, and carried it off to an old pickup truck. Still sitting there in the sand, the experience dripped from me as though I had just come from the water.

In the months to follow I ventured further and further out along the jetty, hoping one day to reach its end. One morning a Hawaiian diver approached me as I was inching my way out among the rocks. In a friendly way he told me to be careful, that

Kamo swam beyond the jetty, and that I could be carried off and eaten. (Kamo Hoa Lii was the king of the shark gods who lived in the Honolulu Harbor. He was Pele's favorite brother and the most celebrated shark in Hawaii.) The diver assured me that I would be safe if I stayed close to shore where the bottom could be seen. Sharks, he said, don't like the shallow water. Nearly all that the turtle inspired was wiped away by that news. Thereafter, my swims along the jetty ceased when I neared its end where the bottom began to drop away to deeper water.

The Hawaiians took pride in displaying their catch and I was always interested in what they had caught. The following summer they permitted me entrance into their small tribe. Their talk always seemed to be about sharks. It was a teasing camaraderie that made light of sharks, though I sensed they were fearful of them for such talk made me uncomfortable. I envisioned Kamo circling in deep water waiting for the diver who would wander too far from shore. Despite the endless talk of sharks, I felt safe with the Hawaiians and began to swim out with them to the end of the jetty and a little beyond. There, they would leave me to dive among the rocks until they returned, and I would swim back with them to shore where they would display their fish and tell their stories. The strongest and the bravest always speared the biggest fish and with every outing, they further entrenched themselves as my heroes.

Another year on the beach found me comfortable with the deeper water. But with the portent of Kamo, progress was slow. One morning the men had gone out into the water and I stayed on the beach watching where they would swim. The grandmother of one of the spearfishermen was there, as she often was, making hats out of palm fronds. She had given me one of her hats earlier in the summer and I wore it whenever I went to the beach. She said that soon I would be out spearfishing with the men, and that she could see the ocean on my skin, and that it was the place I would always be.

I was ten years old that summer, and in September our family left Hawaii, never to return, eventually settling in Arcadia, California, a suburb of Los Angeles. It was an uprooting from which I never fully recovered.

The little reef is in fifteen feet of water not far from where the *Nirvana* is anchored. Having little interest in macro photography or pictures of tropical fish, I bring no camera. From the beginning I was always in search of big creatures. In that pursuit I missed out on much of the macro ocean world for which studious devotion is required if one is to photograph their tiny, detailed universe. It occurs to me that since I left Hawaii as a boy, this is one of the rare moments when I want no more than to simply observe the world of tropicals in shallow water. There is a certain childlike pleasure in the observance of the small. They inhabit their own cheerful little kingdom oblivious to the larger world of tooth and blood. The parrotfish, triggerfish, butterfly and angelfish nibble away at rock and reef, flitter among the stone garden as hummingbirds or butterflies might dance about a flowering bottlebrush. These fish never seem to settle anywhere, or travel very far. Their lives appear to be quite busy, and equally as meaningless. Yet there is something undeniably charming and peaceful in the confines of a tropical reef. And in pursuing this pocket playground I see myself spending many an hour here in my later years, where the life of ghost shrimp will keep me thoroughly occupied and content. Such reefs are the proper place for young children and old men to escape the civilized world.

# DAY
# 4

We depart for La Paz and are underway before the sun. On golden sea and under burning sky we turn into the Cerralvo channel and pick up a moderate breeze blowing off the land from the west providing *Nirvana* with a fine beam reach. Jack is genuinely happy under sail, tinkering incessantly with the sheets. Sailing is the ideal marriage of the linear mind with the forces of nature. While racing down from the States against fifty-eight other boats this old cruiser, a Cal 34, led the entire race until outside Turtle Bay when a sail ripped on the self-furling jib. Both Jack, and Pam who regularly races sailboats herself, are expert and move about the boat with competent ease. The task of helmsman, when they are busy raising and lowering the sails is given to me. Which is fine. The foredeck is no place to be in foul weather. When sailing in a straight line, which is generally the case, we put the helm on autopilot, sit back in the cockpit and enjoy the day.

Dark volcanic peaks along the Baja shoreline silhouette against a cornflower sky, leaking wispy clouds spilled from the palette of Georgia O'Keefe.

The lapis water ripples under the bow, and the contrast of sea, sky and land are as vivid as a morning dream. The eye reels from such beauty, yet one cannot help but notice there is scarcely any sign of life above or below the surface. In eight hours of passage we have seen a total of three sea birds: two frigates and a lonely gull winging its way inland. In the afternoon while a single frigate wheels high in the azure sky, something dark moves beneath the surface. Mola Mola, I say, but now I see them, small mantas, mobulas, a school of eight. Normally, these mobulas are of no particular interest, but I am so anxious to see something, anything large in the water that I scramble for my Nikon and housings, all of which are buried deep in the bowels of the boat, stowed for sea over a month ago. The Nikon must be fitted into the Aquatic housing with the proper lens, housing port dusted of lint, film popped in, the dive gear bag broken open.

At last I am in the water positioned in front of the mobulas, their three-foot wing spans gracefully soaring in the liquid atmosphere; they resemble in every way the giant pacific manta ray we seek at San Benedicto except they are about an eighth their size. I drop down into a hazy twenty feet of visibility. Maybe a silhouette shot from underneath. After two passes and being picked up by the boat and dropped in again, I manage to get close enough for a shot of seven mobula flying in formation. But the camera doesn't fire! I check all switches then look into the port and find the lens cap neatly in place. In the meantime Jack and Pam have lost sight of the mobulas in a building wind chop. Chagrined, I climb on board, and Jack, who views me as a serious underwater photographer, doesn't know what to make of such a blunder. When finally my own laughter is inescapable, he joins me, his bellows convulsive, turning to coughing fit.

Finding a cove in the late afternoon, ten miles north of La Paz, we drop anchor. Jack is anxious to spear a fish so he takes the spear gun along with Pam and I out to the most northern point of the cove before the sun sets. Making the jump, I drift down into the torpid water to a shallow twenty-foot bottom, where out of the dim haze pour a school of fifty parrotfish. They are followed by streams of sargent majors, angelfish, cabrilla, Mexican hogfish, giant damselfish, triggerfish, butterflyfish, pompano and surgeonfish. "This place is alive," I tell Pam when I am back on the surface. "There should be some decent fish here for Jack to spear; you can feel them in the depths."

In forty minutes Jack spears two cabrilla, his first fish on this leg of the trip. The cabrilla are a respectable fifteen pounds, but given the size of the fish population and the depth Jack can dive, I expected he would see something larger.

I have given up entirely on spearfishing, not for any moral or ethical beliefs, but because I cannot eat sea food of any kind, having consumed a highly toxic fish while in Fiji which permanently damaged my endocrine system rendering me, among other things, hypoglycemic.

That is not to say I don't miss the stalk. I had been doing it for a long time, beginning in earnest when I was twelve years old, two years after I had left Hawaii and taken residence in California. Though the water was not as clear as Hawaii, and certainly colder, the fish were larger, and having never seen a diver, far more accessible. In the summer of my thirteenth year, I managed to spear a ten-pound halibut in the sand off the Newport jetty in fifteen feet of water. It was the largest fish I had seen in the water, and lying there in the sand, was easy pickings. Later that same afternoon I found a spider crab with a three-foot spread that could, in all probability, have been picked up by hand, but was big and unwieldy with such formidable pinchers that the pole spear was the obvious choice. That night our family of four sat down to a dinner of fish and crab and so impressed my father that it gave profound validity to the idea of hunting for sustenance. The year was 1954 and although a long way from the warm waters of Hawaii, California was on the cusp of the Underwater Age.

The Underwater Age had begun in a vague and rather intermittent way with the introduction of goggles by Japanese female divers, the Ama, in the late 1800's when they came to California to dive for abalone. Later, the Ama appeared in Italy in 1911, which stirred the European's curiosity for breath-hold diving. But interest waned until shortly after Guy Gilpatric produced his book, *The Complete Goggler*, in 1936. Soon after that, around 1939, goggles become available to free divers in all parts of the world, which, in many regards, were the true beginnings of the Underwater Age. In and around that same time the first facemask was patented by Maxium Forget in 1937 and a few years later, Owen Churchill secured the American rights for the first swim fin from Luis De Coulier. It was all coming together around 1940-41 when World War II put the explorations of the seas through free diving on hold.

After the war, from 1946 onward, men and women around the world began to explore the shallows of the oceans and seas on breath-hold dives. The natural progression produced spearfishing clubs, which in turn produced the first United States National Spearfishing Meet held in Laguna Beach, California in 1950.

In 1954, I was too young to drive a car, and caught rides to the ocean where I would hunt the jetties of Newport Beach and the shallow reefs of Corona del Mar throughout the summer. During the winters I built pole spears, the early hunting tool of its day in California. It was nothing more than a six-foot pole with a five tined frog gig secured at one end and a loop of surgical tubing fastened to the opposite end. One would run a hand through the loop catching it between thumb and forefinger and then stretch the rubber tubing up the length of the pole to within a foot or two of its end. Then, by slightly releasing the grip, the pole would spring forward, giving an effective range of about three feet.

I would prowl the shallow reefs with the pole spear looking first for fish, then discovering abalone and in the process, encountering moray eels. Moray eels grow to over five feet in length with a thickness of a weightlifter's arm, and range in colors from green to brown. They prefer to hole up in ledges and caves with just their head exposed. Because they generally remain stationary, morays must push water through their mouths and out their gills to breathe. This they do by opening and closing their mouths, exposing a formidable set of needle-sharp teeth. In the early days of diving, the shark myth was not as predominant along the Pacific Coast as it was in Hawaii. Though the unknown of the deep water played a significant role in sustaining the shark myth, it was never emphasized because so few sharks wandered into shoreline reefs and kelp beds. Any unexplored wilderness is usually accompanied by a myth or two that incarnates danger. The early hunters who explored the reefs and kelp beds were the first myth messengers of the moray eel.

Stories of eels were passed on by word of mouth or by way of articles written in the early dive magazines that delighted in such tales. One particular story came out of a magazine that described an incident involving a free diver who had speared a moray eel with a pole spear. When he tugged on the spear the eel, as large as full-grown man, exploded out of its cave and charged the diver. In panic, the diver swam off with the eel in pursuit. The eel caught up to him but did not bite at his feet. Instead, it continued to swim past his legs to his torso, and finally reaching the diver's head, arched out of the water like a great serpent and struck with every intent of biting the man's face off. The fellow lifted his arm to protect his face and the eel lunged down and caught the elbow, nearly biting it off.

This was the sort of lore that sustained the moray eel as a true menace to the reef hunter. Shortly after reading that story I was sitting on the rocks in Dana Point, long before the marina was built, intent on prying up some abalone. An old fisherman happened along and told me the place was full of eels. My imagination conjured hundreds of eels rising out of their caves and holes, mouths opened wide just below the surface, waiting for my bare belly to expose itself. After agonizing for an hour I jumped in, flailed around for ten seconds, and clambered back up on the rock, done for the day.

Abalone was abundant in the 1950's and easily accessible to those who would wade out at low tide, willing to turn over large rocks to which the delicacy would be fastened. Abalone is a snail and it is the muscle, or foot beneath the shell that secures it to the rocks, that is eaten. The foot is an exceedingly powerful muscle that when clamped down is difficult if not impossible to dislodge while underwater on a breath-hold. Thus one has to use diligence when slipping the flat iron bar between the muscle and rock so as not to forewarn the abalone that something is amiss. While the outside shell has all the appearances of a rock that is part of the reef, the inside, once the muscle and guts are removed, is a pearly iridescent green, pink and blue. The Chumash Indians, during their reign along the California coastline up until the early 1800's, used the shell to make jewelry, a purpose it is still coveted for. The meat itself is unremittingly tough and has to be pounded with a tenderizer before being dipped in egg then breaded and briefly cooked. When garnished with a bit of lemon, it emerges from the pan a thoroughly delicate treat.

In the early fifties the great bounty of abalone was due to a quirk in the natural order of the ocean universe. Prior to the 1900's abalone was the principal food source of the sea otter, which ranged down the entire coastline of California. At the turn of the century the otters were all but wiped out by Russian fur traders. Thereafter, with no predator to harvest their numbers, the reefs fairly crawled with abalone. By the time free divers entered the water in the late forties and early fifties, they were stacked one on top of the other. Finding abalone in those days was considerably easier than spearing a fish. Though more work was entailed in its preparation, it was nonetheless a coveted prize for the dinner table and a rather generous reward for the limited skills I possessed as a hunter/gatherer. By the age of fourteen I could pick up a limit of five in two dives.

Prying the abalone free from rocks would cause them to "bleed", releasing a mucus that when smelled by eels, would roust them from their lairs. Often, an eel, frightfully strong, would snatch hold of the abalone just after it was loosened from the rock and an underwater tug-of-war would ensue, the eel twisting and turning on itself, writhing with power, as the diver tried to hold on to the other end. Early on, I would, without much reluctance, give up the abalone, but later, after becoming warily accustomed to eels, I was not nearly so generous.

The ocean territory was new and I was a youngster experiencing a world few had seen, doing things few had done. There was a sense of high adventure and of developing skills that permitted me to gather delicacies that rarely reached the palate of the common man. Additionally, I was becoming aware that something unique was happening to me; the ocean had become a teacher and I its student.

Later the world, and particularly the Japanese, developed a craving for abalone, and scuba sport divers began to take the easily accessible snail in the early 1970's. They along with a handful of free diving spearfishermen who turned their skills to commercial enterprise using hooka (a compressor-fed air line attached to an otherwise unburdened diver, which permitted him to freely work shallow water for hours at a time) ravaged the abalone. These commercial abalone divers essentially wiped out the population by the early 1980's. Today, there is a moratorium along much of the California coastline and its offshore islands making it illegal to take abalone. Perhaps one day it will recover if it can withstand the poaching that is difficult to police along the lengthy coastlines of California and its islands.

The water off California is cold, in the mid- to high-sixties during the summer. Wet suits first became available in 1953, but were too expensive— around a hundred dollars for a shorty. However, after a few years the price came down and I bought a full wet suit kit for $29.95 and glued it together. The wet suit changed everything for the West Coast diver. Now instead of spending minutes in chilly, uncomfortable water I could spend hours. Almost instantly I began to see fish larger than my pole spear could handle. Now fifteen years old, I purchased a spear gun called The Hammerhead, which was touted to be more powerful than any other over-the-counter gun, and was, in fact an-after-market muzzle made by Bel Aqua (a company owned by Bill Barada, one of the first accomplished writers for *Skin Diver Magazine*). Properly equipped, I ventured out further to deeper reefs where the fish were large and the specter of Kamo loomed. Kamo slowed the journey into deep water to one of cautious fits and starts. Lured by the promise of larger fish, which possessed a certain mystery, uncertainty and apprehension with regard to their power, I, despite Kamo, was drawn inexorably into the deeper water. As long as I could see bottom (the voice of the Hawaiian would caution), I could maintain a level of comfort. On days the water was exceptionally clear I would venture further out from shore into deep reefs not normally traveled. So it was that I and others like me slowly worked our way out into the dark water.

At age sixteen, having worked after school, I purchased a car and began to dive the reefs of Laguna Beach in earnest. In that same year I experienced a rite of passage that was probably overdue, that of spearing a large eel and bringing it to the surface. Having seen others spear eels, I knew they were terribly strong and, once speared, would twist and turn on a steel spear shaft, easily bending it into pretzel shapes that were impossible to straighten. On a rare dive trip to Catalina Island aboard a small boat owned by the father of a friend who wanted to learn more about diving, I found my eel. Or rather the friend did, and it was he who wanted me to spear it. I was willing, though I didn't want to destroy my spear gun in the process, so instead used his gun.

Because eels extend their heads from caves, they make an easy target. The difficulty is not in spearing them but in being able to pull them out into the open before they can retreat into the cave, taking the spear with them, making it difficult if not impossible to retrieve either the spear or the eel. This eel was quite large and, after spearing it and pulling it out of its cave, all hell broke loose. Six-feet-long, the eel was too powerful to hold off with the spear shaft, and so it pushed me backwards, teeth gnashing, and body twisting violently around the spearshaft, a ball of writhing fury an arm's length away. I couldn't let go for fear it would swim free and, as had been done to others, bite my face off. When I pushed the barrel of the spear gun near its mouth it bit down repeatedly, its teeth breaking off on the aluminum barrel. The eel thus occupied, I rose to the surface for a breath. Swimming the eel to the boat, I threw the whole twisting mess, spear gun and all, into the cockpit. The eel went berserk, driving the father up on the cabin as it thrashed and banged, summarily destroying what was left of the spear gun and the varnished deck, as the son and father looked on forlornly.

The passing of such rites was probably necessary, but I was left with an ill feeling when it was over. This was compounded later when I threw the dead eel overboard. It was the first time I had killed an animal without any intention of eating it, and the act left a lasting impression. I never again killed a creature without intending to eat or share it.

Continuing to free dive the shore-bound reefs of the Pacific Coast through my teens, I grew comfortable with all aspects of diving in shallow water. The more comfortable I became, the more risks I took, wedging myself down into narrow crevices to get abalone, or wiggling my way through an underwater tunnel whose end would reveal more abalone. In the course of these hunts for abalone I would find lobster. Soon lobster became the object of my pursuits. I was beginning to understand how the ocean worked, where game could be found in relation to the variables within the environment: tide, surge, current, temperature of the water, time of day. Slowly I grew to recognize how each of those factors and their combinations influenced the inhabitants.

During this period I became faintly aware of the development of another form of perception. It was a kind of knowing that seemed to transcend the normal sensory modes of comprehending the underwater environment. Drifting along on the surface more or less detached, with the object of the search held in the back of my mind, I would feel a vague impulse to dive, as if called in a whisper, and invariably, at the end of my descent, come upon some previously hidden cave or hole holding the very thing I was searching for, be it fish, abalone or lobster. Initially I was astonished, then, as time went on and these impulses continued to bear fruit, it further confirmed this hushed voice to be valid and have substance. It was the beginning of what I came to understand when writing about it many years later, as a form of intuitive intelligence. At the time I assumed other divers had the same sort of experience. It was not something easily explained much less understood, so it came as no surprise that this form of perception was never brought up in discussions with other divers. Over the years this sixth sense continued to gain power until it became an accepted part of my experience underwater. Because it arose out of a seascape that was already mysterious, there was no reason to believe that events and moments would not manifest in equally unexplained ways. There was a fascination attached to its workings and I often toyed with explanations; perhaps I was more observant than I believed myself to be, or I was absorbing information I had no awareness of, and it was this that was directing me. In any event, I was cognitively sensing and observing this new wilderness beyond conscious awareness.

While my activities in the ocean appeared magical, my life outside the ocean was difficult. Moving

from Hawaii I went from school to school before
settling in Arcadia. There, I became asthmatic in
the smog-filled San Gabriel Valley, and acquired the
bad habit of carving my name in desktops and anything else that would yield to the will of a knife.
Much of those first years after leaving Hawaii were
unclear, like walking through a dream without a
notion of where I was or what had transpired. Often I was punished for behavior for which I had no
inkling. "Out of control" was the term most frequently used. I do remember, quite vividly, the two
years spent in junior high school. The first day at
school symbolized the entire experience. I was walking to my first class with an armful of books when
I met the gaze of a man who was dressed like a
student. He had reddish hair and needed a shave. I
could not take my eyes away from him. As we were
about to intersect he swung a meaty arm down,
hitting my books and scattering them twenty feet
down the hallway. Staring down at me with brutal
cold eyes, he asked what I was looking at. Dumb-
struck, I could not take my gaze from his eyes as
he raised his arm again, this time to hit me. A
teacher stepped out of a classroom door and instructed "Stoney" to move on. It was the first of a
series of humiliations and later fights that would
occur throughout the seventh and eighth grades.
The mere sight of the place as we came upon it by
bus each morning, its unpainted, cement gray,
chain-link fence, having all the appearances of a
penitentiary complete with bars over the windows,
caused me to slip low into my seat, waiting until
everyone else was off the bus before I would get up
and depart.

Bullies smell fear, and there is no escaping them.

It is an instinct quickly cultivated and exploited. One day, tired of the humiliation, after having been shoved down from behind on the playground, I lashed out with fists flying, and bloodied the face of an eighth grader, reducing him to a crying child. It was a strange sort of liberation. Soon I was fighting everyone: older kids, teachers and my parents. By the time I entered high school I had established a reputation as unpredictable and quick to fight. But something had invaded my soul, something I could not fight off with fists or an attitude. There came the vague notion that the school, the system of education, was trying to steal something from me that was important, that had value.

In the 1950's the constructs of education and relating to the world were quite rigid in their linear approach, and did not provide alternate avenues with which to understand the subjects presented in school. (Not until I began to write several decades later did I realize that my intuitive sense of the ocean was in fact the way I perceived much of the world; and it was this that I felt was being stolen.) For a time I struggled with the learning process but could not master it, and soon rebelled against the system by participating less and less. More and more I became a fighter, looking now for bullies to bully. Cronies would follow me around on a Saturday night in the hope I could find a good fight. I wasn't always successful, and over the course of four years broke my nose twice, broke a knuckle and a finger, and was always on the mend with cuts and bruises. Suspended from high school for fighting on several occasions, I eventually wound up in minor trouble with the law, and after several automobile accidents, had my driver's license revoked. My parents, no doubt at wit's end, sent me to a YMCA camp on Catalina Island in the summer of my seventeenth year. It was a homecoming of sorts and the child of Hawaii was, for the first time in seven years, daily embraced by the sea. That summer became the most blissful of my adolescence.

Prior to that same summer of 1958, I had gone in partnership on an Aqualung, which amounted to a bare tank with a J valve, which when pulled would allow for five minutes of additional air once the tank ran out. I would dive until the tank was empty then pull the J valve and make my ascent. The regulator was a one stage, double hose affair (that malfunctioned at eighty feet during its second year of use). Aside from instructions by the sales clerk, "don't hold your breath, and follow your slowest bubbles up when you return to the surface," we had no other information on the safe use of the Aqualung. Apparently, it was enough for I dove with the regulator in shallow water half a dozen times before taking it with me to Catalina. There at the camp I was introduced to Jon Hardy, who was a few years older than me, and the resident expert with the Aqualung, and who, years later, was to become one of the premier scuba divers on the West Coast. Jon took me down to ninety feet and checked me out. I had never been that deep and the sensation of breathing under the water was both strange and miraculous from one who had always held his breath. Initially, I was never quite sure the next breath would be there, but when, after a time I became comfortable, the dive was pleasurable and certainly unique. However, I quickly came to realize that in exchange for that breath I gave up my place as an active and intimate member of the underwater community. I had become an observer who seemed to be sitting outside the experience I knew as a free diver. The Aqualung provided time; that was both its gift and its curse. For without the urgency to absorb and accurately perceive my surroundings in the length of a minute and a half breath-hold, I found my observations going the way of lazy preoccupation. The Aqualung altered my approach to the sea, as well as the sea's approach to me. I was unable to "sense" my surroundings in the way I had been accustomed to and the ocean inhabitants reacted to me more as an intruder rather than a member of their community. Upon returning to the mainland at the end of summer, I set the Aqualung aside for occasional use and continued to explore the ocean as a free diver.

By my senior year in school there was no one left to fight. I was attending half days, working nights as a shoe salesman, trying to find answers to questions I couldn't even formulate. The sea remained my escape and while friends planned out their colleges and careers, I would wander down to the beach on my days off and do some diving.

I attended junior college in the hope that some sort of option might reveal itself. But motivation was weak, for I had fallen in love with sports cars and dreamed of being a Formula One driver, and thus selected the Mt. San Antonio Junior College, not for its academic standards or even offered courses, but because it had a nicely banked winding road on which to refine my skills in a newly acquired MG TD. In the year and a half I became a competent driver but not much of a student. Life remained confusing off the road and out of the water, and, looking back, the bulk of my time was spent in wait. Waiting for someone, a mentor, a wise man, someone who knew something of the world and could confirm it to be the illusion it was, and that this life I was living, this life that would become my future as it was my past, was utter nonsense.

I could not hold out to the harsh consequences of my existence, having neither the strength nor the will for such isolation, and soon caved under the sheer weight of consensus reality. It really wasn't a conscious decision, it just happened as water happens when naturally seeking its own level. I simply could not reside in the rapids of my existence any longer and sought a more comfortable level.

At the age of twenty and leaning decidedly towards a self-destructive life by way of racing cars, I asked my high school sweetheart to be my wife. We married and I settled into a part-time job teaching peewee swimming at the local YMCA. We scraped by for a year before being swept up in the chase for gold in the form of real estate at the end of California's rainbow. I could see where big money could be made, but had none of my own to invest. I went to school, acquired a real estate license, but thoroughly failed as a salesman. The best I could come up with was as a salaried employee of a company that insured title to properties.

In the interests of my marriage and commitment to make money, I put away what appeared to be the toys of childhood and sold or gave away my dive equipment, resigning myself to an hour commute to a large office building in downtown Los Angeles. The truths imparted by the ocean, dulled and eventually forgotten, were replaced by the sort of lifestyle I had for so long held in contempt.

# DAY
# 5

Amid gossamer clouds blowing apart in an early morning southerly, frigates work high on a thermocline. I drink tea by myself on the bow as a large vessel looms in the channel going south to La Paz. At first glance I suspect it to be some kind of cruise ship, ever popular in the southern and northern latitudes, but this is no cruise ship. There is an oversized wheel in the stern. It is a commercial fishing boat, a purse seiner, the largest I have seen. Jack joins me and we estimate the vessel to be at least two hundred feet long. "Almost the size of a small destroyer," says Jack, who spent nine years in the navy on a nuclear submarine. The fishing boat trudges past as Jack speaks of global overfishing, and the remarkable efficiency of such vessels, and how they are stripping all life in their wake. He mentions global fisheries taking close to a hundred million tons of fish a year. Idly, he wonders how much longer the Gulf can sustain the fishing pressure. How much fish can it give up before it passes a point of no return and is forever lost? Having made no comment on the subject, I sit gazing at the ship. Finally, Jack is quiet and together we watch the ship disappear and the future of the Gulf with it.

Pam calls us to breakfast in the cockpit. Absently pushing the food about the plate, my mind cannot release the ship. It is taking more than the future. It is stealing the heart from this once perfect wilderness. In that stark and terrible realization I am overcome and begin to choke back tears. Jack is uncomfortable with this display and avoids eye contact. Pam suggests I go right ahead and cry. But I am disabled in this area and continue to suppress the emotion.

Later, when I have composed myself, Jack asks, "Why now?" I seemed to be so accepting of the plight of the Gulf before the boat passed. A legitimate question. Intellectually, I had accepted the destruction of the Gulf from afar, removed as I was from the direct experience of that devastation.

It has been happening in earnest for over the last ten years, since Mexican fishermen discovered the power of the gill net. Through heavy tourism and hotel trade alone they were making more money from fishing than ever before. There was no authority to police their activities and soon they were netting every fish that swam in the entire Gulf. In this same time frame the Mexican Government gave permission to Japan to run their high-tech fishing vessels into the Gulf, and in a short three year period, before Mexico was able to withdraw permission, the combined efforts reduced the Sea of Cortez to a lifeless pond relative to the thriving sea it had been a few years earlier. Over time the Mexican gill-netters ran out of quality fish and now are content to harvest anything that swims, from bat rays to pufferfish. It didn't happen all at once and I had gradually come to accept the sorry fact that the Gulf would never again be as it once was. However, reading about a rape is one thing; actually witnessing the effects of that brutalization is quite another. The heart and mind are able to hold the beauty and power of a thing remembered, but with each new day in these waters the memories of the past are being replaced by the reality of the present.

It is difficult, if not impossible, to express the loss of something that once so nurtured my heart and spirit, and so thoroughly altered my life. I am reminded of the stoic silence of Native Americans as they witnessed the systematic destruction of the lands they held sacred for thousands of years. What can anyone say in the face of such trauma?

Those who participate in the befouling of the land, air and water prefer to confine their arguments to an intellectual discussion, i.e., the so many tons of fish-yields up or down, proper harvesting is beneficial, etc., etc., etc. But the real value of a natural environment cannot be expressed in intellectual or quantitative terms. It goes far deeper, touching the very fabric of our being, the very threads of our attachment to this planet.

We are connected to the planet in much the same way we are connected to the mothers that bore and gave birth to us, fed and nurtured us into conscious beings. There are many notions as to this source of our connection to the planet. Some would simply say that the bond is direct and ongoing as evidenced by the earth we walk upon, the air we breathe, and the resources we consume. Thus we are in a very real way a manifestation of the planet's life force, its spirit, its soul.

Tragically, in the last few hundred years, a mere heartbeat of mankind's presence, we have declared war on the environment. In that time, we have caused incalculable destruction, wrecking absolute havoc to the air, land and sea. (Dr. Richard Leakey, famed conservationist and paleontologist, estimates 30,000 species of life vanish from our planet every year at the hands of the human race.) And in this campaign we appear bent on severing the last threads of our connection to the planet. Today, we float free of our roots and have not a clue as to the source of our chaotic existence. That fishing boat was far more than the reaper of fish, it was carrying off the last filaments of mankind's attachment to this once magical body of water.

We make La Paz by late afternoon and tie up at the Marina de La Paz. The old streets and town remain relatively unchanged since I first passed through twenty-three years ago. The Mexican people remain remarkably untainted by American influence, for there is nothing much here for the tourist, no pristine beaches or slick hotels. It remains a fishing port that is cooled in the summer by tricky westerlies that blow off the Pacific and find their way through the valleys and into the harbor. The town has aged slowly and gracefully, and the people have retained their charming and generous ways. There is little thievery or mugging, for they are not contaminated by greed. I remind Jack of this when he suspects our cab driver of foul play when driving off in the opposite direction we intend. The cabbie is merely taking a short cut and swings back onto the main drag as Jack settles into his seat. We have dinner in the center of town then walk the clean, uncluttered streets back to the marina. Enroute, the young and old exchange eye contact and shy smiles as we pass in this gentle, slow paced haven of safety and good will, living up to the name of La Paz, peace.

# DAY
## 6-7

J ack leaves for the States in the morning on
business and will return tomorrow night. In the
meantime we are anchored in La Paz, the one-time
oyster capital of the world.

The eastern shores of the Baja Peninsula were
once considered the best pearl fishing on the North
American continent. Early explorations of the Gulf,
including those of Hernan Cortes in 1535, reported
the presence of pearls. The pearl beds were easily
located by scanning the beaches for mounds of
shells discarded by the Indians who used the oyster as a source of food. The abandoned shells were
thrown into piles that became large enough to be
seen offshore. The Spaniards employed free divers
who could reach sixty feet without fins, and thoroughly harvested the shallower beds.

During the next hundred years pearling became
a profitable venture and was exploited with vigor.
When the Jesuits came into influence in 1697, the
pearling industry was curtailed until 1768 when
the Order was expelled from Baja by the King of
Spain. But by that time the riches had all but been

harvested. A small resurgence occurred around 1830 when a French trader developed a market for the discarded shells in France. The shells were fashioned into buttons, cutlery handles and the like, but this ended when the shells turned brittle and flaked as older shells were retrieved nearer the bottom of the piles. From the 1850's to the 1940's a mild revival occurred when Russian pearl dealers made their way into La Paz and motivated the merchants to take an interest in the industry. And though they all but enslaved Yaqui Indian divers to do work that stretched nearly the length of the peninsula, the results from their efforts were minuscule. By the middle of the twentieth century the oyster was finished.

In Pam's travels among the shops for souvenirs and jewelry, she finds no evidence of the pearling industry or its by-products, a sad commentary to man's thorough ravaging of a resource.

# DAY
## 8-9

Been in La Paz four days. The delays are frustrating. Though the offshore islands hold little promise of exciting dive activity, I long to be in the water. Relative to my trips down to the Gulf twenty years ago, this one, so far, has been uneventful. Jack returns this evening and it is decided that rather than resupply and head south for Cabo San Lucas and then to San Benedicto, we will go north to Espiritu de Santos Island and then to Los Islotes where lies a sea lion colony. I am in agreement with this decision for I have no desire to reach the wild waters of San Benedicto on frail legs and a poor breath-hold.

# DAY

# 10

We depart La Paz on the outgoing tide, heading for Espiritu de Santos Island. Beyond the adventure and sheer will required to undertake this trip, both Jack and Pam are seeking something that will more clearly define either who they are or what they are to do with the remainder of their lives. Pam's life is in flux; she loves Jack but their life together has been on and off for years. She is viewing this expedition, among other things, as one last opportunity to reconcile differences, and perhaps begin a life together. She speaks of moving and buying a house. Right now her life resembles a kite in a strong wind held to earth by a string, and she is in the throes of realizing she must reel in some of that string before the winds of change sweep it from her hands.

For Jack this journey is no less than one of self-discovery. Having come out of nine very structured years as a nuclear specialist on a submarine and now has a high-paying job working outages for nuclear power plants across the country. He has made considerable sacrifices to be here so that he might observe life from an entirely different perspective. He struggles with the shift from his knowable linear world to the non-linear world of nature beneath the sea. It is difficult to give up one thing that is familiar for another that is virtually unknown. I watch him in his daily battles with the hemispheres of his brain, the left unwilling to give in to the right, the right yearning for the new wisdom of the water and an opportunity to stretch its synapses in the natural world of its birth.

This morning while Pam is below, Jack and I are in the cockpit and he asks what he should do on this journey. What should he look for that would enable him to further understand the ocean and allow him to enter into it with a less cluttered mind? I advise him to seek no instant remedy, have no expectations, simply to try participating in each and every moment. He runs these suggestions through a mind-boggling array of interpretations, his facile mind again the center of its occupation. I listen as he verbalizes, knowing as he does it is not for my ears at all.

Two hours into the motor sail the engine's water temperature gauge indicates overheating. Jack believes that something may have been sucked up into the filter. I am on the wheel and he instructs me to kill the engine so that he might pull the filter and clean it. We are in a narrow passage a quarter mile from a reef outcropping rising six feet out of the water. I want to pass the rocks first and be well clear of them before we stop. Jack has a habit of smiling in a patronizing way whenever either Pam or I have a suggestion that is in conflict with his own judgment. He is smiling now, but I insist, and the temperature is not yet very high so he shrugs in compliance.

We put some distance between the rocks and us before killing the engine. There is no wind whatsoever, and the current appears minimal so we rest upon the glass sea while Jack inspects the filter. He pulls and cleans it and in short order we are underway again. Within five minutes Pam, who is now at the helm, alertly notices that the temperature has risen sharply to 230 degrees and she kills the engine. No cooling water emits from the exhaust, which indicates the cooling system is down. We are not going anywhere for a while. Shortly, a current picks up and begins to push the *Nirvana* towards the reef outcropping. Within an hour we are nearly on top of it. There is little choice in the matter but to lash the skiff to the side of the Nirvana, fire up the outboard, and make for the nearest refuge a mile away. I have done this once before with this same boat, with the same problem, after blowing the cooling system off Point Conception on the Central California coast.

It takes over an hour to trudge into a cove and just beat a blow building from the south. In no time the cove rolls with swells. Jack, who is six-three and one hundred ninety pounds, and I, at six-one and a one hundred seventy pounds, squeeze into the engine room, which is not really a room at all but a few feet of passageway on either side of the diesel engine, to dismantle the water pump. Jack does not label himself a mechanic, but he is unintimidated by the workings of a motor and will attack any problem, secure that it can be solved and the broken part repaired or replaced. I, on the other hand, am intimidated by anything mechanical, and for all purposes other than handing Jack tools and holding a wrench now and then, am utterly worthless in the engine room.

Winds of thirty knots now whip the boat around and I am woozy when finally we come out of close quarters with the water pump that, we soon learn, has pulverized its impeller. Jack rebuilds the water pump, while Pam prepares dinner. After dinner Jack and I crawl back into the bowels of the boat and reattach the pump. It is eleven o'clock before we are through and fall into bed exhausted.

# DAY

## 11

In the morning we sail north along the east side of Espiritu de Santos and Partida islands, whose ocher- and chocolate-rich earth striations along the high cliffs and chiseled plateaus, appear to have been lifted from the Grand Canyon. We arrive in the late afternoon at the small rock island of Los Islotes, a quarter mile long and no more than a few hundred feet wide, upon which rests an active sea lion colony. Dung-covered shear escarpments are packed with resting pelicans, frigates, sea gulls, a lone heron, red breasted bobbies, cormorants and a turkey vulture. In the water sea lion pups frolic in groups of twenty or more, on shore rest half a dozen males. An alpha male barks at all who come within shouting distance as his harem of several dozen females lie in languid repose on the low lying rocks. All this life suddenly becomes an anomaly relative to what we have observed so far on this expedition. The sea lions barking and playing in the shallow water, the birds wheeling in the azure sky, suddenly the Gulf is alive and breathing its wild and restless breathes again.

These California sea lions range from as far north

as Vancouver Island, British Columbia to the Galapagos Islands off Ecuador. Their estimated population is around 150,000, half of which are located on
the Galapagos. The frolicsome pups appear to be
quite young and were probably born in the early
summer and are now six to seven months old. They
will nurse until the next pup is born, in about a
year. After spending their first week with their
mother they begin to gather in their own groups,
as they are now, to play and explore the world together. The pups, filled with energy, are far more
willing to play than their mothers who appear quite
content on the dry rocks basking in the warmth of
the winter sun.

When we enter the water and swim towards the
rock island the alpha male leaps from his perch and
charges into the water. In a matter of moments he
makes a rush at us (their top speed underwater is
more than 17 miles an hour) with a full compli-
ment of underwater barks and explosive bubbles
issuing from a wide-open mouth. The seven hundred-pound male veers off in the last instant, de-
lighting no doubt, in his ability to make us flinch
as he barrels by. The alpha male is formidable, and
turning, stakes out his territory by patrolling forty
feet of water near to where he entered from the low
rocks. If we venture too near as I do, he rocks his
head from side to side in a peculiar and obviously
aggressive manner that leaves little doubt of its
meaning. I move elsewhere, and soon he returns to
his harem on the rocks, leaving us with the pups.

The pups are the size of wet border collies weighing around fifty pounds apiece. They dart about
with the agility of hummingbirds, zipping in and
out, up and down, coming to my facemask and peer-

ing in, their eyes wide with curiosity. One wraps its fore flippers, which are remarkably strong, around my arm and pulls me to it. Unlike seals, which use their hind flippers for swimming and their fore flippers for turning, the sea lion propels itself along using its fore flippers, which accounts for this strength. The pup tries to pull me into it and I let it, feeling its muscled chest against my own, its eyes inches away from my mask, peering in, seeking intelligent life. Seeing none, the pup releases me from its grip and spins off in search of more frolicsome friends.

Breath-holds come easy on the shallow sea floor at fifteen feet. I look up for an image of light and sea lion to compose itself. While the idea might be sound, the application is next to impossible. The pups have converged on me. One has my snorkel in its mouth and is yanking away, another is biting and tugging at my swim fin, still another is gnawing on my strobe light. To attempt serious photography is folly, so laying the camera aside I join in the play. The pups enjoy biting hands and arms. The bite is gentle, probing; they are wild animals exploring an odd creature, much like a human baby explores the world with its mouth. We dive and spin and roll for twenty minutes until a large female appears and aggressively scatters the group which reforms a few minutes later. But I am too slow for their high-speed play and they tire of the novelty. Through collective communication they quickly gather themselves and dive away into the depths.

Neither Jack nor Pam have been in the water with this many sea lions, and are overwhelmed by the intimate interaction. Later Jack comments on the ineffability of being accepted so completely by wild animals. Marine animals, unlike their terrestrial brethren who are wary and have an instinctive distrust for man, will readily interact with man, particularly the young. Even the usually shy harbor seal (who, in their close proximity to shore, have seen more of man than other more ocean-going seals), has embraced me under the water. The Atlantic spotted dolphins of the White Sand Ridge off the Little Bahama Bank make interaction with humans an almost daily practice. The list of interplaying marine animals is long: elephant seals, harbor seals, whales, eels, turtles, fish, and today sea lions.

It grows late in the afternoon and we are in need of an anchorage so cut short our play and pull anchor.

We sail south to a typical Baja cove—deep, with high walls, and a low apex that catches the prevailing wind, keeping our bow steady at anchor in Ensenada Grande. There is one other boat in this peaceful cove. We sit in the cockpit, each with a single cold beer, our daily allowance due to the restraints of our tiny refrigeration unit, enjoying the golden hues of sunset catching the stratified cliffs, coloring them in rich siennas and rusts. In this glowing solitude Jack jumps up and goes below to turn on some music. It's an interesting reaction to the scene playing before us, and I suggest he listen instead to the silence of the Gulf. He willingly obliges and shuts off the music.

Perhaps it is no more than an issue of generations. Jack, like the majority of young people in our culture, has a need to feed the external stimulation that has been bred into his life via TV, music, video games, etc. It seems they scarcely hear it. We had drugs, they have din. Such a din would be unbearable for anyone from the 18th century to the birth of Christ and beyond. A hundred years ago there were far fewer people and much more space. A single family had fifty acres to themselves. Today those fifty acres must be shared with a hundred people, all of whom, it seems, have arrived with their personal ghetto blaster.

Are humans meant to live in this way?

Though we inexplicably resist and vehemently deny such dependence, it appears we are not physically, emotionally or psychologically equipped to operate very far outside the physical landscape of the natural world. If given the opportunity, mankind would surely covet a large area he could call his own space and may even recognize it as an essential requirement to a good life, as are equal portions of quiet and beauty, love and affection. All are elements under which humans can enjoy a measure of balance and harmony in their lives. The solitude of a wilderness possesses, among other things, the aspect of cleanliness; it is in the air and water, and when breathed and drank, will wash away the stress imparted by the conditions of civilization. The stillness of a wilderness can slow the mind to a peaceful walk, quiet the insecurities and incessant dialogue of instruction, speculation, projection, analysis and fear. Peace and harmony cohabit a wilderness and welcome all visitors. To spend some time in the quiet of seashore, or on a windswept hill, or in a grove of trees, and breathe in the place, is to know this to be true.

# DAY
## 12

**M**ile-high winds push cotton ball clouds south-ward as we head into the wind and six-foot seas. While this northerly blows we have few alternatives but to visit the sea lions at Los Islotes for we can anchor on its lee shore in relative protection.

We arrive to a group of sixteen pups huddled together in a tight ball. This behavior is called rafting; I have seen adults raft out in the open sea off California, but never here. The pups accept us into their ball of fun while the females stay on the periphery of the circle, nipping, jostling and occasionally mounting one another. The pups charge us then slide by in the last instant, just grazing us as the alpha male did yesterday. Curious, they dip under our arms, seemingly looking for strokes. Like yesterday they nibble on snorkel tubes and stare directly into our facemasks. However, the energy is quite different today. The place is alive. Pam and Jack feel it too; magic pervades the water.

After shooting a roll of film and swimming back to the boat for another camera, I return to the pups and settle down near the shoreline on the shallow bottom. Going up for a breath, a single pup becomes interested in me and reaches out with his flipper and brings himself into my arm. He pushes his chest into my shoulder and arm, giving every indication he wants to be stroked in the chest and belly. It is difficult to resist and I gently rub my gloved hand down his silky chest and muscled torso. There are those who would say the emotion of affection is not involved here, but rather a need to be stroked for grooming purposes or some other reason deemed practical. Having no desire to engage the pragmatists, I would, however, invite them to take a close look at such behavior among dolphins and many species of seals. It appears clearly to be an expression of affection, which indicates that emotion of some kind is involved. And why not? We have all witnessed sadness and joy in the family dog. Is it such a stretch to include wild animals?

As a rule, I do not condone the touching of a wild animal. Having long conditioned myself to give them space, even when dolphins make a clear invitation to a touch, I resist. It is ultimately dangerous for a wild animal to engage man in this way. They might come to trust us and that would be a mistake. Or worse, we would give them names, and begin to feed them making them lazy and demanding. They would forget how to hunt, and eventually die, eating the foil in a Big Mac. It is far better to keep a distance.

Still, I cannot pull my hand away.

There are other humans in the water now. A boatload has shown up. Actually several boats and I don't want others to see me touching the pup; they will get ideas.

Within an hour there are seven boats anchored

at Los Islotes. Everything from a mini-cruise ship that unloads four, eighteen-foot inflatable boats holding ten passengers each, to small pangas willing to buck the big swells all the way from La Paz. There are fifty people in the water. This was once an isolated haven for the sea lions. When I first came here twenty years ago, not a single boat made an appearance the entire time we were here. Today it is an "E" ticket ride, Mexican style. Wearing red life preservers, the cruise ship passengers dangle awkwardly in the water, struggling like broken dolls to get an underwater look. One man takes off his swim fin and invites a pup to bite it. Another stumbles onto the reef area and creates an uproar with the sleeping sea lions. Another more active floater is able to pet a pup. A plastic bandage has come loose and a pup picks it up then drops it. I dive and retrieve it before the pup takes a notion to swallow it. An old man with white wrinkled skin reaches out in vain to touch a passing pup. The symbology resonates with the longing of man to connect to something alive and real that lives fully free.

This whole scene strikes me strangely. On one hand the idea of money alone permitting these folks the privilege to invade this once remote sanctuary is bothersome. At the very least some skill should be required and some understanding of the sanctity of wild animals (Hypocrisy noted since I have already touched them.) On the other hand, better to invade a wild sea lion colony than to observe them captured and stuck in some zoo or circus. It is a dilemma that has no clear answer. Man is pushing in on the natural world from all sides, and the animals are disappearing under the weight of our numbers.

I suspect what really disturbs me is the growing realization that the old ways are gone forever. What was once an authentic adventure with all the inherent risks and accompanying sense of wonder is now just another stop on the Princess Cruise. In the middle of all this, Pam is hit with a Portuguese man-of-war. She is severely stung and in pain. Though she was wearing a wet suit, her arms and shoulders were exposed and it is here where the burning welts of contact reside. Concerned that those in the water, bare and blissful, will also be hit (the sea in some way or another is still capable of biting back), I swim over and warn the leader of the cruise ship group, but she dismisses me as a nuisance that is interfering with the more immediate responsibilities of her job.

With Pam laid up and the crowded conditions turning ugly, we pull anchor and head for Ensenada Grande.

# DAY
# 13

A northerner has blown in and from our sheltered cove we gaze out into the Gulf's stream where roughshod seas roll southward, fracturing the horizon's thin line. Once again we're bound for Los Islotes and the sea lions. Clouds of mist diffuse the sky as gray reflects gray turning the water to mercury. Near the mouth of the cove a dorsal fin cuts like a razor across the water scattering baitfish that leap like silver buttons thrown from another sky. I expect Jack to make a jump on the fish with the spear gun, but he declines. Perhaps it is his inexperienced crew that discourages a jump into the sea. He has more to think about than spearing a fish. First and foremost is the welfare of this boat and all possessions on board.

When we jump Los Islotes in the early afternoon the atmosphere is much different than yesterday. The magic is gone, replaced by a disaffected mood. The water is cloudy like the sky, and several males, all over five hundred pounds, make runs at us, barking underwater, spewing bubbles with mouths agape and teeth bared, charging, then spinning away at the last moment.

The males, with their large heads and bodies, resemble their descendants—a bear-like creature that lived on the coast of the North Pacific and took to the sea twenty-four million years ago during the Oligocene Epoch. Their evolutionary relationship to land mammals is readily observable in their skeletons with the presence of leg bones that are encased in the sleek body to the ankles.

The maneuverability of the sea lions is extraordinary. They can change directions at full speed while swimming upside down, then miss rock and reef by centimeters. They whip around us like bees on the fly. There are six males on Los Islotes at present: the alpha male and five subordinate males. The alpha male has a splash of white on his chin, and regally patrols his underwater territory in front of the main entrance to the high ground where the females and young bask in the morning sun. When approaching this area White Beard will begin to sway his head from side to side, as he did when we first arrived several days ago. Oddly, White Beard does not charge us as the other males do. His confidence is such he needs no show of strength. He concerns himself with the more immediate duties of running a full sized harem. He guards the access, breaks up fights between females, watches over errant pups, and chases off males who wander too close to the harem. He is also an indulgent father. Later in the water, a playful pup has bitten White Beard in the tiny flay of skin over the ear (this piece of skin is the easiest way to distinguish a sea lion from all other seals), and will not let go. White Beard spins and rolls and the youngster hangs on like a tattered flag in a gale. For nearly half a minute the pup withstands every maneuver by

White Beard. Finally the pup runs out of breath and releases his hold to head for the surface. White Beard follows him and gives a belly rub before moving on.

Minutes later, and for no apparent reason, White Beard herds most of the pups on shore, barking all the while. I suspect a large shark has ventured close to the rock, but see no evidence above or below the water. One thing is clear; the energy of the place has changed. No doubt White Beard has the same feeling. We move further west up the island where there is less sea lion activity.

Pam is always on the lookout for sea horses. I have never seen them in the Gulf, but then I have never looked. I tease Jack by wondering aloud if she will find a sea horse before he will spear a grouper. Accepting the challenge, he returns to the boat for a spear gun. He will hunt for grouper while I attempt to burn the last of a single roll of film in these less than ideal conditions.

Again, I find myself in a comfortable position on the bottom in twenty-five feet of water just watching the play of a single pup. This day I am using a strobe and attempting close-ups. The flash goes off when the pup is but two feet away. It abruptly swims off, dives to a fist-sized rock, picks it up in its mouth, swims back over to me still sitting on the bottom, and drops the rock on the Plexiglas port of my housing, clearly communicating its displeasure with the flash. Stunned, I head for the boat. The day is over for me in terms of photography. It was a strange day and unwise to force a personal agenda when the sea so clearly communicates its mood.

Jack, off hunting up some dinner with the spear

gun, returns to the boat with a twenty-five-pound cabrilla, exclaiming, "They were everywhere at the seventy-foot level. It was like diving in a museum. It must have been like this when you first dove the Gulf. Big fish make everything different." He continues, "They give power to the place, a meaning that feels so old." He has tapped into the feeling of the Gulf, but a twenty-five-pound cabrilla at seventy feet after two weeks of hunting is a sad and woeful reward. He then takes me aside so that Pam will not hear, and tells me he blacked out on a deep dive. He was down at the seventy-foot level, which is quite deep in these dirty waters, and on his return to the surface lost consciousness near the top. Shallow water blackout is not uncommon among free divers who have extended their limits. Having created an oxygen deficit on the dive, when nearing the surface a vacuum is created pulling blood from the brain (like standing up quickly and getting dizzy) and the diver is overcome and loses consciousness. Jack passed out near the surface and found himself coughing up water as he regained consciousness while floating on his stomach. He appears to be all right. But it was a dangerous lesson. I have never blacked out but have had what are called the "sparklies", flashes of brilliant light exploding in the head just before black out. It is the last warning for a deep diver.

Diving to depth is less a physical undertaking than it is a profound psychological excursion into the unknown. When I first began to dive to depth as a teenager, the barrier lay at twenty feet. There the water was dim and cold, and the pressure on the body and ears was pronounced. These indications warn the body and mind that one is trespassing into ominous territory—dangerous territory—where the breath-hold becomes a flimsy vehicle on which to ride, and has one invariably turn prematurely to the surface. So it was in those early days when twenty feet was all one needed to find fish, abalone and lobster. With each year I gained about five feet of depth on my dive until reaching forty feet where I was comfortable on almost all shoreline reefs. When I began to dive the Gulf and deeper dives were required to hunt fish, my limit was pushed to sixty feet. Much later, when in my late forties, I was able to crack the hundred-foot barrier with regularity when diving the ultra-clear waters of Fiji.

By the late 1980's and early 1990's, the commercial fisheries and sport fishermen had all but wiped out the big grouper, and deeper dives were required to find the few that were left. The spearfishermen of the 1990's arrived on the scene with the depth barrier pushed to seventy feet and psychologically were able, in a relatively short period of time, to hit those depths and beyond, many going over a hundred feet. Jack is in extraordinary shape and has already overcome the psychological obstacles of the deep dive in only five years of diving. Today, depth is no longer the factor it once was for the novice diver. Nonetheless, diving to depth remains a risky business. A hundred feet may be a long way down, but once down, can be an agonizingly long way up.

In the early afternoon we travel to a cove further south, Bahia Cardonal, and anchor up in the light of dusk, as wild manic brush strokes of filmy clouds sweep across a sky that graduates from a smoky orange horizon to ash gray. Night is on the brink and from a distance there comes the sound of water explosions. Jack witnessed this event last year and has brought us to this cove expressly for this evening's show. In near darkness scores of pelicans are slamming into the northern shore of the bay. They are herding unseen bait toward us. The sounds of the birds hitting the water are like gunshots, as everywhere around us the pelicans make their low-altitude plunges. In silhouette off the afterglow of last light they rise for moments then fall away, diving bricfly, disappearing into black water. For twenty minutes they work the bait. As the light finally fades altogether they have pushed beyond the boat and are still echoing explosive plunges. This is the Gulf as I remember it thirty years ago— on-going, never ending flight or fight, life and death, drama upon drama. Exhilarated by the pelican feed, we are left spellbound.

# DAY
# 14

Sailing southeast between Isla Gallina and Espiritu de Santos Islands then through the San Lorenzo Channel, we head for Cerralvo Island. Midway through the channel, as Cerralvo looms large before us, Jack surmises that we are eight miles away. He is fooled by the clarity of the air and I confidently assess the distance to be more like twelve miles. When we check the chart we find the island to be nearly twenty miles away. The pristine desert air that deceives the eye is the same that provides such breathtaking sunsets. The one tonight sustains like a musical note ringing into evening, clean and untainted, igniting the high clouds in spiritual glow, then slowly bruising them into silhouette against a leaden sky. It is in these dark shades that we enter an exposed cove on the west side of Cerralvo.

Though anchored in a cove exposed to the northerly flow of wind and sea, it lays down nicely as night falls. A Mexican shrimp boat has taken refuge in a cove further south. Jack hops into the skiff and runs down to buy a kilo of fresh shrimp. While I cook them up scampi, he wonders if the Mexicans

don't get sick of the gringos with their plastic sailboats prancing about the Gulf, taking up anchorages that otherwise would be available to commercial vessels. Despite the annoyance, the shrimpers
are usually gracious and often give the shrimp
away, or trade for girlie magazines, which are illegal in Mexico. The Mexican fishermen treat North
American visitors far better than they themselves
might fare in the United States.

# DAY
# 15

In the morning under a blue sky and a searing sun, we head north two miles to a rock outcropping a quarter mile offshore. It is a likely spot to find pelagic yellowtail and wahoo, maybe an amberjack. Upon my suggestion Jack makes a jump outside the rock, then inexplicably heads inland. He is accustomed to diving deep for grouper on the bottom, but here he must stay close to the surface where the pelagics run in open water a good fifty yards outside the rock. I frantically wave but he doesn't see me or hear my shouts.

Beneath the boat swims a five-foot-long wahoo, and Jack is elsewhere. When finally I get his attention, he swims back to the right location and shortly pulls off on a wahoo. Underestimating the clarity of the water, he misjudges the distance and the spear falls short. It is the only shot he will have this morning.

Suiting up, I drop in, and the place is alive with great schools of Gulf anchovy. They appear as tightly packed jewels of light, and are the reason the wahoo are here. While I am down, three sierra mackerel make a rush at the bait. Their silver bodies flash into the bait that explodes in fragments of light, then congeals into itself, healing the wound of space. The sierra strike again and again as I make several deep dives looking for pargo and grouper which had been in great abundance when I was last here seventeen years ago hunting with Jerry and Dan Higman. Expecting to see evidence of big fish with the flourishing bait, I instead find nothing.

The wahoo have vanished as they are wont to do, so we reboard the *Nirvana* and head for the back side of Cerralvo, where, in that same dive trip seventeen years ago, we found pargo, over eighty pounds, grouper, also over eighty pounds, and big amberjack, over a hundred pounds. It was here I saw my first giant pacific manta ray. What a breathtaking sight, swooping in over us, blocking out the sun and then moving on, like an ocean apparition watching over its domain of big fish and wily sharks. It must have been one of the last, for the giant mantas soon vanished altogether from the Gulf, no doubt harpooned for shark bait and I never caught sight of one again.

Jack jumps in fully expecting to come up with a pargo or grouper in short order. In an hour he reports no sightings. Finding this difficult to believe, I make a jump myself. Within moments it is clear that there are no big fish here at all. The usual tropicals flit about vacant reefs; the bait is scattered, lazy and unfed upon. The place is dead.

Moving down the island, we continue to dive. It is disheartening to revisit reefs that were once filled with magnificent creatures and now are barren. Like coming upon a once grand forest and discovering it to be stripped clean of all trees. Perhaps

more than the visual loss is the absence of energy
that only wildlife can give to a place. Unlike the
air in which a forest breathes, water is dense and
so conducts sound and energy with far more facil-
ity. It is this lack of energy, the absence of life once
felt, that is so dispiriting.

I return to the boat grieved by the state of this
island, once one of the more prolific in the Gulf.
Later, I ask Jack why he continued to dive when it
was obviously a waste of time. Though he saw no
fish, he believed they might appear around the next
reef or bend in the island. We talked about a diver's
intuition, feeling the environment beyond the eyes.
Jack has an excellent mind and a quick grasp of
the linear world, and I suggest he let go of that
world and allow the ocean to enter him without
analysis or extended thought. "It will tell you what
you need to know," I say. "Let the mind take a rest.
Learn to trust the other intelligence, your intuition."

That was the sort of advice I should have heeded
when, after marrying, I believed that diving was a
childhood indulgence and should be put aside. In
the course of that grand misconception, I was away
from the ocean for five years. In that time I was
gainfully employed, wore a suit, a tie and wingtip
shoes, had a house, a car, children, and was over-
wrought with a distemper I could not identify. Depressed and drinking too much, my relief came
through the game of basketball, which I played in
maniacal fashion. While others in the same business with the same responsibilities and the same
commute to the same city seemed to thrive in such
circumstances, I was barely hanging on. To what, I

had no clue, understanding nothing.

In the summer of 1966 I borrowed some gear and went for a dive at Salt Creek, south of Laguna Beach. Swimming out to a reef a hundred yards from shore, I initially expected the ocean to feel alien and perhaps even a bit threatening; after all, I had been away for five years. The water was particularly clear, and in that startling clarity lay invitation. The placid water conjured schooling fish, lobsters and exposed abalone, instantly washing away feelings of anxiety, and replacing it with a lost sense of wonder. Moving into deeper water, the thirty foot-long kelp stalks, like great amber trees, rose straight up from the bottom. In this liquid forest drifted big calico bass, and beneath them nearer the bottom sheepshead larger than I had ever seen, a half a dozen over thirty pounds, wandered like grazing wildebeests. The sight of such fish stirred the hunter and I fell into that state of mindless drift where past and future fall away leaving me suspended in the immediate moment. Having not experienced such a state in a long while, it jarred me from the doldrums of my existence and swept me into the immediacy of the unknown. In such lofty territory, all that I had done in the world of man seemed insignificant and far away.

In the course of a failed attempt at snagging a lobster, I came across a small octopus sliding along the rock face of the reef. When I tried to pick it up it changed color, blanching pale pink, and blowing a jet of ink in my direction. I lifted it from the rock, held it as it held me, tentacles working around and through my fingers. The delicacy of the creature, the complexity of it, was mesmerizing, as if I was seeing it for the first time—a witness to a hidden marvel—the patterns on its skin, the fine edged suction cups, the tiny, probing end of each tentacle. This small octopus awakened me to all that I had been missing. All the small treasures missed and miracles uncovered. I placed the octopus back on the reef and watched it slide into a crack so narrow it defied logic.

I spent several hours on the reef. My spear gun was too small for the big sheepshead, but I managed to spear a calico bass, grab two lobsters and a limit of abalone. I was delirious with accomplishment, cleansed as if the depth and its pressure had squeezed the impurities that had found their way into my heart and flushed them into the sea. I felt more alive on that reef than I had felt since I abandoned the ocean five years before.

Reborn is an overused term these days, but there was no better explanation for the impact the ocean had on me that day. I had returned to a sacred place in myself—the boy in Hawaii and the teenager of the reefs. Making the long swim back to the beach, I contemplated my life. It would have to change. I could not ignore the message of the octopus.

Within six months I sold my house and moved the family down to Dana Point to be near the water. Eight months later my wife and I separated, she taking the children back to the suburbs while I moved into a one-room apartment in a dingy complex of drifters and ner-do-wells in Dana Point. Though I was back in the water, I was still trying to sort through the confusion of my life, vaguely aware of the new path I had set upon, yet having no idea in which direction my next step would be.

With a longer commute, seeing my children three times a week, playing basketball, and courting a woman, I was busy but directionless. In many ways my life was unchanged. However, the ocean called to me in misty tones that I would not, could not, deny. I was able to get in a couple of dives a month that barely satisfied my longing.

My body had become strong through basketball, and with the strength came boldness, and with boldness came risk. One afternoon, after locating several abalones down in a V-shaped crevice, I wiggled down to where I could just get the ab iron under one, pry it loose, and with my fingertips lift it free, then squirm my way out of the wedge to freedom and air. Having pulled three in this fashion, the fourth was deep into the V and I was able to pry it loose, but it slipped from my grasp and fell to the bottom of the V. Wiggling down to where I could just reach it, I realized too late I had solidly wedged myself between the rocks. There was nothing to grasp, no protruding rocks, nothing to gain purchase to lift free. Already I had expended energy trying to get the abalone and was out of breath. In the last moments a thin crack revealed itself along the wall of the V near my face, and I jammed the abalone pry bar into the crack and was then able to push myself free.

So it went over the course of several years. As I probed deeper into the reefs, my confidence returned as did my intuitive feel for the sea.

My interest, as always, gravitated to big fish. The big sheepshead I had seen that first day back at Salt Creek continued to swim in my imagination. Sheepshead are a thick, meaty fish with a large head and prominent jaws used to crush mussels, crabs and other crustaceans. The males, somewhat larger and far more colorful than the drab females,

have a bright-red body attached to a black head
with splashes of white on the lips, bottom jaw and
belly. Their meat is an acquired taste, having an
odd texture much like crabmeat. But it is the largest fish to inhabit the coastal reefs of Southern
California. The small spear gun was inadequate for
this tough skinned fish, motivating purchase of a
longer, more powerful spear gun. The spear gun,
bought for a hundred dollars, an unheard of price
in 1967, was a Sea Hunter, with far greater capacity than was required for sheepshead, turned out
to be an over-built disaster. The three bands of rubber, each with a hundred and twenty pounds of force
when pulled back five feet to the very butt of the
gun, was formidable when finally cocked. However,
if more than three shots were taken within twenty
minutes, I would quiver with tension in pulling back
the final rubber and was often unable to cock the
gun. The most notable feature of this spear gun was
its penchant for randomly firing the spear shaft
without the trigger being pulled, discouraging com-
panionship of even the bravest souls.

The Sea Hunter, really designed for big game fish,
became the impetus for my first trip down to Cabo
San Lucas with Sam and Leo, whereby they imparted their philosophy of job and life, forcing me
to further question my direction. Upon our return
from Cabo San Lucas, Sam and Leo insisted that I
should have a boat (primarily because they didn't),
and if I wanted to learn how to hunt big fish, it
would have to be at Catalina Island where the white
sea bass and yellowtail swam.

My experience with boats was limited to having
ridden in them. Needing a boat that could be lived
on so as to defer the expense of owning such a

luxury, and one that would get me to Catalina, I
wound up paying too much for an old Owens cabin
cruiser *The Gamine*, twenty-two feet long, with a
gas-eating Chevy engine. The first time I ran over
to the island in pre-dawn darkness, the running
light switches created a magnetic field around the
compass throwing if off by twenty degrees and we
missed the island. On that first trip I came across
a white sea bass and mistook it for a shark. Plainly
I had moved into water where I could not see bottom, out beyond the jetties of Hawaii, and the reefs
of Salt Creek, to the blue edge where Kamo swam.

Here in the late twentieth century, the gods of
sun and rain (bear and owl) have been driven into
oblivion. We of this century claim no gods of weather
and none for animals, but we are misled for buried
deep in our collective unconscious swims the shark,
the last of the animal gods. The sea god lives in
modern man as surely as the snake and the raven
lived in Native American culture. The image of the
shark is not carved on totems or etched in rock but
resides in the caves of movie theaters and in the
household totems we call television. We flock to
worship the larger than life images on the big
screen. It is where we safely go to probe the unknown and sometimes dangerous world that dwells
beneath the surface of the ocean and lurks in the
hidden recesses of our ancient minds. Our culture
has ingrained in us the fear of sharks, lumping it
all in a general fear of the unknown in the ocean.
Cultures have manipulated the unknown into fear
since emissaries from the sun thirsted for the blood
of virgins according to the shamans who made such
interpretations, and ours is no different. For as
advanced as we may think we are, when it comes

to the shark, there is little distance between us and our ancient brothers and sisters.

With the purchase of the boat, I motored into a realm I was psychologically unprepared to explore. In the blue water, with no illusion of protection from reef or kelp forest, the specter of the shark loomed ceaselessly. Silently Kamo circled my frontal lobes. It was larger than all other sharks, for it had been fed from birth with myth and movie, story and lie, until, in the silence of blue water where no bottom can be seen, it swam in wait.

In the open ocean the free diving hunter is exposed from all quarters. It is futile to try and defend oneself in this position. The sense of vulnerability is excruciating, and attack, like a phantom limb, is felt from the exposed blind side. It is impossible to be a competent hunter harboring this sort of fear. Moreover, these fears effectively blocked my ability to "feel" the ocean that had guided me around the reefs, further compounding my sense of vulnerability.

Over the next few years of hunting in the blue water, I discovered the irony of my dilemma revealed in its solution; I had to place my faith and trust in this delicate "feel" and give myself over to it. This left the body no choice but to surrender to its primal need to survive. In making this separation I would induce an urgency to develop a "feel" for the open water simply in order to protect myself. Despite a continued racking sense of vulnerability, I placed my trust and faith in this rather obscure and delicate intuitive feel for the sea. There seemed no other way. Ironically, it was the real presence of the shark, which ultimately forced this feel or intuition to be firmly developed and applied.

In the course of my ocean wanderings I began to come across other blue water hunters, chiefly members of the spearfishing club The Long Beach Neptunes, who at that time, along with the San Diego Bottom Scratchers, were the most accomplished spearfishermen on the West Coast. As a tight-knit, rather obscure community, they were characterized by a strong sense of competition among themselves and a quiet sort of machismo that was reflected in the simple rules governing their actions in the water. All fish must be taken on a breath-hold, without assistance from any other divers, no matter what the depth or the circumstances, and never leave a fish once speared. To use scuba or any other breathing aid to retrieve a fish was defeat.

For the most part, these men and the blue water hunting they practiced existed far outside the mainstream of diving. Few beyond their tribe knew they existed at all. Their only interest outside of spearing the largest and most difficult fish to stalk was to impress one another with their accomplishments and near-escapes from tight situations.

It was with this group that I began to explore the far reaches of the Sea of Cortez (the Gulf) in the latter part of the 1960's and through the 1970's.

Prior to 1972 when the paved road completed the thousand-mile length of the Baja Peninsula, linking Cabo San Lucas with Tijuana, the Sea of Cortez and the land which enclosed it, particularly its western shore (the peninsula), were as wild as the unsettled regions of Africa until the late 1950's. The brutally rugged terrain of Baja kept the Gulf effectively inaccessible to the outside world, and its pristine beauty and rich waters virtually unspoiled.

The few Americans who did reach the Gulf were

generally fishermen who flew down by small plane, and only they and the Mexicans ever managed to land the grouper, *pez fuerte* (amberjack), dorado, pargo (snapper), rooster fish, wahoo and tuna that schooled in this wild spit of salt water. The Mexican fleet, what there was of it, was comprised of shrimpers and bottom dredgers who did not seek out the powerful fish that would invariably tear their nets to shreds. The Mexican fishermen confined the nets to small fish and left the big ones for the occasional hand line.

It was into this virgin water, teeming with big fish and sharks, untouched and certainly unseen by man, that I made my pilgrimage. For a young man with limited means, it was the ideal adventure that was to run non-stop for twelve years.

A hundred miles beyond the American-Mexican border one entered another time. It was not unusual to see *vaqueros* on horseback herding cattle, or feral mules wandering across unfenced roadways. When the paved road ended, one was alone in a harsh and unforgiving desert. To arrive at the shoreline of the Gulf on the peninsula side was an exercise in resolve and preparation, and necessitated a sound vehicle. A breakdown was catastrophic. It took weeks, sometimes months for car parts to be found and then replaced. Much of the adventure was in the attempt to reach the Gulf's waters.

Seven months after the trip to Cabo San Lucas with Sam and Leo I made a run by car on a paved road along the eastern edge of the Gulf to San Carlos Bay. The road through the desert was stark and uninviting with arid winds and unadorned yuccas and far coffee-colored mountain ranges cast with boulders thrown up from the ice age. In vivid contrast the waters of the Gulf were so rich in color one could believe he could dip a hand into its stream and smear its blueness on his skin. This contrasted sharply with the awareness that beneath the turquoise calm a river of blood ran from the mouths of sharks that would shred sea lions, turtles and anything else into pink ribbons.

In San Carlos the hunting for me was uneventful. I was a novice and knew nothing of the hunting grounds or the techniques required for hunting the grouper that drifted in deep underwater canyons. The Long Beach Neptunes were there, and it was through them I was able to secure phone numbers of hunters living near me in the States. Eight months later in 1970, Frank Taylor of San Diego rang me up and proposed a trip. He, along with Jack Pesh, were going to trailer Frank's eighteen-foot open boat down to San Felipe, the most northern town inside the Gulf, then make a ninety-mile run by water to Gonzaga Bay. There we would rendezvous with other divers and hunt what is called the Midriff, the most northern islands in the Gulf, east of Gonzaga.

The road to San Felipe was one of the few paved, and the overland ride, though long at twenty hours, went without a hitch. We launched the following day, and under perfect conditions ran south on a glassy sea, stopping once for fuel in Puertecitos. Then we made our way to the most northern island in the Midriff chain called Salvatierra, though it went by different names depending on whom you asked.

Here, finally, was the grouper, the most powerful and dangerous fish a free diver could hunt. Dan-

gerous because one had to dive very deep for long
periods and then wrestle a fish, whose power was
unprecedented, to the surface. With all this before
me, my only question to Frank as I stood poised to
jump, was if the sharks were aggressive. To which
he replied, "Just get the fish in the boat as quick as
you can."

The water was far different from Cabo San Lucas,
or even San Carlos. The visibility was torpid with
life. Clouds of nearly transparent, minute fish swam
just under the surface; beneath them schools of silver and blue bait fish meandered, and below them
cabrilla, the free-swimming sierra mackerel and
skip jacks. And in the depths rested the lords of
the Gulf, the grouper. Moving cautiously, I inched
my way along in visibility that was less than thirty-
five feet. The lack of visibility fed a fertile imagination that envisioned sharks forever patrolling on
its dim edges.

Within twenty minutes I stumbled across a grouper weighing forty pounds and managed to spear it
without too much difficulty. It was similar to working a large sheepshead out of the rocks and up to
the surface. Still, the grouper was the largest fish I
had ever speared and, heeding Frank's advice, I
swam it quickly to the boat. After depositing the
fish I reentered the water and swam south, as before, but further from the island, out into deeper
water. There I dropped down to fifty feet settling
on a large boulder that rested on a slope, which fell
away to bottom barely visible at seventy feet. Stilled
on the boulder, I watched a black shape rising from
the bottom. It was a fish, as large as a man, its
head the size of the fish I had just speared. The
grouper drew within ten feet and turned broadside.

Letting the spear fly, it struck the fish in the side. It exploded down the slope with an awesome force, the line moving off the reel faster than I could keep pace, dragging me down the slope towards the bottom. In those moments time stretched into liquid warps that fused exhilaration and anxiety into a mind-boggling ride. When the fish stopped running I turned for the surface kicking hard, line running off the reel, light-headed from lack of air, looking for sharks, in way over my head. It was the longest ascent I had ever made, and not one I would wish to make again. On the surface, gasping breaths behind a pounding heart, I waited for the sharks, sure they would come from the commotion. Wanting no part of another dive to depth, and anxious to leave, I gathered up the slack line until it was taut, leading directly to the fish, then yanked hard, kicking furiously until exhausted. The fish gave not an inch. I might well have been attempting to lift a car. After several minutes my breathing settled down and I was left with no choice but to make a dive.

Hyperventilating deep breaths, the last filling to full lung capacity, I descended, pulling myself hand-over-hand down the line to my depth limit of fifty feet, then into the dark unfriendly depths beyond. At sixty-five feet the line ran into a cave with a three-foot opening. The end of the spearshaft protruded from the upper portion of the cave. Grasping it, I gave it a pull. Nothing. The fish did not budge. Pulling again, hard, still nothing. Then putting both feet against the cave for additional leverage, I heaved on the spearshaft and the fish suddenly released, causing me to fall over backward out of breath. The grouper was nearly as large as

me. Impossible to lift it as well as myself back to
the surface, particularly at the end of the breath-
hold at that depth, so pushing off and leaving the
fish, I began the long ascent to the surface. The
same instincts guided the grouper back to the
depths. Knowing that I'd never be able to retrieve
it if it holed up further down, I grabbed the line to
which it was attached and continued to kick toward
a surface that was as distant as another sky. Halfway up the taut line stopped me short, the fish and
I suspended in the mid-water column, swimming
in opposite directions, moving nowhere. The moment was held. Desperate for air and prepared to
release the line, I felt the fish give, and we were
moving again, straining, heart pounding, breaking
through the surface, completely limp from the effort.

Weakly pulling the fish to my hand and finally
securing it, a cloud of rusty blood formed around
me, releasing the sharks from my previously occupied mind. Finding energy in my fear, I swam to
the boat a hundred yards away.

Later, sitting in the boat staring at the single
fish filling the aft section between the gas tanks
and the rear seat, it was difficult to believe that I
had taken such a fish on a breath-hold, and after
having done so, was no closer to explaining how it
was done.

Frank and Jack returned to the boat empty
handed, and I considered my good fortune to be the
product of beginner's luck. But it was not treated
as such by the other hunters we met back in
Gonzaga. In this new world a man's salt was not
measured by the stories he told, but by a single
achievement—fish in the boat. Mike Oceanus and

Bob Donnell, two of the very best hunters on the West Coast, offered congratulations and warmly welcomed me into their tight community.

The next day three boats of divers went out to Salvatierra Island to hunt grouper. The hunt did not go well for me, and while I did spear a fish, it was not nearly as large as the one the day before. Nor were the other divers having much luck, and realizing early that the fish would be scarce, Bob Donnell indicated that he would swim to another island about a mile and a half away, and that we could meet up with him over there. "Maybe I'll pop a yellow on the way," he said. In my mind it was a dangerous swim over open water, and if he did spear a fish and was by himself, he could have problems with sharks. Bob made the swim, speared a yellow-tail which he strung to himself, then speared another. When the boat arrived several hours later, he quietly deposited the two fish and continued on with the hunt. The moment left a lasting impression, for clearly, if I wanted to hunt and experience the full effect of roaming freely about in the ocean, I would have to do it in the fearless fashion exhibited by Bob D.

In the years to come I came to know Bob D. and dove with him frequently. He was not a careless or foolish man, nor was he as free from fear as I first imagined him to be. He understood that the only way to hunt effectively in blue water was without fear, for fear obstructed the ability to read the environment and eventually become integrated into it. It was also a common belief that fear drew sharks, as it draws mean spirited dogs to those terrified of them.

To exorcise the shark from the myth of my childhood would require actual encounters in the water with its flesh and tooth. The shark had to exist outside my mind where I could put a name to it, see it, feel its energy and power, and begin to understand its true nature.

Guardian Angel is the largest of all islands in the Gulf. It sits high in the northern section of the Gulf some thirty miles from the nearest land and said to be infested with rattlesnakes. Few boats other than shrimpers ever visited the island. The underpowered fishing pangas of the Mexicans were far too fragile for the volatile seas driven by strong, unpredictable winds that could blow from any direction. Guardian Angel was so named because at its most northern tip is a protected bay called Refugio, sheltered as it is on all sides including the northerly entrance where lies a long, low island, the home of a large population of sea lions. Refugio Bay on Guardian Angel Island was the destination of Frank Taylor, Bill Brown and myself in the fall of 1972.

Ours was the second expedition of spearfishermen to reach Refugio. Beyond the logistics of such a trip, luck had to play a significant role for anyone to succeed. The boats used were small, for they had to be trailered down on poor roads that could not bear heavy loads. The light boats were not capable of withstanding strong winds and seas, which could easily abort a carefully planned expedition. Additionally, if one were to get into trouble, there was no help in those waters—no Coast Guard or radio contact of any kind. You were on your own.

We pounded down in Frank's boat from San Felipe to Gonzaga. Spending half a day looking for fuel, finally locating thirty gallons in a ramshackle ghost of a fishing village inhabited by a mad hermit who said he had been waiting for us for eighteen years. The fuel was older than sand, equally as dirty, and we had to filter it through our tee shirts before pouring it into the fuel tanks. The following day we set out for the island. The wind blew hard from the east directly into our faces and seas swept over the bow burying the small boat up to the windshield. Trailing behind us were Bill Green and Dwayne Smith who had driven to Gonzaga and launched an inflatable, and though we broke their seas, they too were taking a beating. As we ducked yet another wave that blew over the bow and into the open cockpit, Frank, an Annapolis graduate and Navy commander, turned to me who knew next to nothing about Gulf waters and asked if we should turn around. Unhesitatingly, I barked out a yes.

Returning to the peninsula, we made camp on an isolated beach intending to try again early the following morning. At the edge of dawn in a stillness that could seize one's step, we departed. Taking full advantage of the break, we sped over a glassy sea and in two-and-a-half hours, reached the island.

There is something enormously exhilarating about seeing something few have seen. This majestic island rose in vertical, jagged edged escarpments, maroon and primordial out of the Capri blue, both sea and island as wild as the day they were born. Rock formations stood as spires remote as the moon, monolithic edifices of another older time that the light had washed clean and pure. Above us, thick flocks of gull and pelican wheeled at the strange sighting of boat and man, their cries ringing in the pristine air. The heart, knowing well beyond the mind what country had been entered and, perhaps in anticipation of what would be encountered beneath the surface, skipped a beat, stealing the breath.

On the most northerly outside edge of the island, we anchored the boat and suited up. I dropped down through clouds of minute fish that obscured visibility. Beneath them, layer upon layer of baitfish hovered, each school larger than the last. Turtles and yellowtail meandered in the mid-water column and in the depths, darkened by the layers of fish above. Gigantic shadowy shapes of grouper prowled among fallen boulders. It was difficult to relax and maintain a breath-hold in such water. At fifty-five feet I settled on top of a twenty-foot-high boulder, and from all around, grouper, larger than could ever be imagined, well over a hundred pounds, drifted up from the depths to the base of the boulder. Utterly fearless, the mammoth fish eyed me with curious disdain. When I rose for a breath they would drift off and then gather again when I returned to the boulder. Over the course of an hour some came to within ten feet of me. Frank and Bill dropped down to the boulder and beheld the grouper, and we named the place the Round Table, for the grouper possessed the somber nobility of knights gathering for council.

We were in no rush to spear a fish, having settled into the dream, the dream every hunter from the plains of Kenya to the jungles of Borneo has shared—that is to come upon a place teeming with animals, never seen nor touched by man. There was something deeply inviting in this wilderness, as if conferred by a higher order, at once humbling and stirring. At the core of my feelings, not yet fully realized, the thing observed would change as I would change in ways unknown.

The beauty was everywhere, but it was the power of the place that transfixed. Large animals move differently than small ones. Accustomed to ruling their domain, they are rarely challenged. The strong have no enemy; the weak have long been weeded out. All that remain are the superior residents: the knights, queens and kings, who move with regal disdain, and observe as a lion or a cape buffalo might observe, fearlessly and with indifference.

As I lay on the boulder, a six-foot shark scurried in from the periphery. Without the scent of blood to encourage, it drifted off and out of sight. Here, the hunter and the hunted were interchangeable, with never a clear line distinguishing the two. This was wilderness in its purest form. It was not difficult to understand why men went deep into jungles, climbed to the peaks of high mountains, and sailed dangerous seas to far places from which they might never return.

I had never been more alive in my life than in those moments under the water on that boulder.

We did not spear fish that first day, but could not restrain ourselves on the second. We had come a great distance with considerable effort to hunt the biggest fish we could find, and we had found them. However, none in the party had ever speared fish this size. Our equipment was untested, and my experience and disposition as fragile as the equipment. Because so few hunters had speared fish this large and so little information had been passed on, we, for all intent and purpose, were the first, or so it seemed. All that I really knew about hunting grouper was to try and make a kill shot, and failing that, attempt to turn the fish to prevent it from holing up. Judging by the size of the fish, I was quite confident I could achieve neither.

Despite misgivings, I dove to the boulder at the Round Table and lay in wait. Several grouper moved near the base of the boulder but not quite close enough for a good shot within the length of my breath-hold. Four times I dove the boulder and waited, and on the fifth dive was able to get within range and let the spear fly. The fish, like a runaway train, barreled off with instantaneous power, towing me along the bottom with such force that had I turned sideways my face mask would have been pulled off, giving me no time to consider if, in the interests of my own safety, I should let go. (This rush of speed, initially frightening, came to be in later years, an exhilarating and manageable ride). The fish stopped running after holing up in a cave at sixty feet. Breath gone, I rushed to the surface, adrenaline leaving me jittery and unable to regain my breath for nearly five minutes. In that time I gathered up the slack line so that it ran directly above the cave. Regaining my breath, I pumped up and dropped down. The grouper was bleeding, its dark blood leaking through cracks in the roof of the cave. Reaching the entrance which laid close to the bottom, I squeezed in and found the end of the spearshaft in the low light and gave it a pull. Nothing budged, the fish in the dark of the cave could scarcely be seen, and was wedged in solid. I tried to reach further and get a hold of the gill plate, and had a grip on it when a strong notion came over me. I instantly released the gill plate and backed out of the cave. Turning, I very nearly ran into a shark that hovered five feet away. It was a thing of awesome presence: a sixteen footer (by all accounts), species unknown, heavy in girth, wide across the head, with stout pectorals. (Aside from whale sharks, this would be the largest shark I would encounter in the Gulf.) Looking directly into its smiling mouth, I was oddly unafraid. The shark moved slowly and unthreatening over my head and around the cave, while I remained reasonably safe on the bottom, protected by an enclosure of reef. When finally I needed a breath, the frail sense of security evaporated as I was forced to release from the bottom. Rising in mid-water was to become vulnerable, and when I was in that position, the shark slid away from the bottom and angled beneath me, its dorsal so large I had to lift my fins to avoid hitting it. The shark followed me halfway up and began to circle ten feet from where I lay on the surface. After a few moments, it settled back down on the cave and made lazy loops atop the blood spoored cave. Lifting my head from the water, I looked across the surface for other divers, but none were about. The boat was anchored a hundred yards away, and I considered swimming to it and waiting. Putting my head back in the water to check on the shark, I found it had vanished. After waiting several minutes it still didn't return and I dropped again on the fish. Inside the cave I heaved on the grouper in near frantic gestures, but could not dislodge it. In need of air, I backed out, turned to ascend and almost plowed into the same shark that had moved to within a foot of my back. I had never felt its presence. Quite possibly my anxiety had prevented me from sensing it as I had previously. The shark startled as I jumped, thoroughly unnerved, and now it moved with agitation. I lifted gently from the bottom and pushed steadily to the surface while it circled back toward me then lost interest as I gained altitude, and returned to the blood spoor. I had had enough and quickly headed to the boat, calling in the other divers. Though familiar with the unwritten law that no matter the circumstances, one must go to any length to retrieve a speared fish, I was at a loss as to how this would be done.

The shark was still circling the cave when we brought the boat over. It was decided to run the boat at high speed back and forth in the hope it would scare off, but it remained unmoved by the gesture. Left with no choice, I had to drop in with a scuba unit while divers covered me from above. It was a defeat to use scuba, rather than free dive, but the shark was too big and I was too intimidated to continue making myself vulnerable by free diving around a bleeding fish. I also began to doubt my ability to work the fish out of the cave at that depth on a breath-hold. The scuba made it easy; I was able to work on the fish as the shark circled, extract it, and bring it up without incident.

We had no scale but all agreed the fish weighed well over a hundred pounds. Later in the day, Frank landed one about the same size. For the next three days we covered most of Refugio, and in my explorations came across a grouper that was well over two hundred pounds, twice the size of the one I had landed. I was within three feet of it but did not pull off, for we had established a limit and would only spear what we could carry back to the States in ice chests.

Near the end of the week we discovered a shallow reef in forty feet of water that held more grouper than the Round Table. We dove and interacted with these mammoth fish but refrained from spearing any. I had brought a super eight underwater movie camera and was content to spend the days shooting footage of these magnificent animals so in possession of their realm, so far away from man.

It is one thing to spear a big fish out in deep water, it is quite another to be the first to do so. Over the next five years we never knew what to expect in the Gulf. Sharks were always a factor in every jump, and though they continued to circle my frontal lobes, it was not with the same fervent preoccupation. We would see them, often big, but seldom aggressive. They would swim in after a fish was speared, but rarely challenged the diver for the fish once it was in hand. Over time I grew confident, even reckless. Often big sharks were seen near sea lion colonies, which was always dangerous, for it indicated they had developed a taste for sick or wounded sea lion, which was more or less the profile of a swimming free diver. But if big fish were there, and it felt right, I would dive the sea lion colony. It was as if I were confronting whatever fear I held and at the same time stretching my powers to feel sharks before they would appear.

One afternoon, years after the first Guardian Angel trip, my confidence was shaken when diving Coronado Island off Loreto. I had speared a yellowtail and was casual about pulling it in. A dark shadow came very close across my left shoulder and the shark hit the fish when it was just five feet off my hand. I had a drag line and yanked back hard on it, for I didn't want to lose the spear shaft and point. Half the fish went with the shark, the other half drifted to the depths. The entire episode lasted six seconds, yet was replayed later by the hours. I never felt the shark coming, never knew it was there, and it caused me to reexamine my capacity to sense the presence of sharks, a reminder that would repeat itself often in the ensuing years. Sharks are in the main, predictable, but there is always the odd exception. The rogue shark, perhaps the most dangerous of all, is usually a weakened or older shark that can no longer compete with healthy sharks for food. In this deprived state it will prey on anything that appears sick or injured, as free divers seem when swimming on the surface. Rather than first bumping its victim as a healthy shark would do to determine the state of its prey, the rogue can afford no such luxury and, driven by hunger, will simply bite at the first opportunity. Thus I could never relax or feel confident that I was somehow immune from their constant if unseen presence.

Throughout the 1970's blue water hunters ruled the Gulf like the Masai ruled the East African plain. From the beginning it felt like the waters of the Gulf were sacred, traveled but once for the first time. Such journeys change men. Civilization harbors a great deal of past and too much future in the form of security, money, women, material goods, getting ahead and falling behind. In the Gulf, civilization and all it represented was replaced by the immediate present, where all pretense of self and past and future were forgotten, erased from consciousness, washed clean by the sea itself. My mind, body and spirit had, for the first time as an adult, room to breathe large breaths.

The Gulf swam through me and swept me away from myself. The more time I spent in those waters the more difficult it became to return to life in the

States. Life, real life, had been redefined. All else appeared, if not false, then superficial. Hunting in the Gulf became my religion as it became the religion of the other hunters. I watched all manner of man change from the experience. Some had difficulty in returning to a culture that demanded less, exchanged little and seemed incomparably tame. They lived for the hunt and the hunt was in the Gulf; everything else became killing time between jumps.

I returned to Guardian Angel Island on seven different occasions, and led other spearfishermen to the Round Table. We all kept to the one fish limit. But as I have recounted in my book, *Secret Seas*, when we began using the Mexicans' converted shrimpers as liveaboards, we unwittingly led the Mexicans to the hunting grounds. Marking the spots and taking bearings, they would return, unbeknownst to us, with American line fishermen and within a fifteen-year period, wipe out all the big grouper in Refugio Bay. The loss, coming with a large measure of guilt, was incomprehensible, staggering and terribly sad. To this day it is difficult to believe that those majestic fish, in numbers uncountable, are forever gone.

# DAY
# 16

J ack wants to jump the rock a quarter mile off Cerralvo in the morning to look for wahoo, so we return to the anchorage of last night. The seas build during the evening and Pam has a difficult time in the galley. Nevertheless, we eat a tasty lasagna with a cucumber salad for dinner. As the seas continue to rise Jack sets a stern hook to minimize the roll. We are getting five-foot swells in the cove, and twice during the night Jack goes topside to adjust the anchor line. It is a sleepless night for all.

Up at dawn, the skies the color of dull steel, we are staring into the teeth of a major weather front. Six-foot swells roll in and crash on the beach one hundred fifty yards behind the *Nirvana*. Undaunted by the change in weather, Jack is determined to jump the rock for wahoo. Out of the rather dubious protection of the cove, the seas run seven feet. These are not the rolling swells of the Pacific, but near vertical walls of water fetching out of the narrow passage between the peninsula and Cerralvo from the north.

Reaching the rock where the swells have increased to ten feet with occasional twelve-footers, Jack asks if he should still make the jump. Pam looks at me before I can answer and voices her concern. "This is crazy."

"It's do-able," I say. "I mean I've seen worse." Pam shakes her head; she can't believe we are going through with this. I excuse myself to go down in the head. This will be my last chance for a while. While peeing, I look out the porthole, which is battened down and for the most part, very nearly under the water. Pam is right; a jump here is crazy. We could lose Jack in an instant, never be able to pick him up. I had jumped into water just off Catalina to film dolphins in far lighter seas than this and the boat lost sight of me. I drifted, waving at the boat sometimes not a hundred feet away. It took two hours to find me and only because the boat practically ran me down. On another occasion a neighbor in the slip next to mine watched his stepson fall overboard when the boom swung unexpectedly. Unhurt, he waved from the surface, smiling; everyone on board laughed as they swung around to pick him up. In moderate seas they never found him.

In the pitching boat I lurch my way topside to the cockpit where Jack and Pam are arguing. I recant and agree with Pam; the jump is too risky. Pam breathes a sigh of relief and thanks me unnecessarily. My initial response was born long ago when in the Gulf, great obstacles were overcome through acts of will alone. Often necessary in the early days of trekking into these waters, but inappropriate here. Jack accepts my judgment and we abort the jump. However, now we have another problem that reflects the foolishness of the scheme; we must hoist the inflatable aboard in what are now raging seas and powerful winds, and secure it to the deck. The plan is for me to steer into the heart of the wind and seas while Jack and Pam muscle the skiff up on the foredeck near the bow by way of the jib halyard. Appropriately, I have been given the job that requires neither courage nor balance on the pitching deck. I must hold concentration though, for if the boat swings even slightly in these seas, it would have serious consequence. The waves could easily turn us sideways and roll the boat, washing both Jack and Pam overboard.

At one point, Pam is on the bow as the boat drops into a wave trough that produces an oncoming wall of water that towers over her by fifteen feet. She crouches low, gripping the railing with both hands, awaiting the wave that will surely envelope her. But the *Nirvana* rides up and up and up and over the cresting wave that blows its ten-gallon froth over Pam, losing her in the frosting of this reckless sea. She emerges drenched but relieved to still be on the deck. Together she and Jack hoist the skiff on board, the wind catching it once. It flies off, crashing into Pam and nearly throwing her overboard again. But they get it down and secured, and have distinguished themselves. Jack is fearless, and a show of courage is almost expected. Pam, however, is an unknown, and her bravery and skill impress me. What is more remarkable she never makes a show of her skills. It appears she has a better grasp of the fine art of sail trimming than does Jack, and it was she that spotted the rising water temperature and averted what could have been a serious problem. Later, I learn she is also a technical rock climber having achieved a 5.9 climb at Joshua Tree.

We head off for Partida in heavy seas, and I, having been seasick twice in my life, am becoming ill enough to take a pill. I don't lose it but it is close; bets are taken that I would.

# DAY
# 17

After anchoring last night in Partida, we head up to Los Islotes. About a dozen sea lions are in the water; the males are aggressive and will not allow us near the shore. As we get close to them there is a lot of underwater barking and air expulsion, head shaking from side to side and mock biting. We get the message and return to the boat when Jack is hit with a Portuguese man-o-war across his right bicep, chest and face. He is in severe pain and Pam, who is also lightly hit, swaths Jack in vinegar-soaked paper towels. My left ear is a bit tight from deep dives on Cerralvo, so we content ourselves to watch the sea lions interact on the shoreline.

Ear trouble is a free diver's malady. On an average day a free diver might make sixty to seventy-five dives. (A scuba diver usually makes one or two dives a day.) Each time down, the ears must be cleared via the Eustachian tube, three to five times depending on the depth of the dive. Building pressures can often squeeze fluid into the Eustachian tube, making it difficult to force air up and into the eardrum to equalize the inner ear pressure with the external water pressure. If the diver is unable to equalize the pain becomes too intolerable to dive. Until 1978 when I was guiding a trip to Guardian Angel, I never had trouble with my ears. After spearing a grouper that had holed up in fifty-five feet, I was forced to make repeated dives to try and wrestle it out of a small cave. A dozen dives later I was having to continually clear my ears, and never having had an ear problem, did not recognize the symptoms. By evening I was in excruciating pain in both ears. It was the second day of a ten-day trip and no treatment was available. The pain was unbearable and had me eating little and sleeping hardly at all. After the fifth day I became somewhat delirious and was taken ashore at Bahia de Los Angeles during a windstorm. They dropped me off with the idea I might catch a ride back to the States. The wind was blowing offshore at sixty knots, and there were no light planes leaving. When I tried to catch a ride by car, people stared scornfully and backed away. It occurred to me later they probably thought I was strung out on drugs. I wandered out on the airstrip, sat down in the middle of the runway and began to sob in pain and delirium. Somebody finally rescued me and found a boat that would take me back to the dive boat. At the end of the trip, when finally I was able to get to a hospital, they discovered my eardrums to be so distended that they wanted to take photographs for medical journals. In lieu of the permanent status afforded my eardrums in the memoirs of medical mishaps, I demanded instead for relief. Within thirty minutes after an injection, the pain was gone. Having not slept in almost ten days, I found myself in an awake dream state, where the music of Souza played in

my head, and wild hallucinations came upon me in
clarity so profound I remember them to this day. In
the months that followed I lost eighty percent of
my hearing in my left ear and fifty percent in my
right ear. Eventually, I regained my hearing, but
my left ear has never been the same. When diving
deep, it is highly susceptible to a middle ear block-
age and is now slowly going deaf.

Near dusk we head south with a light wind on
our beam. A half-mile out of Los Islotes the wind
and seas increase. I suggest that, what with a beam
reach, we raise a sail. On a lark, Jack unfurls the
jib and kills the engine, and we enjoy the breeze.
Soon the seas build and the wind increases. Instantly we are in five-foot seas and twenty-five-knot
winds. There is too much sail out and the jib becomes fouled when we attempt to roll it in. Jack
drops the main and sails on the fouled jib.

Night falls and we are without anchorage. The
seas are coming out of the west directly into the
normally protected anchorages. We must settle on
the best available while sailing on the jib, and enter a cove black as ink, feeling our way to its apex,
sliding by other boats at anchor. With the rolling
seas and possible wind changes during the night,
Jack must be prudent in his assessment of a safe
anchorage, all this under sail, with little room to
maneuver. Jack settles on a spot and we let out all
sheets and, with lines whipping in the wind, drop
anchor.

We are anchored in only twelve feet of water and
Jack remains anxious throughout the night. This
is the price of responsibility, not one I would covet.
Sailing, of late, has become more of an effort than
the diving. These last days have beaten us all up.

Nicks and bruises add up and lack of sleep takes
its toll. Strange maladies play out on boats. Pam
has somehow driven a piece of wire filing through
the nail of a finger and into the flesh. She can't
pull it out and infection is beginning. Jack, as fit
as anyone, is decidedly slowed by the man-of-war
hit, and my lower abdomen has been in pain for
the last day and a half. Jack mentions that I don't
look well and I confess my illness. Pam concludes
by my symptoms that I have a urinary tract infection as a result of severe dehydration experienced
four days ago. I was suited up ready to jump and
had to stop and make adjustments with the camera that required breaking down the housing and
removing the camera, all in a wet suit in the heat
of mid-day. Sweating excessively, I neglected to re-
place the lost fluids, so now the pain mounts and I
take antibiotics for the same illness she suffered
before my arrival.

# DAY
# 18

In the morning under gossamer clouds we sail out of Partida and into a soft west swell. We are heading south to a cove outside of La Paz that offers more protection from the west winds. Jack had a restless night, fearing we might bottom out on low tide, but his fears went unrealized. We are all tired and look to rest up this day. After finding suitable anchorage we have decided to lay low and confine our activities to meals, sleep and reading. Or so I am led to believe.

Jack, forever restless, is anxious to hunt. Getting him to just sit and relax is futile; better he launch the skiff and make a jump. Several hours later he returns and reports no sightings of grouper or cabrilla. He speaks of the depth of his dives and how long he stayed down, but little mention of the fish or their habits. He refers to his wristwatch that in addition to giving the correct time, is also a depth gauge and measures time on the bottom.

I have never used a depth gauge. Over the years the depth of a dive became a knowing. I could know almost to the foot how deep I was at any give time. Technology has wormed its way so deep into our lives that we can't conceive of operating without it, allowing it to perform functions that are thought to be beyond us. How could such a thing take over so fast? Jack is unaware that his wristwatch is undermining his ability to use the finest computer he will ever possess—himself. However, it is stealing more than information. It is preoccupying his attention from the world of nature under the water to the world of linear time and space. The natural world is not constrained by such properties, and to operate effectively in it one must be willing to yield to the realization that his connection to the environment runs deeper than the culture and the technology, deeper even than his personal beliefs. The voice of the natural world speaks to the core of man's intuitive knowledge and calls us to use this inherited intelligence.

If Jack were to surrender to his intuition, there would no doubt be a period of adjustment that would include moments of vulnerability, but a sense of himself as a part of the natural world would begin to develop. The use and play of untapped knowledge and its accompanying view would offer him a far broader perspective of nature, and provide him with an internal map for its exploration.

The scuba diver who brings his linear world of technology into the wilderness with him must divide his attention between the two, or he might well get himself into trouble. The breath-hold diver is free from these encumbrances, moving as a bird on a thermocline, observing the subtle world of the ocean often missed by the scuba diver; a nubble of lobster antenna among the maze of reef and cave; the quarter inch of a single eye of the halibut protruding above a vast flat of sand; the tick of a fish tail in a darkened cave; the faint lip of a scallop lost in the reef; the camouflaged eye of the octopus filling crack and rock. Behavior is observed, connections made between species of fish and their environment. Pieces of the ocean puzzle float loosely at first, then slowly begin tying into one another, becoming not fragments of information but a web of connection. One ultimately discovers one to be a strand within the web, that nothing floats free from anything else; all is linked to one, one is linked to all. There comes the inescapable realization that to harm the web in any way ultimately destroys oneself.

# DAY
## 19

S everal hours after sunrise, with the wind coming out of the north, we head into the channel
that is the entry into the Bay of La Paz. On the
outgoing tide, the current runs about four knots.
Motoring at six knots, it will take us well over an
hour to reach Marina de La Paz. The going is slow
and the most dominant presence, apart from the
sky that in the northern vector is dark and ominous, is the sound of this small city. There is a grind
to it. I think the sound comes from traffic noise,
but it is indistinguishable when heard from the water and melds into an omnipresent sound that is
insidious in its invisibility. It is the very same sound
I would hear after returning from many months at
sea in California. There, the sound could be heard
ten miles from land, a sickly rumble as if God were
clearing His lungs. It was the sound of industry
chewing up the resources; the cries of children and
the aged strangled by steel hands, of butterflies
caught in the whirling blades of lawnmowers. The
grinding would grow louder as I neared the Long
Beach Marina, and once in my slip, I would stay
sealed up in my boat for days until my psyche could

conjure up the barriers needed to go out into the day and meet the world. Eventually, when the sound of the grind became absorbed into daily life and I could no longer hear it, I knew it was grinding on me.

In La Paz, Pam is off for the airport and Christmas at home. Jack and I restock supplies, and I call my wife, Margaret, whom I haven't spoken to in three weeks and hear in her voice the longing I feel. She will be here in six days to spend Christmas on the boat as we sail from La Paz to Cabo San Lucas where we will resupply and then depart for San Benedicto in the Revillagigedos.

# DAY
## 20

Rather than hang around the city, I suggest to Jack that we go north and anchor up near Los Islotes. I had located a cave on the last trip that produced filtered ambient lighting for the sort of images I am looking for. Jack is enormously accommodating. Anyone else would politely tell me that four and a half days is enough in one place and I would not have argued. Yet underwater photography, for me, is always a state of discovery—the never ending search for unique lighting and subject.

We leave La Paz near noon on the outgoing tide. A mobula crosses our bow near the entrance of the harbor, wing tips in the air, a shadow drifting across the surface. The sea surface is calm with scarcely a breeze. We motor up and anchor near dusk in a long and narrow bay called Cardonal.

# DAY

# 21

The overcast sky, like granite scree, has stolen all hope of sunshine. Wind out of the west indicates a front will be upon us soon, and without light I shall be unable to photograph the images envisioned in the cave, so we remain anchored.

During the afternoon, Jack and I take the skiff to the northeast end of Cardonal with the intention of hiking to a large cave high on a peak several hundred feet up a red ridge overlooking the bay. Mounds of ancient oyster shells, some as small as silver dollars and others the size of dinner plates line the shore. It was piles far larger than these that Cortes spotted from the channel in his search for oyster beds, sending long boats and divers to further exploit the resource. Along the shoreline are stonewalls three-feet high, just enough to prevent water from coming over the top at high tide. The pattern of the walls is unusual and first appears to be a fish trap, but is probably only the remnants of an oyster operation.

I prepare dinner and Jack keeps me company sitting in the cockpit. He appears more settled than the previous three weeks, content to watch the sunset without having to describe it aloud. Perhaps the absence of Pam has affected him, for he has made a quiet turn and a charming innocence is revealed beneath the cultural mask. In the evening, meandering through the *Nirvana*'s small library, I come across Henry Miller's book, *Henry Miller On Writing*, the very book that twenty-six years ago inspired me to attempt to collect my thoughts and put them down on paper. As usual, Miller's work evokes inquiry of a profound nature and Jack asks me, having just read the book himself, "What does it take to live life fully? A life of the mind? What?"

"Passion," I say. "Passion for whatever you do."

"That might be easy for you to say," he replies. "Passion comes easy for you."

"What is so difficult about passion? You have a passion for sailing, for adventure. Passion is easy. What is difficult is to be true to your passion, to be willing to give up everything else and follow it."

"Not everyone can do that."

"No, not everyone can do that. But not for the reasons you might believe. People don't trust enough in themselves to find their passion. They tend to believe in the wisdom of others: parents, teachers, politicians, figures of authority. Believe in yourself, despite what others say or what the world believes. Embrace your passion fully. Surrender to it as you would to a lover. Allow it to speak and then listen to its voice. Carry out its desires. The process will empower you and lead you to your bliss."

"Are you in bliss right now?"

"Hey, I'm on a boat in the Sea of Cortez, about to take underwater photographs of sea lions. What can be more blissful than that?"

# DAY
# 22

The wind has dropped and the gray skies have given way to cornflower blue, with traces of cotton candy clouds running south on another wind.

We have returned to Los Islotes for a specific shot, the cave with a narrow entrance facing south, catching dramatic light between 11 A.M. and 3 P.M. The entrance to the cave is eight feet across, fifteen feet high from surface to bottom, and there always seems to be one or two sub-adult males hiding out in the inky shadows near the rear. I position myself inside the cave near the entrance with my back to the rear so that I might catch a sea lion framed just outside the entrance bathed in light rays. I'm in the cave not a minute when two males rush from behind, spooking the hell out of me. Their momentum carries them into the light outside the entrance where they spin around and blaze past me, eyeing me with disfavor on their return to the blackness. In these close quarters I am careful not to brush up against the walls of the cave for it unleashes loose sediment that fouls the water and thus the photograph. Having overweighted myself in the shallow water, and in a vertical position, I expel air quietly through the snorkel and simply settle to the bottom feet first to gain the angle for the shot.

This is how I blissfully spend my day. Up and down on a breath-hold as sea lions come and go into the cave. Several hours into the dive there comes an explosion of sorts next to my head. My first thought is that a boulder has fallen from the ceiling of the cave, for the concussion is pronounced. Spinning around, I see nothing on the sea floor, no boulder, not even a small rock, and no evidence of sea lion. In the afternoon it happens again, and this time I catch one of the males opening his mouth and discharging an explosion of bubbles directly behind me.

Up and down, getting shots. Burning rolls of film, swimming back to the boat for a bite to eat and a film change then back to the cave. When the cave empties I wait, kicking steadily for over an hour to keep from sinking. The light has long changed and the angles of its rays have lost their effect, yet still I wait. Finally, when I return to the boat it is 4 P.M.; I have been diving five hours.

# DAY
# 23

The following day at Los Islotes the clear skies have been overcome with cloud cover. This day the water is as cloudy as the sky. Moreover, the sea lions are edgy and White Beard makes passes at us when we near the rookery. Nearly all the pups are on shore and whenever one attempts to play with us, White Beard shows up and drives it away. Several of the younger males are mock fighting under the water. Five pups looking for a little fun have slipped away from their guardian and found me. One is gnawing on my arm in a gentle manner, and I expose my fingers to which it nibbles ever so gently. I rub its belly and it moves in pressing to get close. Suddenly, White Beard shows up barking in a menacing fashion, herding the pups back on the beach in no-nonsense body language.

Later, Jack asks if the sea lions pose any threat to man. Only on rare occasion have they bitten divers, under severe circumstances when the pups are believed to be in jeopardy, and on one occasion of outright harassment. Generally, they confine their aggression to posturing and barking. Certainly, if a male or female sea lion had a notion to intentionally harm a human, they could with little difficulty. Charging into a man at a high rate of speed would inflict serious injury, but for the most part, wild animals of the sea do not attack unless it is absolutely necessary. Generally, they spend their days in social interaction, often demonstrating clear signs of affection. We have seen White Beard stroke heads and necks of females with a flipper, or rest his flipper casually on a shoulder of a female. These displays are never for very long, usually interrupted by his single-minded pursuit to continually establish territory among the other males.

When I come within fifty feet of the rookery, White Beard enters the water with amazing speed, and I think he is going to rush me, but instead does a very strange thing. He appears to be vomiting up balls of food that sink quickly. Closer inspection reveals that they are stones! A half dozen or more. The pups investigate along with me. We all sniff around the bottom until the old male rounds up the young ones and herds them back to shore.

Science has not the slightest idea why sea lions and other seals swallow stones. There are a number of theories but none supported by hard evidence. Some biologists suggest that the stones may help grind up food that is swallowed whole. There is the belief that perhaps they crush parasitic worms in the sea lion's stomach. Another theory has been forwarded that the stones might be ballast, or perhaps a way to ward off hunger pangs, which I doubt. However, seals do fast for long periods of time, two to four months a year depending on the species. They rarely drink fresh water and appear to get all the moisture necessary from the food they eat. My guess would be the stones are swallowed to clear the throat and stomach of fish bones that might get lodged anywhere en route to the digestive tract, then thrown up again to clear the debris. For along with the stones I saw what appeared to be the bony remains of a fish. In the end, it is just another mystery to ponder.

It is time to depart the sea lions. Jack is off spearfishing and returns to report his first grouper sighting. He does not take a shot for we have just restocked the boat and have no need. For all the effort he has put into hunting, he shows remarkable restraint.

The first Guardian Angel expedition was a breakthrough, and I returned to the States brimming with confidence, having faced my shark and resolved a measure of my fear of them. With this newfound confidence, I was able to elevate my concentration, so necessary in the stalking of white sea bass. It was only then that I began to understand the fish's subtle connections to the ocean environment around Catalina Island.

The white sea bass was a fish of mythical qualities among the big game spearfishermen. A fish of stunning beauty with a fluorescent purple back mixed with moss green at the edges, its colors graduating to silver just above the lateral line and continuing down to a belly that was snow white. As extraordinary as its colors were, they became absorbed in the lightless fathoms and blended perfectly with the hue of the depths, rendering the fish almost invisible. To see a white sea bass swimming at eye level was to catch a luminous ghost that had absorbed the available light of a dim sea and reflect it back to the viewer. Unlike other large pelagics that were fueled by untiring frenetic energy, the white sea bass moved with effortless grace, giving the illusion of gliding through the water rather than swimming. The very large appeared to shoulder their way along, their bodies swaggering under muscled bulk. A member of the croaker family, the white sea bass is the only deep-water fish that emits a distinctive guttural sound. Many a hunter has chased its surreal croak until the sun went down, never seeing the fish. It is a wary and intelligent creature that vanishes upon sensing the slightest disturbance in the water—a fin splash, a slight noise from the boat, bubbles escaping from the snorkel, even the faint noise of the human ear clearing through a pressure change.

Those who hunted the fish were a strange lot. They hunted alone; they were in the water as the sun came up and they were there after it had set. Cold and fatigue were their companions. They were meticulous with their gear. Their spear guns were handcrafted pieces of work that were extensions of themselves. There was little room for error when opportunities were few and the shot but once. It was an engagement that called for discipline, endurance, concentration and considerable knowledge. In the late 1960's the white sea bass averaged forty pounds and was four and half feet in length, though often fifty-pounders and occasionally sixty-pounders were caught. The world record at the time was held by a tireless hunter, Yas Ikeda, at seventy-two pounds.

The white sea bass was a grand mystery. To understand the fish was to know the depths and nuance of the waters of the Pacific along the Southern California coastline and its attending islands. To trek into the blue water with the underwater equivalent of a bow and arrow on the length of a breath-hold was to embark on an ancient path, for hidden within that realm lay secrets revealed only in the primal hush of the hunt. The fish would become my medium into these magical places. I never realized that once I had entered, the ties to my father's world would be forever severed and I could never return.

Though I dove almost every week with experienced divers, the fish themselves were ultimately my teachers. If my snorkel leaked a bubble, the calico bass would tell me by instantly drifting away at the sound. Or, if my descents reflected movement, the calicos would not be visible at all, having long departed the area. If the calico bass was my teacher, then the white sea bass was my master, and it was the master whom I courted at every opportunity. I endeavored to fill myself with the fish: knowing where it fed; and where its food source could be found; its patterns of travel in the morning, afternoon and evening; the influences of a continually changing environment, including current, water temperature, tide, visibility and thermoclines.

There were two approaches in stalking white sea bass. The first and oldest method was to first understand and then locate the pathways the fish traveled underwater. Much like the pathways of wandering herds across a vast plain, these underwater pathways would change as currents and kelp beds changed, thermoclines fluctuated and food sources shifted, so there was never a firmly fixed pattern. Usually a pathway was found by observing the movement of other creatures under the water. The bat ray, for example, often travels the same pathway as the white sea bass, usually on the far edge of a kelp bed that overhangs a sand bottom. Once a pathway was located, the hunter would then dive to the depth level of the pathway and hang a few feet inside the kelp and wait the length of a breath-hold for the fish to pass by. The ascents and descents were made with minimum body movement, gliding down and pulling up on the kelp stalks with little fin movement. In this way he would not arouse any fish in the area and for all purposes, became invisible.

Up for a breath, down for a breath-hold, unmoving, in utter silence so as to feel one's heartbeat and know the heartbeat of the sea. Do it long enough and the beats become indistinguishable; the hunter and the sea become one. Often small fish would gather around me as though I were just another kelp stalk in the ocean terrain, fluttering about my face and dancing between my legs, all traces of Carlos having vanished.

The second stalking method, if not developed by Al Scheneppershoff, was certainly employed by him with more vigor and refinement than any other hunter, and with enormous success. Al was a powerful swimmer who put more faith in his legs than in his breath-hold. He was constantly on the move endeavoring to locate whites from the surface. Al's approach to hunting whites was as aggressive as it was difficult because it required perfect technique in the descent. If flawed in any way, the white would sense the hunter and move off, leaving him with poor position and an unlikely opportunity for a good shot. This method afforded more sightings of white sea bass but fewer opportunities for a shot.

Al's approach to hunting was unique and we all tried to emulate him in one way or another. When I went diving with him I tried to learn all I could, but was never able to keep up with him. I was in awe of his skills; his dedication and aggression were legendary. Once Al and a group of hunters went out to hunt albacore, a deep-water tuna that runs far offshore, sometimes a hundred miles from land. After searching all day and coming up empty they were heading home in the late afternoon. Suddenly the skipper spots a school and gets on top of it. All the hunters are scrambling around, getting out of their street clothes and into their wet suits, for the water is cold. All except Al, who, buck-naked, jumps in ahead of everyone, stalks and spears the only albacore of the trip.

Different conditions, and variables within the conditions, usually dictated the method used to stalk the white sea bass. If visibility was poor, then one would usually dive and wait along the pathways. If the visibility was excellent or pathways could not be found, then Al's method would be employed.

Hunting white sea bass was an exercise in discipline. The fish were extremely wary and would depart an area over something as insignificant as the squeak of a human ear clearing at depth. A hunter of such fish might spend three to five hours a day in the water for weeks and never release a spear shaft. There were divers who had hunted white sea bass for years and never seen one. Yet once the fish was understood in all aspects of its nature, one could find them with relative success. Their general habitat of a sandy bottom among a sprinkling of kelp trees was widely known. The precise location among hundreds of possibilities was another matter altogether. Once a location was discovered and the hunter had developed the skills to move without detection, then the possibilities of landing a white sea bass were quite good. Over the years I had internalized the fish and knew it perhaps better than anything that swam in the sea.

In the course of my weekly travels to the island I quite naturally came across other hunters and in time began to hunt with them. They were highly skilled and considered the best on the West Coast, some the best in the world. Bob Donnell was to become a national spearfishing champion; Mike Oceanus, Larry Brakovitch, Bob Stanbery and Dale Coty belonged to the spearfishing club, The Long Beach Neptunes; they and others like them were as much an aspect of the seascape as man had ever been in the brief history of the Underwater Age.

These hunters knew the ocean in ways few did, including commercial fishermen. They could read the surface or a weather front or a current line quickly and efficiently. They knew specifically where to find yellowtail, white sea bass, black sea bass, calico bass, barracuda, halibut and lobster in a thousand different spots that included all the offshore islands and the entire Southern California coastline from Santa Barbara to San Diego. It appeared they took great risks on the water, but in fact rarely did.

White sea bass generally fed and moved at first light, and again in the evening from dusk to darkness. It was usually during these periods that the hunters would take to the water. While diving with Bob Stanbury, Bob Donnell and Dale Coty, with darkness rapidly swallowing up the last light, I was off by myself on a small kelp bed fifty yards off the island waiting along one of the pathways. A forty-pound fish, near invisible in the lightless water, cruised by slightly below me. I dropped a bit for angle, and the white sensed me and veered off. (Spearfishing is a one shot event. If the fish is missed, the spear shaft must be retrieved, the line restrung, and the bands of rubber recocked. By that time the fish is well down the island. Additionally, if the shot is not well placed, the fish will run strong and usually wrap or circle a reef or a kelp stalk which, as they power off, will pull out the spear, leaving a hole in their body from which they would eventually die.) In the dim light I lined up what would be a quick shot, the fish putting distance between us, and snapped it off. The twenty-foot shot dropped several inches before striking the fish in the gut—poor placement, an area of soft tissue. The white, not mortally wounded, ran hard straight out to sea. Little tension could be placed on the line for fear of pulling the spear point out. Keeping a delicate tension, I slowly caught up to the fish and then stayed some twenty feet behind so as not to frighten it into a burst of speed. Swimming with it, I waited for the fish to tire. It swam for forty-five minutes, and in that time night fell. Finally, the tension on the line went slack; the fish was done and I eased in carefully to slip a hand into its gills. A half-mile off shore, tired and with the bleeding fish, I was not looking forward to the kick. A hundred yards into the swim, a powerboat raced by, not fifty feet away. I shouted; the boat slowed and made a turn. Shouting again, he found me. Coming alongside, he looked at me, puzzled, then gazed out searching for a boat, but in the dark saw nothing. He wanted to know what I was doing out here in the middle of the ocean. Rather than responding to his question, I asked for a ride back to the island. He said sure, and when I came aboard he saw the fish. His wife and two children were with him and he turned to them and said, "I'm glad you're along because no one would've ever believed this." His daughter, no more than seven years old, looked at the fish, which was quite a bit larger than her, looked at me leaning against the gunnel in a hooded black wet suit and replied, "I would have believed you, Daddy. He comes from the stories you read me at night."

Soon after Guardian Angel my personal life began to change dramatically. Having abandoned all pretense of gainful employment and quitting my "career job", I had no prospects for the future other than hunting the waters of the Pacific and the Gulf. I moved off the *Gamine* and in with a woman, Carol, with whom I would spend the next twelve years. I lived off unemployment and when that ran out, began selling off much of what I had previously acquired, including some land out in the desert. I had not been unemployed since I was fifteen, and in those lazy days to follow it came to me that I was no longer living for the prospects of tomorrow, but rather in the moment of the day. It was the early 1970's and the world of suits and ties, and the structure of society in general, were blowing apart. The old religion—to always hold a job—was discarded in favor of the new religion—the search and exploration of the self. New alternatives of thought and perception were examined through the works of Ram Dass, Alan Watts, Krishnamurti, Aldous Huxley, Joseph Pierce and later, the Tao. Concepts such as work as play, life as death, time as static, change as time, less as more, reality as illusion, and dreams as reality, swam through me and rested in comfortable places.

Through their books, these men joyously validated beliefs I intuitively knew but had been scrambled in my linear mind. It was wholly uplifting to realize I was not nearly so crazy after all, that the silent agreement among us to ignore who or what we really are, was indeed true. There was much to learn and as I did, things began to make some philosophical if not metaphysical sense. Eastern mysticism, along with the Native American concept of a Great Spirit that revealed itself in the natural world, spoke to me in its ethereal voice, and began to give meaning to regularly witnessed events of the supernatural which might have been defined as miracles, or God's work.

I am not comfortable with the term God, for it implies an elderly gentleman with a long gray beard wielding power from the heavens. God, or the Great Spirit, as I define it, is the presence of mystery, magic and power that resides in all living things. Thus God's work could not be ignored any more than the direct experience of a white sea bass appearing in that scant minute-and-a-half on a breath-hold dive in the middle of the ocean could be ignored. As this magical world revealed itself into a kind of understanding, it was the observance of connections within the ocean universe that confirmed the presence of the Great Spirit. These webs of connection linked sea creatures great and small, fast and slow, fixed and free swimming. It brought together the minutiae with the gargantuan, those with the largest brains on the planet to those with no brain at all. These connections perhaps best revealed themselves in my ability to know the whereabouts of the hidden, and see the camouflaged beyond its cloak, yet having no idea as to the source of this ability. These clear instructions I had been following became murky when I tried to verbalize them. Now through these readings, the sensing, feelings and observations I previously could not put a name to were defined and revealed as an aspect attainable within the realm of human experience. My self-doubts as a witness and instrument of the natural world fell away when those perceptions were finally validated as perfectly reasonable.

My growing confidence encouraged further explorations, and new insight became the fabric that tied together the observation with the experience, the subtle to the obvious, intuition to perception.

The direct experience of the natural world supported the concepts presented by the likes of Ram Dass, Watts, Huxley and the rest; nothing exists separately and unto itself. All matter of life and energy is united, interdependent and inter-related. (And though human beings often appear to display a complete disregard for life in all its forms, they are nonetheless a part of this process which we call living.)

To spend time and intimate moments with these life forms deepened and infused a sense of relationship with all living creatures, and made clear my connections to them. Eventually the relationships became spiritual. By that, I mean the physical connections transcended into something else, a deeper connection that was recognized somewhere other than the mind. It was felt in no particular place, a knowing of another kind. Such bonds, I was coming to learn, were unavoidable and an essential aspect of my deepening relationship with the sea.

For the first time since I was a boy on the beaches of Hawaii, I felt I had found my way. I was on the right path, that much was certain. What was not clear was exactly what I should be doing on this path. It did not provide, so far as I could see, a way to fulfill my financial and moral obligations to my children, for soon the money would run out and I would have to return to a way of life from which I had grown apart. The prospect was too unbearable to contemplate.

The 1970's were heady days. In the fall and winter we were pushing deeper into the Gulf, and in the summer were working the white sea bass, yellowtail and black sea bass off the islands of Catalina, Anacapa, Santa Cruz, San Clemente, and the Coronados off San Diego. The only element that slowed us was underwater visibility. A hunter needs reasonable visibility (at least twenty-five feet, preferably forty feet on the offshore islands, and thirty to fifty feet in the Gulf) or the undertaking becomes difficult or even impossible as the visibility drops.

When the water was dirty and deep, tales of Kamo would whisper to my frontal lobes. Bob D. once revealed that occasionally he was spooked in dirty water. (It was a comfort to hear that from him.) His advice was so sound as to make it ridiculous in its simplicity. "If you are feeling spooked, then get out of the water." He didn't elaborate; there was no need.

The ebb and flow of sharks, and my fear of them, was as variable as the tide. Just as I was beginning to feel secure some event would come along and influence my notion of them. Case in point was a dive off Pukey Point at the Coronados with Bob D. and Larry B. Bob had just speared a yellowtail and a big hammerhead shark came twisting out of the murky water. Bob brought the fish to his hand and swam it back to the boat without incident. I went along, wanting no part of the shark, believing that we would move to another area. Instead, Bob returned to the same spot where Larry had remained and reported that the shark was still around. Bob, in a rather off-hand manner, instructed me to dive down and chase it off. Still very much the novice, I deferred to his judgment, and so assumed that if he said the shark could be chased off by the likes of me, then of course it could and would be done. I dove down to forty feet when the hammerhead appeared near the sixty-foot bottom. As soon as it eyed me it began to twist and arch its body and shake that prehistoric head in a manner that left a message of no uncertainty. I eased to the top where Bob asked if the job were done. I replied that the shark didn't seem to want to leave. Bob gave me a rare look of disapproval, took a breath and dropped down, his fins all but disappearing in the gloom. Then they stopped, hovered a moment, and in the next instant Bob turned and was ascending. His singular comment upon reaching the surface was, "We're out of here."

My hunting skills had made an impression with some of the Long Beach Neptunes and I was asked to join the club. Never much of a joiner, I was nonetheless hungry for their cumulative underwater knowledge and signed up. They knew where to find the fish, and they had access to hunting equipment that was in a state of continual development. Hunting big fish in the 1970's was, for the most part, a trial and error process, for the fish of the Gulf would make off with spear guns, and tear up spear shafts and points, causing the hunter to both lose his gear and the fish.

A wonderful old spearfisherman, Charlie Sturgill, was one of the pioneering divers. As early as 1929, he was feeling around submerged rocks in tidal areas for abalone and began using a facemask of his own design in the 1930's; he was regularly bringing up abalone. A top-notch tool and die maker, Charlie became the primary source of equipment development in the Los Angeles area in the 1970's, and was responsible for retooling much of the spearfishing gear: spear shafts, spear points, muzzles, heavy gauge wish-bones that secured the powerful bands of rubber to the notches in the spear shaft. Any diver, novice or veteran, was welcome at Charlie's home and all were treated as equals. There was rarely a time when there weren't half a dozen guys hanging around his garage talking hunting and equipment. Like me, they lived in homes, trailers and boats. Some had families and jobs, but never seemed to be working; every activity centered around the ocean. It was a lifestyle that, in one degree or another, consumed us all.

During those wild and unpredictable times my connection with the sea grew deeper, as I wrangled less and less with the sharks in my head. At times though, I was still spooked, oddly, more in the Pacific than in the Gulf where I had seen sharks regularly. The portent of sharks, particularly the great white shark known to inhabit the Pacific waters, created more havoc in my imagination than the reality of the sharks in the Gulf.

Meanwhile, my skills as a blue water hunter were

reaching their zenith. The Long Beach Neptunes presented their King Neptune Award to the hunter who could land at minimum, a forty-pound white sea bass, a twenty-five-pound yellowtail, and a hundred-pound black sea bass. It was a feat rarely accomplished, and was usually done over the course of many years. It was my good fortune to have landed all three fish in two successive weekends at the same spot, Church Rock, on the east end of Catalina. I speared a sixty-six-pound white, a twenty-seven-pound yellowtail and a two hundred and fifty-one-pound black sea bass to become the eleventh recipient of that award.

Every fish has its own tale and the black sea bass was the most dangerous and unique fish on the West Coast for no other reason than its size, which ranged from sixty to over five hundred pounds. One diver, Mory Rothstein, speared a black sea bass off Santa Cruz Island in 1969 and the fish took him down. He was found unconscious on the bottom with his gun, and the line to the fish cut. He never regained consciousness.

The danger in spearing any big fish over forty pounds is if, in gathering up the line that is attached to the spear, the fish, in nearing the surface, decides to make another run, which they often do, and the loose floating line loops around a weight or cinches around a wrist. Forty-pound fish are too powerful for even the strongest of divers, and in the limitation of a breath-hold, the diver is at the mercy of the fish.

My single experience with loose line involved a small, eighteen-pound yellowtail. The spear went clean through the fish and speared another of the same size. I had two fish on one spear, and was at-

tempting to bring them both in by way of letting
out line and hoping they would tire without placing too much tension on the line. The second fish
was poorly hit and eventually came off, and when
it did I began pulling in the line. It was a small
fish and I was casual with the line, allowing it to
gather around me rather than staying up current
and free of it, which is the proper procedure. When
the fish was fifteen feet from the surface, a two
hundred-pound sea lion bolted in and hit the fish,
taking off with it at high speed. Line looped around
my wrist, cinched tight and pulled me down. I had
no knife to cut the line and all I could do was quickly
gather up slack line and try and pull the fish out of
the sea lion's mouth. Having not taken much of a
breath, I was completely out of air when I managed to pull the fish free. At that point my only
interest was in reaching the surface. Swimming
hard and not three feet from the surface, I was
yanked to a halt at the wrist. The sea lion had hit
the yellowtail again. Though I could nearly stretch
my arm to the surface, I was unable to reach it,
and had no strength left to engage in another tug-
of-war with the sea lion. I was into the throes of
blacking out when, inexplicably, the sea lion released the fish and I was able to reach the surface.
Floating on my back and heaving breaths, concerned that the sea lion would hit the fish again, I
pulled up the line as fast as I could, still floating
on my back until I had the fish and line draped
over my chest and stomach. The sea lion continued
to come after the fish while I had it in my arms,
forcing me to kick it away repeatedly until I had
made my way back to my boat.
    The morning I landed the black sea bass, I was

rigged for whites, using all nylon cord instead of stainless cable so it wouldn't cut the fish. My spear gun was equipped with a reel, which did not hold enough line usually required for black sea bass. The fish was down at fifty feet facing out to sea when I made the drop. With rigging that was fragile for a fish that I estimated weighed over two hundred pounds, it was important to place the spear just behind its pectoral fin where the fish was vulnerable. This I did, and then watched in awe as the black took off. It was so big that its tail action did not explode into movement but made great sweeps taking it straight out to sea. By the time I reached the surface, the reel was spooled and I was being dragged, helpless to do anything but hold on, out to sea. The fish towed me a good three quarters of a mile from the island, out where sportfishing boats were trolling for marlin. During those moments, it occurred to me that I had made a serious mistake. If somehow I could stop the fish, how in the world would I bring it up, no doubt bleeding profusely, and swim it back to the island without attracting sharks of every kind? I knew that Bob Stanbury had speared a black sea bass off of San Clemente Island and it had towed him for miles out to sea. Finally letting go of his rig, he swam for shore late into nightfall, scarcely making it back. As questions continued to mount, the fish, for no apparent reason, turned and headed back towards the island. It settled into sixty feet of water and I tied off the line to a buoyant boat bumper then swam back to the boat for another spear gun. After putting a second spear into it, I began the job of pulling it up to the surface. Kicking furiously, I would pull in a couple of feet, rest, then kicking again, pull in a few more feet, always keeping the line free and away from my body. Twenty feet from the surface, the black made a run back down to sixty feet, taking all the line with it. Twice more I worked the fish up to twenty feet and twice more it made a run. Finally, two-and-a-half hours after I first speared it, the fish was landed.

A moratorium prohibiting the taking of black sea bass by line or spear was imposed when it was learned in late 1970's that their numbers were decreasing dramatically. However, for about an eight-year period, when spearfishing equipment was sturdy enough to tackle such fish, it was the ultimate physical challenge for the breath-hold diver.

Blue water spearfishermen were experiencing a period of unprecedented success during the 1970's, and their confidence in the water was at an all time high. There was the feeling that all worlds beneath the sea could be conquered. Fear was falling away, skills were developing at a rapid pace (principally because the fish populations were so large), and equipment, developed by Charlie Sturgill, was holding up to the power and force of these tremendous fish. We were riding a wave crest that was unparalleled.

One afternoon it all came crashing down.

A month before, Bob Stanbury had asked and I had accepted a spot on a trip to Guadalupe Island to hunt for blue fin tuna. Two weeks before the trip was to depart, while finishing a dive up with Al Schneppershoff off an Oceanside kelp bed, I blurted out that I would not be going on the Guadalupe trip. To this day I don't know what possessed me to suddenly say I could not make the trip. I had been having misgivings about it, but it was more about money than any strange feelings. Or so I thought. At any rate, I told Al my spot would be open. He called Bob and he took it.

Three days out of San Diego, Al was attacked and killed by a great white shark. Al Schneppershoff was arguably the best hunter among us. If it could happen to Al, it could happen to anyone. A profound sense of vulnerability and disillusionment affected the blue water spearfishing community. Few spoke of Al's death by way of shark attack. All knew that the possibility of attack existed, but the subject was rarely discussed. Fear is a strange and powerful entity, and if denial permitted the diver to make his jumps, then that is what he did. But when someone with the stature of Al is killed, denial becomes a broken crutch on which to rest one's confidence. Al's loss was shattering and the collective erosion of confidence touched everyone who pushed the limits in the blue water. With that single incident the sharks were let loose to feed our anxieties and patrol our defenseless imaginations.

Certain areas of deep blue water were avoided after Al's death. Open water drop-offs on the east and west end of Catalina were passed up, as was Farnsworth Bank which had great white shark sightings on numerous occasions. Hunting was curtailed to the edge of the kelp beds, and the idea of hunting tuna in Mexico was never discussed.

# DAY
## 24

Outside the cove, the wind blows thirty knots from the south. We are anchored in Ensenada Grande two hours south of Los Islotes. This day we are going nowhere, so I catch up on my notes while Jack scouts for fish out on a point.

In the afternoon I make a jump for no other reason than to get wet. The shear cliffs of this cove descend into the water and straight to the sand at forty feet where boulders from another age rest in piles on the bottom. Fish begin to materialize while I settle on a boulder; small butterflies and sargent majors in large schools greet me, then run off and spread the word. They return with parrotfish, a mobula, golden cabrilla, sierra mackerel, small cabrilla, damsels and the usual Sea of Cortez fish I have never identified. This is as many fish as I have seen at one time on this trip. Up and down, the fish wait for me on every descent, like children, cautious yet curious to see what I am all about. If I stay absolutely still on the boulder, they come very close, within inches, only to jump to safe distances at my slightest movements. Shortly, my curiosity nudges me off the boulder and has me prowling into ledges and holes, where rock scallops are found squeezed into crevices, delicate lips quivering in the current. These are not the football-sized scallops that once filled the Gulf twenty years ago. Mexicans using hooka mined the Gulf clean of those big scallops within five years. Still, this little haven seems to have maintained much of the prolific flavor of the Gulf, and I take pleasure in its company. Two mobulas drift by, sense me and bank away. Three more fly in from open water, stopping directly below, while I rest on the surface. Shortly, I drift across a small underwater canyon where a half dozen fifteen-pound cabrilla hover near the floor surrounded on all sides by walls of fallen boulders. They are all that remain in the way of good eating rockfish now that the grouper are gone.

Later, I mention the cabrilla to Jack who is having trouble finding fish. Somewhat miffed, he asks, "Why don't you dive with me once in awhile and show me where I can find these fish." He assumed from the beginning that I would be making spearfishing jumps with him and giving advice and refinements on techniques. To a degree I could be schooling Jack with the nuances of the stalk but haven't, for any advice I could give him at this stage would be minor in terms of what he now needs to understand.

Already a competent diver, Jack, in many respects, has already hit the wall in terms of linear ocean information. Now is the time for him to begin to feel his way into the water. Similar to learning to dance by getting "a feel for it" rather than following a diagram of steps sketched on the floor. In the same way the best musicians distinguish themselves by virtue of their "feel" for the music.

It goes far beyond the sharps and flats of the mind and into the realm of feeling and intuiting, and perhaps more than anything, into the belief that one can come to understand something in great depth without endless analysis. If Jack would allow himself to open up to that place beyond the mind, trusting in the subtle messages of the intuition, he would soon discover he does not need me at all.

In the fall of 1974 the last of my money ran out and I was flat broke. Actually I had been broke for some time, and Carol was fed up with supporting a fish hunter who could bring sumptuous meals to the table and little else. Additionally, I had not made a child support payment in months. With the reluctance of a one-legged surfer about to drop down a twenty-foot face, I leapt back into the world of suits, finding a job with another title insurance company, this time as a salesman.

I made the transition with disturbing ease and within a year, was their top salesman. Soon I was able to afford a fine house high on a hill in Laguna Beach that overlooked the Pacific where, on a clear day, Catalina Island was visible forty miles away. Before long, I was living the American Dream in the perfect beach community. The home in Laguna was a dream house of sorts, and Carol was forever furnishing it with one thing or another while I quietly descended into the world of possessions.

The suit was not a complete sell-out; within a year I had the job down to four days a week, and diving the reefs of Laguna filled up my week. There were lobster, abalone and fish, all within a ten-minute car ride. It was like a trip to the supermarket. Over the course of seven years, I would come to know each and every well-stocked reef and rock from Crystal Cove to Salt Creek. Although the lobster boats were trapping more lobster than ever before, there remained reefs where the trappers would not take their boats for fear of losing them. And so there was plenty to go around for the small tribe of free divers who resided in Laguna. Though we rarely went diving together, secrets were shared about newfound reefs that would be chock full of lobster and abalone. Over time we knew each and every cave that would yield lobster, and how to direct a diver to it, i.e., "There's a cave inside the reef on the northeast corner on the sand just west of the second breaking reef off Cress St."

On one such reef I discovered a tunnel four feet high with a sand bottom that was crammed with lobsters, and slithered up to my waist for the easy pickings. At the far end of the tunnel, another opening provided enough filtered light for me to work by. After picking up one lobster, the light suddenly dimmed. Filling the back end of the tunnel was the largest moray eel I had ever seen. Its girth filled the entire tunnel and it was coming directly towards me. Never completely comfortable with eels, I knew enough to hold my ground, anticipating that it would characteristically back off. But this eel with mouth agape, came right for me at eye level, forcing me to back out of the cave, a behavior that indicated it was protecting the lobsters (which eels will eat on occasion, but not as a common food source). Up on the surface, after regaining my breath, I went down to the cave and peered inside. The lobsters had backed towards the far end of the tunnel but were still there in numbers. No sign of the eel, which was strange. I did not take a full breath-hold that would allow me to cover the length of the tunnel and backed out to resurface for another breath. Feeling something brush my head as I cleared the entrance, I looked up; all six feet of the eel was draped above the entrance of the cave, camouflaged within the seaweed, its mouth inches from my face. The idea of an eel laying in ambush for a man was an unsettling notion, and I lurched away from the entrance thoroughly rattled, and headed for the surface. I lay twenty feet above the eel as it eyed me from its perch above the entrance, convincing me without too much trouble, that there were other lobsters elsewhere.

The next time I met up with one of my diving chums, I told him about this fantastic cave filled with lobsters. He dove it a few days later and met with the same eel and its strange preoccupation, scaring the hell out of him. In the fine tradition of hunters everywhere, he in turn passed it down to the next unsuspecting victim with the same result.

Shortly after moving to Laguna I sold my boat, the *Gamine*, and with it went the frequency with which I dove Catalina Island. Though each summer my vacations were spent there with Bob Donnell, Bob Stanbury and Dale Coty working the island in the evenings for white sea bass. During one of those summers, a great white shark came in on Bob Ballew at Church Rock on the east end of Catalina. I spoke with him directly after the encounter. He had seen the shark while on a breath-hold dive about the same time it had seen him and came into him while he was near the bottom. Able to ascend up a large kelp stalk that served as cover, he hid in the floating kelp bed on the surface, drawing the kelp around him as the great white circled just below trying to sniff him out. The shark knew he was there but was unable to separate him from the kelp. When the shark finally gave up and drifted off, Bob waited twenty minutes before having to make a swim over open water to his boat. Understandably, he was shaken but gamely attempted to hide the after-effects of the experience. Over the next few years Bob became, in my view, obsessively preoccupied with sharks. (Perhaps he had always been absorbed with sharks and I had paid no attention to it.) He was one of the few spearfishermen who would go out into the channel between Catalina and the mainland to spear blue sharks. Which never made much sense because these sharks, like most, urinate through their skin, making their meat inedible. Moreover, unless a brain shot is made, sharks having no skeletal system are difficult to kill with a spear. (A spear is most effective when breaking or damaging the skeletal system of a fish rendering it incapable of utilizing its muscle power.) Once speared a shark will twist and roll endlessly, bending spears, twisting cable, ruining points and in general, wreaking havoc on expensive stainless steel equipment. Consequently, no one hunted sharks for the activity was ultimately pointless. In Bob's case, it may well have been his way of dealing with a terror he could not face directly. Over time, Bob would have more shark encounters than any blue water hunter with whom I was familiar. He was with me when I speared my first white sea bass at Ship Rock, and we did some diving together, but perhaps because of my own dread of sharks, I came to believe that his fear was such that he would attract sharks, and I avoided diving with him after his encounter with the great white.

The sighting of the great white, and subsequent sightings, were continual reminders of both Al's death and our own vulnerability in the water. Naturally, as we pushed back out into blue water, shark encounters became inevitable. Harry Ingram would be attacked by a great white in the same area where Al was killed. More sightings of great whites by spearfishermen along the offshore islands of California had us all jumpy. The most recent was in the summer of 1997 by Dave Long while out hunting white sea bass off the back side of Catalina. There have been no attacks at Catalina, but several divers using tanks and hooka in the northern islands have been attacked, one fatally. Great white sharks became part of the seascape and we never dove the deep water without them drifting into our consciousness.

The seductive lifestyle of Laguna Beach wasn't nearly so difficult or painful as I imagined it would be. In the evenings I would go up on the deck of the split-level house with my glass of white wine and watch the sun set over Catalina. Telling myself how perfect this life was, how wonderful to have everything, but.... There was always the but. I knew that while I was living everyone else's American Dream, it wasn't mine. Though my self-betrayal was but a dim awareness, in the dark hours of night a voice would entreat ever so faintly, and I would invariably turn to that pleasant and ever numbing world of rock and roll, flesh and drugs, and obliterate the voice that might beckon me away from such trappings.

To further deny my deceptions, I would take excessive risks in the water, going into caves and holes

so tight that I would have to let the air out of my
chest to squeeze through. The deeper into material
oblivion I descended, the more reckless my underwater pursuits, finally culminating one night while
diving the San Clemente reef with Larry Brakovitch.

Larry had found a tunnel that dropped vertically
into a reef for fifteen feet and then turned horizontal for another ten feet where it opened up into a
large cavern filled with perhaps a hundred lobsters.
We had hit the mother lode! The tunnel and its
angle were tight, making it a spooky drop at night
on a breath-hold. Scarcely pausing, I plunged into
the tunnel, turned the corner following the beam
from the underwater light, and emerged into a cavern. Lobsters were everywhere: on the walls, on the
ceiling, crawling around on the floor. It was like
nothing I had ever seen before on the California
coast. Picking them up, one, two, three and four,
tucking them under my arms, then feeling the tight-
ness in the throat that signals the need for air, I
turned for the exit of the tunnel. The slender beam
of light had no overall view of the cave and the en-
trance/exit was lost in the convolution of reef. I was
unable to find it. The lobsters, suddenly the least
of my concerns, were dropped from my arms. Sup-
pressing panic, I scoured the rock walls with the
light but still no exit. I then did a very stupid thing
and turned off the light, believing that in the pitch
black I would see moonlight through the opening,
but of course the angle of the tunnel prevented that
from occurring. I turned the light back on with relief, for if the light didn't go back on, which had
happened before, I would be spending my last few
moments in utter darkness. Now completely out of

breath, to the point where in order to trick my body with the building carbon dioxide, I let out half my air supply so my body wouldn't crave a breath for another fifteen seconds, and frantically groped about the walls, of what was becoming my tomb. At the very bottom of my breath-hold, I found the exit and made my ascent through it and then another twenty feet to the surface.

Thoroughly spent, I lay on my back heaving breaths for ten minutes. Larry, believing I had just made an error in judgment, went down into the cavern with a degree of caution. He returned in three minutes heaving breaths, having had the precise same thing happen to him. It was tricky business, we agreed—the exit was hidden and one had to keep an eye on it at all times. Deciding to give it another try, I went down for no other reason than to relieve myself of an approaching terror for underwater caves. Dropping into the tunnel and then into the cavern, I continued to look back and get a fix on the exit, having no intention of venturing very far from it, but the lobsters had moved and were bunched up in a corner, climbing one on top of the other at the far end. Swimming over, I picked up two then checked my bearings. No exit. Couldn't find it again. The place was a death trap. I dropped the lobsters and started searching. My breath-hold wasn't good. The last dive had taken its toll. Finding the exit disguised among jutting rocks, I slipped up into it and to the surface. Neither Larry nor I ever returned to that glory hole in the San Clemente Reef.

Laguna Beach in the 1970's in its upscale hippiedom embodied the original Hotel California, and was a mecca for that sort of lifestyle. Timothy

Leary was busted for drugs in Laguna during that decade. I had fully embraced that way of life and was becoming increasingly dulled by it. My job was a breeze, yet I felt worn down and depressed. I was struggling in what anyone else would have labeled an ideal life. Out of these personal distractions came an idea for a book.

In 1977 there was upwards of an eighty percent drop-out rate among certified scuba divers. (I don't think that figure has changed significantly in twenty years.) No other industry, particularly in leisure time activities, would tolerate losses of this kind, but the diving industry was, for the most part, made up of divers not businessmen, and their view of sport diving was limited to the short term. That is, they sold the scuba certification, and the ocean experience became a by-product of the certification program. Their philosophy was to have the new diver buy all the equipment, and then certify them as capable of using the equipment. Generally, the program would include one or two open ocean dives and perhaps a couple of beach dives. After that, it was up to the new diver to find his or her way through the great body of water that filled both the sea and their minds with all sorts of real and imagined obstacles. Unable to grope their way through the maze of mind and water to a clear and comfortable position from which to experience the ocean, they dropped out.

A book on becoming comfortable in the powerful entity of the ocean, which initially felt and had every appearance of being an alien environment, seemed to me to be the solution. Struggling with the written word, it took me a year to complete *The Inner Experience of Diving*, later retitled, *Diving*

*Free.* Though a small and rather crude book, I nonetheless believed that it would be the salvation for
the dive industry.

Unfortunately, I miscalculated the macho influence that the majority of dive instructors possessed,
and it was they who would need to recommend such
a book. They had little use for a book that dealt
with fear and discomfort, and one that might destroy their projection of the ocean as a dangerous
place where only the strong, tough and brave ventured. Save for a few individuals, I had difficulty
in promoting the book and could not convince the
dive industry that the concept of the "comfort zone"
would, in the long run, generate a good deal more
income for them for years to come.

The book project was not a complete failure (actually seven years later with the help of Joe Schuch
at Scubapro, the book and its principles caught on),
for in writing, I had come upon an arena that thoroughly intrigued me and confessed to Carol my
heartfelt desire to write. I believed that eventually
*Diving Free* would be just what the dive industry
was looking for, and financial rewards were just
around the corner. There was talk of selling the
house and buying a boat and living onboard. Maybe
acquiring another, smaller house in the mountains.
Carol's reply was, "Writers never make any money."

A year later we separated, sold the house and
that world collapsed.

A year after that, in 1982, Ernie Dageford, a man
I scarcely knew, in a most profound act of generos-
ity, sailed his boat, the forty-foot Mariner ketch, *Infinity*, over to Catalina and allowed me to spend
four months alone on board, hunting, gathering and
in general, living exclusively off the sea—something

Jacques Cousteau said could not be done by way of a spear gun alone. Out of that experience came the book, *Last of the Blue Water Hunters*.

Four months on the *Infinity* was a major shift from the life I had been living. My time in Laguna Beach had left me weak, dependent, and spiritless, and I walked the decks of the *Infinity* an empty man. The first two months I struggled with the simple tasks of boat management that on many a night, bordered on survival. In one fix after another, constantly in over my head, my time on board the *Infinity* became a short, tough course in ocean reality. At the end of that summer, Ernie returned and we sailed the boat back to the mainland. It was like coming out of detox at a rehab center, and I knew I could never return to the life in Laguna Beach.

On the trip back came the realization that I had no desire to live a life on land. The sea had returned me to myself and I was determined never to lose my way again; I began to recreate myself from the bottom up. The only way to achieve that goal was to deliver myself permanently to a way of life at sea.

Unlike past years when there was no money and I was eventually sucked back into the culture by way of financial crisis, now there was money from the sale of the house in Laguna. Furthermore, I had embarked on what I believed to be a viable source of income—writing—and beholden to no one, was anxious to get on with the book.

Six months later I purchased a thirty-foot sailboat, *Native Dancer*, an old but well-built 1969 Newport 30, with the intention of living on board and writing in the winter, then sailing to Catalina and diving throughout the summer months.

Other than dive gear and a typewriter, I had given up the possessions of the Laguna Beach life, and unable to obtain permission to live on board my boat, became an "illegal liveaboard" in the Long Beach Marina. If caught, I would have been thrown out on my keel, so I maintained a low profile around the marina, spending much of my time inside the boat. In the fall, winter and early spring, holing up alone, I wrote in the mornings and worked on the boat in the afternoons, developing rudimentary carpentry skills along with the basics of sailboat rigging. In that first summer, I considered my seamanship so poor as to be a hazard to myself and to others, and to singlehand over to Catalina was to invite disaster. Enlisting a crew for the crossing then sending them home, I settled into the same routine as on the *Infinity* the year before: writing in the mornings, doing boat chores in the afternoons, and in the evenings scouting areas to hunt for white sea bass in the fourteen-foot skiff, *Low Now*.

Regaining a sense of myself, I began to reestablish my connection to the sea (due in large part because I was spending several months at a time on the water rather than a week or two). In this regard there is no greater teacher than the wilderness, for it makes you pay for every mistake, every act of carelessness, every incident of poor judgment. And early on I made a bunch: wrapping the prop in my stern line while repositioning myself during a storm, having my skiff drift off one fine afternoon after slipping a poorly tied knot, leaving lights on and draining the battery. The list is endless. The topper was when I unknowingly busted a plug on the fresh water supply and went to sleep for the night, only to awaken in ankle-deep water in firm belief that the boat was sinking. This was not Laguna Beach. At sea, I was forced to pay close attention to every action, for each had consequence.

Eventually, my senses grew sharp and I began to detect problems before they fully materialized: a strange pitch in the engine or bilge pump, a flickering galley light. Little warnings discovered early were investigated and corrected. The sea spoke to the boat and I learned its language: a shift of wind swinging the aft end, the sound of an anchor line tightening, the whistling of the halyards; all the boat's creaks and grunts carried meaning. Alert and energized by the power of the sea's language, the frenetic, abstract world of man gradually fell away to a quiet, confident knowing of both the boat and the environment.

Quite naturally this level of awareness carried over to free diving and hunting, and pushed my limits in the water up to and beyond the level that had been reached before Al's death. Regularly, I wandered off into remote areas of the island to hunt whites and yellows, often to the far west end of the island to the wash rock that punctuated the edge of deep water where ran the great white sharks which frequented a sea lion colony that lay around the corner. Whenever the sharks would swim into my mind, I would block the images from playing out their drama, eventually forcing the issue to come down to either diving with complete freedom or not diving at all. Within a single season I was able to free myself from the long, paralyzing hold that Kamo had had on me. There were still times when the water didn't feel right and I would follow

Bob D's advice and get out, honoring a growing intuitive sense that further entrenched itself in the
nuances of the underwater language which spoke
ever so softly whenever I entered the water.

By the third year, I had thoroughly internalized
the white sea bass and the hunting grounds surrounding Catalina Island. I was able to see the fish
in my mind's eye and feel its presence beyond my
own vision. I came to know its habits and pathways
as I had never known them before. Stalking became
more an exercise in being guided. This intuitive
process seemed to fail only when my strong desires
to find the fish overpowered the subtle directions
of its whereabouts. The grand irony was that, for
me to find the fish, I could not strive in that pursuit.

The idea of sensing or intuiting my way around
the ocean gathered more substance and meaning
as I began to write about these experiences. It was
as though I had tapped into an unknown place in
myself and through writing, was able to pull con-
cealed knowledge from the right hemisphere of the
brain to the more accessible left hemisphere and
the clear light of comprehension. There were pieces
missing, for I still was unaware of how I knew what
I knew, but the writing of it seemed to coalesce this
way of perceiving and I became confident in the
ocean's voice, and more accepting of its mysterious
and conflictive paradoxes.

Over the next six summers I came to intimately
know the major kelp beds and reefs from Italian
Gardens to the West End, over much of the lee side
of Catalina Island. Three years into my wanderings
I found a pathway that produced big yellowtail on
almost every jump, all over thirty-five pounds, a

place near the west end of the island that, to my knowledge, had never been discovered. Why the yellows would run along this one spot, or why they were always so large, was a mystery, but for several years this area produced extraordinary fish. Then nothing, which is often the case for big fish. They move from area to area looking for food sources, probably allowing the food source to regenerate in four or five years, after which they would reappear.

A yellowtail, built like the business end of a javelin, is pound for pound more powerful than a white sea bass. Though tasty, it does not compare in flavor to the white. Yellowtail rarely spook at sound or movement the way whites do, thus the stalking techniques for them are different. However, they do become wary when the body language of the hunter reveals aggression. The stalk is almost formulaic in its approach: locate the fish from the surface, drop down parallel to it, hang at its depth level, and never turn towards it. Generally, the fish will become curious and swing in front of the stilled hunter for a better look. If the fish hangs beyond the range of the spear gun, the hunter remains unmoving save for a slight hand wave with fingers wiggling. This often is enough to arouse its curiosity and entice it to eventually swing into range. Once speared, yellows will inexhaustibly fight the line in the grand tradition of game fish everywhere. A forty-pound yellow is extremely powerful and can easily drag a man under, so the difficulty lies in returning to the surface for a breath while still controlling the fish as it attempts to entangle the line in kelp to pull the spear out. The outcome is usually determined by the will and strength of the participants.

The more in sync I became with the waters of
Catalina, the more in sync I became with myself. It
was a life I had always imagined living, and it was
a life I could not imagine living without. Having
thus simplified my existence, I had become comfortable with everything the sea could offer.

On the weekends, civilization crept over to the
island in all manner of boats and abilities to sail
them, often disrupting the harmony of the small
cove in which I was anchored. As was the case one
day early in the second year when two fellows, fearful of a bit of wind, tried to get inside my stern line
and eventually put their boat up on the rocks near
the beach. In that same summer, an absentminded
sailor crossed my stern line with his outboard and
frayed the line. The first good wind and swell that
came through broke the line and set my stern adrift
in the worst possible conditions. Labor Day weekend was the worst. Traditionally, every boat that
was able came over to Catalina, often this being
their one and only excursion out of the safety of a
marina. On one such weekend, I was anchored up
in Doctors Cove, which was rather large, and boats
were neatly anchored bow and stern side by side
the length of the cove. A catamaran came in and
dropped its hook short in front of the most wind-
ward boat. The wind pushed the catamaran down
the length of the cove, lifting anchor after anchor
of the boats at rest. I jumped in and free dove to
the bottom and lifted the anchor over my chain as
it went by with three different chains hung over it.
I was safe, but the chap next to me, seeing what I
had done, was pulling on his scuba unit when the
catamaran set him loose. There were boats bang-

ing into boats, chaos reigning amid anger, and in the end the entire cove turned on the skipper of the catamaran. One fellow came at him with a knife and cut his anchor line, setting him permanently free from us all.

And so it went from weekend to weekend.

After the boaters left, I more or less had the island to myself, and resettled into daily chores that ended in the early evening with a white sea bass hunt.

Each new season brought me closer to a thorough understanding of the white sea bass. Every year they would school in different areas of the island, and once those areas were located, it was just a matter of stalking them. Having found them for five consecutive years, eating what I caught and sharing the fish with others or trading for supplies, it came to the point that when the owner of the restaurant with whom I made the bulk of my trades would request a twenty-, thirty-, or a forty-pounder, I could usually produce the fish in a single hunt on any day.

Having made hundreds of hunts over a six-year period, I find some more memorable than others. Perhaps not so much for the techniques employed, but more for the circumstances under which the hunt took place. One such hunt occurred at Eagle Reef in the early morning. I had found the school of whites a month previously, so would normally dive on a pathway and wait, but this particular morning the visibility was clear and I was enjoying drifting through the kelp forests that surround this extensive reef. The forty-pound white was seen from the surface and I dropped down some distance away and, using kelp stalks as cover, made my way

172 C A R L O S   E Y L E S

toward it. The fish was resting in thirty feet of open water, and between us hovered a large school of baitfish. I eased my way into the bait and using it for cover, attempted to get close to the white. The bait suddenly spooked and exploded away, leaving me exposed. Stopping all movement, I hung there in the water. The white, sensitive to the disturbance of the bait, drifted off without ever seeing me. I rose for a breath as the fish swam slowly out of view, and I immediately began to track it from the surface. Though it moved slowly, it moved faster than I could swim silently, for the hard strokes of my fins would be heard and flush it off entirely. The fish became no more than a vague indication of light in the depths. If I took my eyes from its faint light, there would be no hope of relocating it again. It was in this manner that I followed it half the length of the reef, over a hundred yards, then out off the reef into deep water. Here, boats ran back and forth with engines whining in the windless early morning that created glassy seas over which water skiers were pulled. I could not look up for fear of losing sight of the fish, knowing full well that my black snorkel tube extending a few inches out of the water was all that could be seen, rendering me nearly invisible to the boat drivers. (On three different occasions, I have nearly been run down by boats—missed by inches. Several years ago, a spearfisherman was killed by a boat under similar circumstances.) I continued to follow the speck of light until it stopped in almost seventy feet of water near the sand bottom off the reef. Pumping up and diving, I speared the fish and brought it up in the midst of boat traffic running full blast on both sides of me. I held the spear gun high out of the water so I could more easily be seen; in response, the boats gave me room to maneuver back to the safety of the kelp beds and my skiff.

By the end of the third summer, I had so integrated into the sea that I would enter a school of whites and drift with them for no other reason but to observe. I watched as their skin would suddenly illuminate in sexual arousal, or as they would nudge one another affectionately with their noses, as horses often do. Intelligence flickered in their eyes, and knowledge dripped from their bodies as they moved in their quiet and unhurried way.

Years before I had begun the practice of acknowledging the white sea bass for the gift of itself by stroking it gently so that it would not die frightened after I had speared and brought it to hand. When butchering, I would take the first meat out of the neck and eat it, blessing the meat and giving thanks again for its gift, asking that its power be transferred to my spirit, a ritual that now bore far more significance in light of the intimate relationship I had developed with the fish.

As written in *The Last of the Blue Water Hunters*, "I find there is a distinct difference between the flesh of a wild animal and that of a domestic one. When we think of the conditions under which a chicken, for example, must live and grow, then these differences become apparent. Chickens live in a filthy, crowded environment. They are fed processed foods filled with chemicals; they are dirty and weak—this kind of existence affects every fiber of that chicken's being; it is spiritless and incomplete. The white sea bass is as wild as an animal can be: free and mobile, it roams the underwater wilderness at will. It is alive because it is strong and must hunt for its food, eating other equally strong and wild creatures. The white sea bass is clean, powerful and spirit-filled, a warrior living out its life. This kind of existence must affect every fiber of its being.

"I question why I should accept a life that is any less noble than that of the white sea bass."

Of all the times to hunt it was the evening, a few hours before dark in the dusky, eerie light of a setting sun, that the ocean became most alive, when the free-swimming creatures became both the hunted and the hunter, and the resulting tension was almost tangible. Seawater, five times more conductive than air, carried the coded messages of the sea like vaporous currents of electricity that lifted the small hairs on the back of the neck. In the dimming light, the eyes acquired a keenness previously unutilized as the head rotated like a slow searchlight, looking not with intensity but simply gazing, awaiting revelation from the slightest indication of light or shadow in the misty, indigo water. The creatures themselves were edgy and quick to judge movement as aggressive. The baitfish would hover and then explode away at apparently nothing at all. One was never sure. The pelagics, the yellowtail and bonito, would materialize and, like lightning, strike into the bait as would barracuda and the whites. It was also the time that the shark would awake from his daily slumber and patrol for the weak and infirm.

How wonderfully invigorating it was to feel the ocean in this way. To know that anything at all could happen, any sort of fish or shark could appear out of the pale light and into the electric blue. I was never more exhilarated in the water, never more alive, than during those moments at dusk. It was as if I had entered another portal of the sea, and was seeing and feeling a world that had changed to something other than what it was in the clear light of day.

When I was putting together the book, *Dolphin Borne*, the story called for two divers to be cast adrift out in the middle of an ocean. I needed to know what it was like to spend the night in the open ocean in several thousand feet of water. Taking the skiff far out into the channel, almost four miles, I tethered myself with a thirty-foot line (not close enough to afford a feeling of security) and went over the side. I first did this from six o'clock in the evening to midnight. Then again from two in the morning to sun up, around 6 A.M., I floated in that nether-world with no rock or kelp, and virtually no fish, though several tiny fish found me and hovered close for protection. In the night there was a blackness that gave new definition to the color black. I could scarcely see my hand in front of my face. Yet every movement created phosphorescent sparks of silvery light that careened about my face like buzzing fireflies. The tension of ensuing nightfall was palpable. The feeling of electric tension and utter vulnerability had me twitching and turning like the character in the book. A force was felt. It seemed to rise from the depths and pull at me from the stomach, like a black hole in some faraway galaxy sucking to its core all that was loose. The same was true in the very early morning when night slowly turned to day, and hallucination and otherworldly aberrations revealed themselves. The water became an opaque blue and the visibility appeared to be fuzzy and unreadable. I wrote, "The change was disconcerting because the unseen now lay but a few feet away. Dark, amoebic shapes appeared, some as large as a car as they undulated ten feet below the surface. They came and went, seeming to stay just beyond sharp visibility...more shapes appeared, some smaller, some of equal size." And it was so—those jelly-like shapes appeared until the sun broke the horizon and chased them back to the world from which they had come.

The ocean holds more mystery and power than we can ever imagine, and it would reveal its edges in the evening out on the hunt. Alone in the darkening sea, unknown corridors would awaken in me from prehistoric slumber through which would flow an almost overwhelming sense of harmony and connection. As if an electrical current had been turned on full, juicing my body to extrasensory levels, feeling in the quiet of depth an aliveness that seeped through every hair and pore that could receive the pulse of this dense atmosphere. Often, after such an evening, sleep was impossible and I would lie in the cockpit and stare into the moon and stars until the following morning, then go about my chores as if I had slept fitfully.

In those ideal days of summer the years slipped by, and time was only measured in the cold of winter when hibernating in the marina. Initially, I maintained some friendships from Laguna Beach and had a girlfriend who visited the boat from time to time. But as the months and years wore on and I became more entrenched in my writing and contemplative life, it rendered me less intriguing to women, and soon they gave up the ghost of who I once was. Waking at dawn each morning, I would eat a small breakfast then sit down to write. Writing did not come easy, for events in a wilderness do not unfold or are revealed in a linear fashion. Thus the words all came rushing out like a wave of impressions mingled with crazy information that only made sense when in the confluence of life's direct and rambling experience. *The Last of the Blue Water Hunters* was rewritten thirteen times. When I finished, I immediately began another book, *Dolphin Borne*, which, writing off and on, required seven years to complete.

Over time, friends and acquaintances wearying of my eccentric ways, stopped coming around. Being utterly alone is like death, both uplifting and frightening. Uplifting, because in solitude away from family and friends (who, if they were around, would do their utmost to sustain the old image of Carlos), I had the luxury of time and space to discover who and what I was. In that examination one's self is eventually revealed, digested, cried over, laughed over and finally, perhaps, accepted. Frightening, because I had entered uncharted territory. I was alone in the darkest places in myself, feeling my way through without benefit of a guide or guidelines. In such circumstances one finds oneself down grungy alleyways of their own making that have long hidden deep fears and lunatic aspects. At the end of day there was nowhere to run and hide, and I was forced to confront the demons of insecurity, self-doubt, anger and fear at a time, in many cases, when I was the most vulnerable to their influence.

The hunting, the isolation on board, the writing, all were designed in a conscious way to crack the illusion of self and reveal to some extent who exists behind the mask called Carlos.

Operating in the natural world was an enormous

benefit for that exploration, for it was nature, not people, who held up a mirror to my fears, and my insights, my joys and my difficulties. And its reflection was untainted by attitude, desire, or manipulation of any kind. Nature provides as honest and true a reflection as one can find. To be sure, hunkered down inside the bowels of a small boat for eight to nine months a year for six years is going to reveal a different self, one that is not entirely mirrored off nature, but one that is revealed in a mix of loneliness, self doubt and despair. Contemplation within these realms became as important as my time spent in the water.

In that pursuit I came across a passage by Carl Jung, the eminent psychiatrist, found in Peter Matthiessen's extraordinary book, *The Snow Leopard*.

"The fact that many a man who goes his own way ends in ruin means nothing....He must obey his own law, as if it were a daemon whispering to him of new and wonderful paths....There are not a few who are called awake by the summons of the voice, whereupon they are at once set apart from the others, feeling themselves confronted with a problem about which the others know nothing. In most cases it is impossible to explain to the others what has happened for any understanding is walled off by impenetrable prejudices....He is set apart and isolated, as he has resolved to obey the law that commands him from within. "His own law" everybody will cry. But he knows better: it is the law....The only meaningful life is a life that strives for the individual realization absolute and unconditional of its own particular law."

A great dark weight lifted from my spirit when I

read that passage. It seemed to validate this lonely and obscure path I had taken and gave me the confidence to continue in its pursuit, wherever it might lead.

That the "true self" emerged from this period is doubtful, for that was left with the boy in Hawaii and would require intense disciplines to bring forth, if that were even possible. I had neither the desire nor the strength to embark down paths far darker and more intense than the one I had endured for so many years. I was content that if the true self did not emerge, then certainly a "truer" self evolved. In the end, I was reasonably free of the debilitating constraints of the culture, and reemerged into the liquid world from which I was born: of the sea, in the sea, pure and simple. I had come to recognize the presence of Spirit in all things, leaving no doubt that I and all of mankind were inexorably connected to the living universe of the planet. I came to embrace the simple life on board a boat and was content to live that way forever.

# DAY
## 25

Returning to La Paz, we pick up supplies and I am rejoined with my wife, Margaret, who is waiting at the airport. She will accompany us on our short run to Cabo San Lucas. We leave on moonrise and this departure holds special meaning, for now we head south, and will maintain a southerly course until reaching our final destination, San Benedicto Island in the Revillagigedo archipelago.

The wind is to our backs and the seas smooth. Or so it seems to Jack and me. Margaret, unaccustomed to the roll of swell, hovers on the edge of seasickness. Jack wisely puts her on the helm, and the concentration required to keep the boat pointed in a general direction is enough to quell her queasiness until she is able to go below and find sleep. We pass Cerralvo Island on the east, lit by a full moon casting a heavenly light, bright enough to read by. The moon's reflection dances across the sea surface as if the sea itself were conjuring up another source of illumination deep within its void. Preferring the watch from eight until midnight, I gaze over the transom where the boat's wake carries the moon's reflection off to the east and west.

The boat courses through the luminescent water as if in the night the *Nirvana* has found her wings and chooses to run faster than the wind can push her.

# DAY
# 26

After an uneventful sail of ten hours, we arrive in Bahia de Los Muertos, the very bay where I began this trip twenty-five days ago, and drop the hook. Since we last passed this way the number of campsites on the bluff have doubled. Americans seem to be everywhere on the land, but few are in the water, and I wonder why they come if not to plunge into the Gulf.

With Pam home for Christmas, I was doing the cooking, and though Jack was quite reassuring in this regard, with Margaret on board we are treated to our first decent meal in over a week. Jack, delighted with the pesto and pasta dish put before him, raves about it far too long into the night.

# DAY
# 27

We leave at daybreak for Los Frailles just south of Cabo Pulmo. It is a short run and we are accompanied by fin whales for a time and mobulas that breach in their helter-skelter way, wings akimbo, doing somersaults and back flips, sometimes reaching fifteen feet in the air. One can scarcely look out towards the water and not see a mobula in the air. Beneath the surface the water must be quenched with thousands of them. I have seen them en masse under the water before, not far from here near Rancho Buena Vista. We were picking lobster off a reef near the beach when a school of uncountable numbers wheeled in perfect formation and then spun away into the blue. A single show, one time only.

In the late afternoon we anchor in Los Frailles. I first dove here in 1972 after Carol and I drove our VW bus down soon after the road opened the length of the Baja Peninsula. There were no buildings here, nothing other than an unoccupied half-built cinder block hut. We stayed a week, finding lobster and big grouper off the rocks at the north end of the bay. I make a jump to see what is left of the grou-

per, but there is no sign of any rockfish whatsoever. The water feels cold and there is a green hue
to its color, much like the turbid waters in the Pacific Northwest. The entire area that was once so
prolific is barren, save for a strange gathering of
silver perch that seem to thrive in the empty water, for they are everywhere to the exclusion of all
else.

Declining a return trip in the skiff to the *Nirvana*, I elect to swim the final half-mile, condition-
ing my legs for San Benedicto. The silver perch pool
beneath me mirroring my swim from the surface.
Diving down to them, they scatter off in all directions and then reform as I surface. When I reach
the edge of the sand they circle back into the rocks
and boulders and are gone.

There was once a fish camp at the southern tip
of the beach where an underground river runs into
the Gulf. Here, just off the beach, the depth of the
water is several hundred feet. It has been said that
the big fishing boats would point up to the beach,
throw an anchor on the sand, and fish for tuna in
this deep channel forged by the river. I dove there
looking for tuna and had one come along back then
in 1972, I would have been hard pressed to land it.
Any good-sized tuna, pound for pound the strongest fish in the sea, would have taken my reel and
me to the depths. Strange noises emanated from
this water like the deep-throated song of a humpback whale. I assumed the source of the sounds to
have been the underground river pushing its way
into the sea. Story has it that the shoreline above
the mouth of the river collapsed and the fishing
camp that was pitched over it was lost into the sea,
killing the fishermen in their sleep. There was a

huge bite taken out of the land at shore's edge that would indicate the story of the river and the devoured fishing camp might be true. And if so, then perhaps the wailing sounds I heard were those of the lost fishermen.

What I do know to be true is that while here in 1972, a teenage boy showed up with his father, and with a small spear gun, which he cocked while standing in thigh deep water off the shore, speared a fish that swam by his knees. After a great struggle he dragged a thirty-five-pound roosterfish onto the beach and never got his face wet.

This day, twenty-four years later, there are campers everywhere on the beach. I count fifteen large homes and a half dozen outbuildings inland from the beach of Los Frailles. There is a hotel with five large bungalows that I am told go for a hundred dollars a night. There might be a great deal more going on in Los Frailles that I am unable to see from the boat, but I have no desire to go ashore and investigate. Who knows, there might even be a Wendy's or McDonalds lurking in the bush. One thing is certain; there are a great many more campers on the beach than there are thirty-five-pound roosterfish cruising in three feet of water.

# DAY
# 28

T he wind has died leaving loose-loomed weav-
ings of clouds against the brilliant sky. We
weigh anchor at sunup with the intent of making
Cabo San Lucas by dusk, allowing for a stop on the
Gorda Banks.

There is not a breath of air and the *Nirvana* mo-
tors across the glass sea; far to the east a fin whale
moves north. Gorda Banks lies five to six miles offshore in deep water and is nothing more than a
series of deep pinnacles, the highest coming to
within one hundred twenty feet of the surface. Arriving shortly after 11 A.M., we search the area for
a high spot on which to anchor. Jack is proficient
with the GPS and depth finder and is able to find a
pinnacle after a methodical search. As we drop the
anchor, two forty-pound wahoo cruise next to the
boat. Jack hurries into his wet suit, but by the time
he is in the water with a spear gun, the wahoo have
vanished. Dropping over the side, Margaret and I
hang above the bottomless searing blue like wing-
less birds floating high in another sky.

Jack dives deep, searching for the pelagic wahoo.
He, like many of his generation of divers, tends to

concentrate more on the depth of the dive, which in my view, is overrated as a necessary hunting skill. To the novice hunter it must appear that once the barriers of depth are overcome, the difficult aspect of the stalk has been mastered. In reality, the depth one dives is the least important element of a stalk, particularly when hunting for pelagic fish that generally run nearer the surface. Here, the reading of the ocean is critical: the subtleties of the bait, the direction and speed of a current, the depth of a thermocline, the time of day, and a complete knowledge of the characteristics and patterns of the species being hunted. These are the signs the blue water hunter must recognize and properly interpret. To complicate matters, this information is ever changing and must be continually reassessed. Eventually, if the diver is of right mind, the information will flow through without "thought" and be held as a knowing that reveals itself as instinct which directs him along in the seemingly traceless ocean.

On this day, I look for such signs from the surface—bait, a whisper of light, anything that would indicate some kind of high spot or fish activity. After an hour a single fish, small, of no identifiable species, angles toward the bottom. Diving on it to thirty feet, three wahoo materialize to my left. Materialize may be an overused word, but there is no better way to describe how these fish appear out of nothingness. I point out the whaoo to Jack on my ascent and he begins to stalk, but the wahoo are wary and keep their distance. He makes four dives, but can't draw them closer than twenty feet. They tantalize by their presence and he is reluctant to give up the chase. For a half-hour they weave in and out of visibility. In the meantime, a strong current has picked up and further inhibits Jack's effort. Additionally, a wind has begun to blow out of the north. In ten minutes we are struggling back to the boat, which is now up current. In ten more minutes we arrive tired and weakly clamber aboard.

As we pull anchor and put the boat in gear, a terrible noise, like metal breaking into pieces inside a steel drum, erupt out of the bowels of the *Nirvana*. Even I know this is not good. A quick inspection reveals the fresh water pump has ripped itself asunder and lies in a crippled state of uselessness. We have no choice but to sail to Cabo San Lucas.

The wind favors us until the passing of the sun, then dies as the lights of Cabo San Lucas fill the horizon. It appears the boat is as reluctant as I to visit Cabo San Lucas. We flounder for a half-hour, then pick up a westerly that is wrapping up the peninsula. Jack assures Margaret that we will be sitting off the beach in one hour, and she goes into the galley to prepare an enchilada casserole in a bright red dish bought in La Paz expressly for this purpose. We tack our way into Cabo San Lucas under a failing wind. The one hour run becomes two, and when finally we are anchored near a well-lit beach, it is almost three hours later. Margaret's casserole has become tortilla mush. Jack insists it will still be good as she doles out a spoonful that has all the appearances of oatmeal. He takes a bite and nods his head approvingly. Margaret has seen enough and takes the meal, dish and all and chucks it over the side of the boat. Jack follows its flight with fork half raised to an open mouth. He holds the moment as the dish seems to hang in mid-air above the gunnels then disappears with a splash. The fork still at half-mast, his eyes shift to me, unsure if the fork's journey should be completed. I shrug, familiar with her Latin temperament. Margaret returns to the galley to break out crackers and canned soup as Jack's fork finishes its interrupted journey.

# DAY
## 29

Whitewashed walls of the hotels that line the beach of Cabo San Lucas reflect clean morning desert sunlight. Prepared to be disgusted at the sight, I find a certain wonderment to the spectacle. Margaret suggests we "pretend it's a different place." (From the one I knew in 1967.) To which Jack replies, "It is."

We launch the skiff and head for town. Jack makes a phone call and finds that the broken water pump may keep us in Cabo San Lucas for a week or more. This is disconcerting news, for I want no part of this place. Jack and Margaret, however, are enthralled and navigate their way easily among the crowded sidewalks filled with semi-drunk Americans and greedy Mexicans hawking everything from time shares and ATV's to gum and clothes, shoes and hats. Through it all I rant and rave against the dying of another, better time.

A man with straw hats piled on top of his head and stacked on his hands is selling them for one peso. "Almost free," he says. One peso is worth eighteen cents. I wonder about the woman or child who wove these hats, which had to take at least three hours. For everyone to make a profit, she must have been toiling for three to four cents, probably less. An American woman hands me a card, encouraging me to use AT&T when making my long distance calls to the States. When I wordlessly hand back the card, she mutters, "I guess people like you don't have anyone to call."

Overwhelmed by the transplanted chaos, I descend into melancholy, becoming rude to Jack, who doesn't understand. "How can you come from the serenity of the sea to all this crazy and frenetic energy and not be affected?" Jack looks at me and sighs. He, like most, easily accepts the conditions of the environment where he finds himself. He has no knowledge of dogs sleeping on the beach or of amberjack in the bay or lobster on a reef. He only knows the insanity of Cabo, and it seems perfectly reasonable. Jack looks at me again, no doubt projecting what three more weeks will be like with this moribund depressant who doesn't seem to have as firm a grip on land as he does at sea.

He is right. I have no grip whatsoever. There is no escape from the mayhem even out at anchor where mindless jet skiers race madly up and down the beach and around boats from morning to dusk while rap music blares from the beach. Dazed, I sit in the cockpit, absently reading the same lines of a book over and over, longing for the quiet of the open water.

# DAY
## 30

Margaret must return to the States to continue her work as a Rolfer. Today, accompanying her to the airport, I become gloomy, knowing we will not see each other again for another month. She takes the broken water pump with her to the States where we hope it can be repaired and then picked up by Pam upon her return. Once Margaret has left I fall into deep depression. Jack wisely avoids me as I settle in to wait out the week in the cockpit of the boat.

After six of the most revealing and important years of my life living on board the sailboat, having scarcely made any money as a writer during that time, and though frugal and quite able to get by on three hundred dollars a month, I was in debt and tapped out. The book sales amounted to very little, and eventually I was left with no choice but to sell my precious sailboat and forsake the life I was prepared to live into old age. In retrospect, it was probably time to get off the boat. The isolation had accentuated my eccentricities, and while I always had difficulty interacting with the world, now

*My first big sheepshead taken off Laguna Beach in the summer of 1957 with a Hammerhead spear gun.*

*This hundred-pound grouper was taken at the Round Table on the first trip to Guardian Angel Island in 1972. Photo: Bill Brown.*

*The white sea bass is the most challenging fish to stalk. This sixty-six pounder was taken at Church Rock off Catalina Island.*

*A male sea lion, establishing his territory, charges us at Los Islotes.*

*After a five-hour wait, a blissful moment finally occurred when the sea lion and the sun merged in the cave at Los Islotes.*

*"Into the Light": the dolphin silhouette at White Sand Ridge was a turning point in my photography career.*

*Looking to interact, a group of Atlantic spotted dolphins approach me on the White Sand Ridge.*

*The unpredictability of sharks is demonstrated in this wild-eyed frenzy breaking loose at Walker's.*

*This breaching humpback whale left us awestruck on our second morning at San Benedicto.*

Brian Quinn brings up a hundred fifty-pound yellowfin tuna while the sharks circled below on the blood spoor.

*Jack picks up footage of a twelve-foot galapagos on the southwest corner of the island.*

*This black manta, weighing over a ton, dwarfs Jack as he moves in for a shot.*

*Flying Air Manta: Jack catching a ride on the blue edge.*

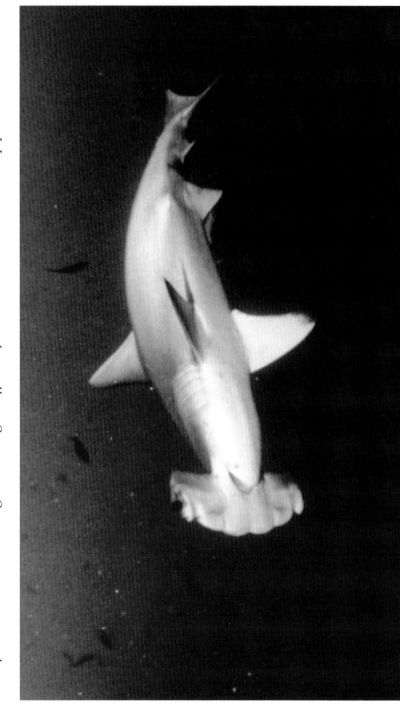

*A ten-foot hammerhead is caught in the lights off one of San Benedicto's southern deep pinnacles.*

*A spooked manta ray takes me to the bottom. Photo: Tom Lyon.*

*Running with the wolves—the hammerheads on the southwest corner of San Benedicto.*

it was next to impossible. It had become a complicated ordeal to carry on a regular conversation. A friend, concerned for me, thought it would be a good idea to get me off the boat, and so dragged me along to a small party. It turned out to be a rather wild affair, at least by my standards; I danced with a pretty girl who was willing to ditch her husband so that we might have sex in the bathroom. There were drugs and loud music that never stopped. When finally it was obvious that I was overcome, my friend carted me back to my boat where I bedded down and waited for sleep. Wired up from the stimulation, I could not sleep for two days.

If I didn't know before, I knew then that I was incapable of returning to a "normal" life.

With a little under five thousand dollars in my pocket after the sale of the boat and debts paid, and unable to reenter society much less be employed, I was left no options but to continue down the path I had begun seven years earlier. I decided to travel to the South Pacific until the money ran out. It was my hope I could find a place where I might continue to live off the sea. I narrowed several choices down to the Republic of Fiji for no other reason than there were three hundred and fifty islands in the Fijian archipelago, most of which were uninhabited, and the odds appeared good that I could find a place where I might make a life for myself.

I wound up on the island of Taveuni in the northern island group. Through the help of Ric and Do Cammick who ran Dive Taveuni, I was able to spend a few days in their compound and dove the nearby reefs for fish, getting acclimated to my new surroundings. I described a particular fish to Do, which was large and had a mouth and body like a snapper, gray in color with a white spot on its back. She said it was a good eating fish, but smart and difficult to spear.

In the course of daily events I met Dive Taveuni's cook, Ruthie, a Fijian woman in her early forties who took an interest in me because I was a free diver who speared fish. Ruthie explained that a good many of island-bound Fijians were spearfishermen and she had never met an American who speared fish. After disclosing my ill-laid plans to her, she generously offered to take me to her island, with the idea that I could find a place among Fijians and spear fish. Saying goodbye and thanks to the Cammicks, I loaded my gear into a derelict, ten-foot wooden skiff with the oldest ten horse outboard I had ever seen. As Ruthie steered, I bailed while the sea poured in over the bow, and we plowed our way south into a fifteen-knot wind blowing off six-foot swells, barely making headway. In no time we were soaked to the bone. Near nightfall we had crossed the Tasman Strait and were in the lee of Qamea Island.

Ruthie piloted us to her humble home hacked out of a mangrove. The ramshackle dwelling of wood and thatch with a twisted corrugated tin roof, made so by the last hurricane that blew through, was humble to the point of poverty. Here lived her mother, Mariah, who, in halting English welcomed me, as did her younger sister, Alice, and her sister-in-law, Lavenia, the wife of Harvey, her brother. I later came to learn that these fine generous people were outcasts, Mariah having married a German man; thus the children were labeled half-breeds. They spoke English and were among a small mi-

nority of Fijians to do so. Nevertheless, they welcomed me into their home with gracious warm
smiles. Harvey arrived shortly with a fish for dinner. After hearing my story, he offered to put me in
a shack of my own on a small beach and bring me
vegetables and water in exchange for a hundred
pounds of fish a week, which amounted, he assured
me, to two big wailu. I would hunt for my own sustenance off the beach and Harvey would take me
out to the deep reefs once a week where roamed
the wailu (an oversized Spanish mackerel, the
southern hemisphere's version of the wahoo).

Harvey, perhaps unsure if I could deliver the
goods, suggested we set out early the next morning
for the deep reefs to hunt the wailu.

In the morning after a night of sleeping on the
matted floor next to a demented rooster who declared the passage of each hour, we headed out to
sea. Several miles from the island, in the middle of
seemingly nowhere, Harvey declared this was the
spot. Looking over the side of the boat, I could see
the reef clearly a hundred and twenty feet down. I
was in the water scarcely a minute before the first
big fish cruised by. The glycerin-clear water fooled
me into believing I was nearer to it than I actually
was and my shot fell short. After misjudging several more shots, I finally speared one that was well
over a hundred pounds and of course incredibly
powerful. Even with a float, I couldn't turn it, and
in its initial run, it tore off into a hundred and
twenty-foot bottom where it and the rigging disappeared into the vast depths. The fish took everything: spear shaft, point and cable, and left me the
gun with only one spare spear shaft and point. This
rig suddenly became precious, for without it I would

be unable to spear big fish. We searched for the fish until noon, but were unable to find it or any trace of my gear. Harvey, no doubt, was having misgivings regarding my ability to spear a large fish, but after re-rigging, I speared two smaller wailu that weighed forty-five pounds apiece, and by his nodding head, I assumed that at least some questions had been answered.

After the hunt, we motored to the eastern end of Qamea, steering along the far edge of the coral reefs that fingered straight out from shore. There was no sign of human life on this side of the island, only ebony mounds of lava smoothed by the sea to high tide and then green jungle. Harvey pointed to a small beach of white sand wedged between a great lava fissure in the island. The sand beach deepened and two thatched huts appeared, one behind the other. He killed the engine and we drifted ashore. The white sand beach, bejeweled with shells and broken coral, gave no evidence of man. Fifty feet up the beach stood an open hut with, of all things, a propane stove. This was the kitchen, and twenty feet behind it a fully enclosed hut of palm frond and wood. Inside was a bed, and even more extraordinary than the stove, a gas-powered refrigerator that Harvey assured me, worked. Harvey had a propane bottle for the stove and enough gas to fire up the fridge. All this had been left by a New Zealander who had abandoned his dream of retirement after experiencing his first hurricane.

Mariah had generously provided me sheets, pillow and a blanket, and after considerable tidying with Harvey's help, the place became livable. With his own tasks before him, Harvey wished me well, returned to his skiff and disappeared around the far point. Sitting on the beach, I gazed out across the Tasman Strait. I was completely removed from civilization, inhabiting a land and sea with which I was unfamiliar, in a culture whose language I could not speak or understand. It was a moment that made my time aboard the sailboat seem almost congested. The past became vague and far away, the future unfathomable.

In that moment a sense of profound surrender occurred. Here I was on a tiny beach in the middle of the South Pacific knowing nothing, not even the sea, and starting over. I had found my way to Eden and the shroud of an uncertain future pushed the limits of my resistance until it dissolved into the white sand and shell shards there on the beach.

The sea was as unfamiliar as the land, and its language, the language of the tropical, was not easily deciphered. The water, as clear as liquid glass, transparent to one hundred and twenty feet on a bad day, held strange fish of every shape and vibrant color. They probed the reefs like butterflies on a magnolia tree. The coral formations were otherworldly, as if grand white statues of Poseidon had toppled from great heights and shattered to pieces there in the shallows beyond the beach. As I had written earlier in *Secret Seas*, "The heaps of shimmering, broken white bones lie in contrast to the browns of the reef, the grays of the dead coral, and the touches of blues and purples of the flowering coral; the rest, the reds, yellows, oranges and greens, were dimmed by the filtered depths. The vast beauty of this oceanic utopia was grander than my meager senses could comprehend."

As for the fish life I wrote, "The water, as clear as air, held vibrating fish of brilliant colors that seemed nothing less than color itself, come alive off a mad man's palette. A fluorescent green floated atop a striking purple that crashed into marigold yellow; a dapple of hyacinth sprinkled over a lavender tail, a brush stroke of fuchsia across a wisteria eye, apricot bellies dotted with vermilion. Fish so surrealistically painted that Salvador Dali might weep with joy."

It was into this new world I entered.

Beyond the sheltered coral swam the larger fish and the reef sharks. Whitetip and blacktip sharks, I discovered upon spearing fish, would allow about thirty seconds retrieval time before they would descend in numbers. Once the fish was in my hand the sharks would slow their movements and, for all intent, the game would be over. These were not big sharks but were uniform in size, five to six feet. The blacktips were more aggressive than the whitetips which, when there was no blood in the water, were as docile as manatees. The blacktips were more territorial and would rush my back on occasion, then veer off as I caught sight of them. I had never been around so many sharks before, and though I had more or less worked out my fears, whenever I speared a fish there were anxious moments until I got it to my hand. After the first month I was able to relax and feel my way through their presence, no longer fearing that I might be mistakenly bitten while carrying a bleeding fish back to shore.

Spearing fish was not the simple matter I expected it to be. Refusing to spear any of the tropicals, which eliminated eighty percent of the population, and finding the remaining fish unusually wary (which I later learned was due to the lo-

cals coming over to this same area to spear fish), I
continued to hunt for the silver snapper that Do
had recommended. But it was cautious and would
always stay just out of range of the small spear gun.
Despite this, I was able to sustain myself quite
nicely with rainbow runners, coral trout (a small
grouper), and small snapper.

The new sea poured into me faster than could be
assimilated. The first few months became a process of internalizing all that was occurring under
the water. The quick, busy ocean world of the trop-
ics began to slow. The obvious, represented in startling form and color that once so overwhelmed,
faded into the background and an intimate sense
of the sea blossomed, revealing among other things,
the subtle hidden among the grandiose and spectacular. With this grew an intuitive sense for the
presence of sharks that enabled me to often get a
feel for them before I could actually see them.
Maybe not so unusual, for this was my first experience since Baja diving among so many sharks, and
it would be quite natural to keep tabs on them in
some form or another. Perhaps I was not as free
from them as I believed. Other than one incident
when I could not get to a fish quickly enough, and
first the blacktips then the whitetips hit it, forcing
me up on a coral head with them nipping at anything that caught the light or moved. There was no
other incident that would cause me to sense them
as clearly as I did. This sensing of the sharks was
not a nervous sort of head twitching reflex, but a
calm realization that sharks were nearby, usually
behind some coral head or other such grand underwater escarpment from which they would suddenly
appear, following their noses in my direction.

It was my habit to alternate the spear gun one day and the camera the next. Usually a speared fish would cover two good meals, and if the fish was large, then I would share it with Harvey and his family. In this routine the days passed into weeks and the weeks into months. Rarely a day slipped by that I did not get in the water. I had found caves which held grouper, discovered a transition zone where ran the pelagics, made my way among sea snakes, lionfish, and all manner of odd and dangerous creatures. Here, the real threat wasn't the shark, but a very small sea snail housed in a black and white shell, no larger than a thumbnail, whose bite could drop a man stone dead in a matter of minutes. The minutiae awaited a misstep or a careless bump to deliver its lethal assault. Despite care and caution, my arms and legs were covered with coral cuts, strange bites and the inevitable infections.

When Harvey came with vegetables and water and often kava, a mild narcotic drink made from the root of the pepper tree, we would talk long hours into the night on subjects as far ranging as religion and drugs, politics and sex. In those inspiring evenings we became fast friends. On Tuesday mornings he would pick me up in the skiff and run me out to the deep reefs to spear the wailu. My breathhold and legs were now capable of taking me to one hundred-foot depths, which I had never done before, the ultra-clear water making such dives psychologically accessible.

Fiji had become home, the present, the only time I kept. The tranquility in many ways exceeded the balance and harmony I had found on my boat. The community of Fijians who would come by the beach in their small skiffs included me in their spearfishing forays. Despite this rapport there existed a barrier of privacy I was not permitted to breach. They never invited me to their village nor encouraged me to speak to any of the women. Though a diver among them, I was nonetheless an outsider, yet I did not consider the exclusion a slight, for I was not particularly interested in becoming involved in the social machinations of village convention or protocol. It was enough to spear fish with the men. (Who, armed with a free shaft hand spear would dive without fins or snorkels in the way man had dived in the early stages of the Underwater Age, while the woman gathered sea shells which they would boil out in large kettles on the beach, eating the meat and later selling the shells to Indian merchants.) For the most part, I would visit with the head man who usually spoke some English, and we would discuss the nature of the sea and how, in its abundance, it had always fed his family and the village, and how, if they continue hunting with the spear, it always would. When I asked him about the scarcity of the beautiful shells that once bloomed on the Fijian reefs, he shook his head. "We used to take the shells from the beach for decoration and dress up," he said. "There was always plenty after a storm. Then the goggles came and we would take more from the reefs, but there was always still plenty. When the tourists came, the Indians (these are citizens from India who had immigrated to Fiji and became merchants and businessmen) began selling the shells and paying us money for them. It was only a few cents, but it was enough to make us greedy and to let us buy sugar and salt and more gas for the engines of our boats. Now there are no shells left, and no money. It would have been better to have the shells; now the young girls have nothing for dress up."

One afternoon after five months of living on the beach, I was returning from deep water after having no luck at the transition zone, which was unusual. Rarely was I skunked on a hunting day. Swimming parallel to a drop-off that fell to a hundred feet, I saw in the distance a massive shape moving quickly along at seventy feet. A whale, I thought, a pilot whale. Moving in line with the animal to get a good look, I soon realized that it was not a whale but a shark—a very large shark, moving quickly, that would pass almost directly beneath me. The realization of the mammoth shark paralyzed me there on the surface. It was twenty-five feet long and by its markings clearly identifiable as a tiger shark, thirteen feet across from pectoral tip to pectoral tip, with a remora on its back that was as large as me. In that shark I saw my death; I felt it coming. I tracked the shark with the puny spear gun used for small fish, knowing it would have absolutely no effect should the tiger decide to rise and do with me as it would. At that same moment it occurred to me how, just minutes ago, I had agonized over my inability to spear a fish, and if I had had a bloody carcass strung to my weight belt, how much worse things might be. The shark turned slightly at an angle when it was directly beneath me and gazed up at my frozen form on the surface. Then, maintaining its baleful stare, it banked off into deeper water and was out of sight in seconds. I moved in next to a reef as if to hide from its great shadow and hugged close so as to lose myself in the coral. In this way I made my way to shore. Long after that episode I sat on the beach, looking out over the placid sea and considered the shark. It was the most powerful, omnipotent creature I had ever encountered. I had been completely at its mercy, and was sure that had I speared a fish, its blood spoor would have generated a much different ending. I retraced my stalking steps, attempting to discover what had caused me to miss shot after shot on fish that normally would have been routine strikes. After a good deal of pondering and coming to no logical solution, I concluded the answer lay elsewhere.

Harvey came to visit and I told him of the shark. He listened stunned, saying it was the Sea God then left quickly in his skiff.

Within a week the news had spread to all villages in the surrounding islands. Three days later, I was asked to be a guest at the most primitive of villages on Qamea. Harvey said later I was the first man on the island in many generations to witness the Sea God while in the water, thus bringing honor to the island and its villages. I would spend many months off and on drinking kava around a small kerosene lantern in sleeping *bures*, recounting the tale of the Sea God to the elders of other villages.

Into my seventh month on the beach, when, through a sheer piece of stalking trickery that gave the illusion I was elsewhere, then made a long underwater swim to wait in hiding beneath a ledge, the silver/gray snapper with the white spot was, after months of stalking, finally seduced into range and I was able to spear it. The fish was a good size for a reef fish, maybe twenty-five pounds, and I gave half of it to Harvey and ate the other half over the course of two days. On the morning of the third day, I was unable to rise from my bed. My body lay ridgid in paralysis. Unable to get up even to urinate, I relieved myself on the floor beneath my bed. Over the course of my stay on the beach, I had acquired several deep infections from coral cuts, was drinking mosquito larvae-filled water, and had lost considerable weight off my already lean body. Believing I had contracted a fatal illness, I surrendered to the inevitable. Though not in pain, strange sensations occurred in my hands and feet.

Three days prior to that fateful day, having physically endured the hardships that this sort of existence will bring, I was struck with a revelation while sitting utterly fatigued on the beach watching the sun set behind Taveuni. I had somewhere along the way, either released or had knocked out of me, my tenacious grip on the life-long concepts that supported my so-called reality. There on the beach, I realized I had let go of the results of my actions, let go of the manipulation of events that would favor me, let go of the pursuits of achievement and joy, let go of sorrow and even death. In that state, it seemed I was able to accept whatever life had to offer and welcomed it into my experience without judging it to be good or evil, worthwhile or trivial. A lightness came and thereafter, I seemed to float through the days with an inner peacefulness I had never known.

I felt free in the truest definition of the word. Or at least felt as free as I had ever been in my adult life. I wrote in my journal, which I faithfully kept, "Let go of the world, let go, let go, let go," over and over, filling three pages so that I might never forget this precious gift and have it slip away. It was a feeling of such relief, as if finally I had found a way into myself that led utterly away from a self-absorbed existence.

Three days later I was waiting for my death. Unafraid, I resigned to having reached the age of forty-seven and no more. I waited peacefully all night, sleeping, not expecting to wake. Morning came and I could move, though with effort. After sitting for five minutes, I stood shakily. Parched, I drank and fixed myself something to eat. Later in the morning, Harvey came and agreed we should probably go to the hospital on Taveuni.

The following day he prepared his boat and ran me over to Taveuni where Do Cammick informed me that the symptoms were those of ciguatera—toxic fish poisoning—common among the islanders, deadly at times. A family sits down for a fish dinner, and next morning they are all found dead. Usually, if one makes it through the first night, one will live. I would live, but my endocrine system was severely damaged. It would come to pass that whenever I ate seafood of any kind, my body would believe it was being poisoned and would affect counter-measures causing me to contract acute hypoglycemia. At the time I didn't know what was going on. The hypoglycemia, or low blood sugar, would give me the shakes, insomnia, and a terrible inability to concentrate. It was all I could do to get through a day. There was no medical treatment for me in Fiji, and unable to live as I had, was forced to leave.

On to New Zealand for five months where I discovered there was no treatment for ciguatera anywhere in the world. I recovered enough to do some diving up in the North Island in the Bay of Islands, speared a kingfish and, believing I had recuperated from my illness, ate the fish and again became severely ill. I went on to Australia to spend a month on the Barrier Reef, but the experience was tainted with the illness that was to last two and a half years, and very nearly drove me crazy in a certifiable way.

The Sea God had proclaimed in a grand display of irony that I would never eat seafood again. It was thus that I never hunted for fish again, and the deep connection I had made with the sea through spearfishing had come to an end.

# DAY
# 31

This afternoon, while wandering the back streets above Cabo San Lucas in search of a bit of the old town, I come across a small house squeezed between two stores that faced a low rent hotel across the street. The owner of the home, Socorro Remero Valle, sixty-six years old, sits on her porch with some of her family watching the world bustle by. She has lived in Cabo San Lucas all her life. As a young woman she rowed the panga while the fishermen fished. "It was a hard life, but there was much tranquility," she told me. She sold fruit to the mariners and fishermen from all over the world who, seeking refuge from the winds and seas of the Pacific, would find comfort at the cape. I asked how things were different now, and she replied, "Before the hotels and the Americans, we had no jail. When someone got too drunk, we tied them to a tree so they wouldn't hurt themselves. The people who work here now and make the money are not from here. They come from other places. Many are bad and steal whatever they can. The jail is big."

Twenty years ago, having left a perfectly good

outboard motor beside a tree in Bahia de Los Angeles, I was told it would be safe if left for a few
days. As things went, I would not return for several months, but when I did the outboard was exactly where I had left it. This was the Mexico I had
come to know and love. There is not a shred of that
Mexico here in Cabo San Lucas, where, it appears,
the residents have fared no better than the Gulf.

# DAY
## 32

Late in the day Jack returns to the boat wired up like he just got off the 405 freeway. He had met up with sailor/diver Terry Kennedy who has spent a good deal of time down at San Benedicto Island. Terry, along with Joyce Clinton, on February 14, 1994, video taped the massacre of the giant pacific manta ray by commercial fishermen. The video found its way to the proper authorities and was responsible for creating a sanctuary in the Revillagigedos Islands, off limits to all commercial boats. It eventually excluded all boats, including pleasure craft. To legally visit the Revillagigedos, one must secure a permit or risk confiscation of one's boat and all property on board. We are without a permit, and although San Benedicto is rarely traveled by the navy, Jack is placing his boat and all gear on board at risk. Terry K. has given Jack a detailed chart of the island, which comes as a much needed reference, for we were headed down blind; in those waters of submerged rocks and reef, particularly around an anchorage, we are grateful for any information.

# DAY
# 33-35

Each day Jack travels into town and phones the States to check out the progress of the water pump while I wait it out on the boat and fall into reveries of the Cabo San Lucas of 1967. I recall lying on the beach after a dive and staring up at the sky as a string of pelicans came out of the west. They followed the edge of the coastline north, and at one point, their noble line stretched from horizon to horizon.

The only pelicans I have seen this time are those who have become scavengers, plunging into the foul waters of the marina to pluck dead baitfish thrown over by the fishing boats. They dive amongst their dead and floating brethren who have supped too long at this poisoned water hole.

Although marooned here, we have found diversion. Tomorrow we will take a boat out seven miles to the west in deep water where tuna have been "boiling everywhere," says Temo Ramirez, a dive operator here in Cabo. We are encouraged by this promising news. Perhaps tomorrow Jack will break his long string of spearfishing disappointments.

# DAY
# 36

Rising before sunup with a planned departure of 6:30, we are not out of the marina until 8:30. Mexicans are never in much of a hurry to go anywhere. Jack has brought a hand-held GPS to assist in finding the exact location of this high spot out in the middle of the blue desert that comes up to two hundred feet around which the tuna are purportedly congregating. A couple of miles out of the marina I am curious about our direction and look for a compass near the helm. There is none. Asking Temo of its whereabouts, he looks down at his watch saying, "This watch does many things; it is also a compass." Jack gives me a look and I smile, not because we are setting out into the wild Pacific with a Cracker Jack compass, but because this is the very heart of Mexico and Mexicans that I found so attractive thirty years ago. They get by so well on so very little.

Three times we stop due to excessive smoke bellowing from the engine compartment and check for fire. It is only a ringless engine gorging on oil. A quart is added and we are on our way again. On every slam of a wave this twenty-eight-foot cutty cabin boat shudders, pieces coming loose and getting re-duct-taped on. The fellow at the wheel knows only one speed, full throttle. Within an hour we come to rest in open water and are told, "This is it, the tuna are here." There are no boils, no birds, no sign of anything. We make the jump, swim around in the blue void for twenty minutes seeing nothing but a single puffer fish. Why or how it got out here remains a mystery.

A large tuna boat is working the water several miles away. Curious, we motor over and from a distance watch a half dozen men work a purse seine net, hauling in maybe thirty fish averaging forty to sixty pounds apiece. So the tuna are here. We jump and look around, but there is no sign of fish. It is decided to return to the high spot. On dead reckoning the skipper, without the aid of the Cracker Jack compass, puts us within two hundred yards of the spot. Jack checks it with the GPS, shaking his head in abject wonder. I mention again that technology is overrated; the best instrument is still man himself. The Mexicans continue to exercise, with great acuity, the instrument of man. While true they may have little choice, there is pride in the performance of the skipper, and his skills are acknowledged by all. They recognize the value of knowing the way without relying on something outside themselves. Upon gearing up for another jump on the high spot, Jack leaves his Do-Everything watch on board. Still, there is no sighting of tuna, and after forty minutes we head back to Cabo.

This is typical of so many hunts, past and present. There is talk of some fabulous dive site, virgin and untouched by man. Bearings are acquired; the expedition is put together at great effort and invariably ends in nothing. This typically occurs more often in these lean times. There were such places of unsullied bounty not twenty years ago, and we did find them. They were everything and more we had hoped for. Now my hopes rest fervently on San Benedicto. Even if it is only half of what they say it is, it will be magnificent.

When I returned from Australia, the aftermath of the ciguatera was severe, discouraging any notion of regular work. Although nearly broke, I was unable (or unwilling) to reenter the culture and secure what one would call a normal job, much less a normal life. Too much had happened over the last eight years. Left with few alternatives, I continued to write and took odd jobs on the Central Coast of California where I connected with Margaret who eventually took me in, and for two-and-a-half years, nursed me back to health.

We lived two blocks from the beach, and from time to time I would wander down to the shore and gaze out over those chilly waters in a state of hopelessness and depression. Unable to eat seafood, no longer spearfishing, and without incentive to draw me to the water other than body surfing, my only solace came in writing. Though still battling the effects of hypoglycemia, I was able, over the course of three winters to put together an unpublished novel begun in New Zealand, a book of short stories entitled *Secret Seas*, as well as a premature effort of black and white photography in a book entitled *Sea Shadows*.

During those same summers I strung together spearfishing workshops at Catalina Island, and though I enjoyed teaching the refinements of blue water hunting to students eager to learn, it grew increasingly frustrating for I still yearned to hunt. After three summers, I gave up the workshops and everything linked to spearfishing.

Upon regaining my health, Margaret suggested I take seriously the underwater photography I had dabbled in for fifteen years. Black and white photography held my interest and though a book was produced of my black and white underwater images, I was not, nor would I define myself as a professional underwater photographer.

After a chance encounter with a singing humpback in Hawaii with photographer Jim Watt whom I knew from my spearfishing days, the idea of serious photography began to take form.

Later the following year, having picked up a housed camera from Jim, I did a trip out on the White Sand Ridge off Grand Bahama Island diving with the Atlantic spotted dolphin. The water was gorgeous, twenty-five feet deep, white sand bottom, warm and crystal clear. The dolphins were as photogenic and friendly as could be imagined. Those on board were photographers from all over the world: Australia, Japan, Hawaii, California. The competition for shots was fierce. Photographing dolphin is largely a matter of good free diving skills coupled with a sense for anticipating the moves of the dolphin by reading their body language. Unwittingly, my experience as a hunter came into play and I was constantly surprised at my photo opportunities. Out of that single week on the Ridge, I was particularly fortunate to capture a rather stunning black and white image of four dolphins silhouetted against a sunburst. That photograph called "Into the Light" gained some attention, and in many ways opened the door for me into the professional ranks. More importantly, it provided the vehicle and confidence I needed for a long-awaited return to the ocean.

It was my notion to photograph big animals underwater while on breath-hold dives.

By virtue of the stalking skills developed for so long while spearfishing, I felt an advantage over photographers who used scuba. However, my technical skills as a photographer were less than proficient. The technology of cameras and photography in general put me at a disadvantage. As it happened I made my decision at about the time automatic cameras were introduced and the advancements in those areas were a great benefit to a technological novice like myself. Also at that time, underwater housings advanced in support of such cameras. So the steps I took were relatively easy and permitted me, in a short period of time, to grasp photography and the underwater technology that supported it.

Spearfishing as I once practiced it, was relatively uncomplicated, having internalized the nuances of the sea and reacted to them with almost a sixth sense. My responses were on automatic, with scarcely any thought involved in the process. Not so with photography. There was a great deal of maintenance with the equipment in the form of a hundred small details that need to be addressed before one enters the water. And there was the constant search for correct light, proper angles, not to mention subject and composition.

Problems, I was to discover, are inherent to underwater photography, as linear thought was a pronounced aspect of it. Yet within those areas in which I was deficient, I eventually found a place to internalize the craft. The process of learning consumed five years before I began to feel it in a way that permitted me to operate in a fluid and instinctive manner. The method wasn't foolproof. Each new situation created its own set of challenges, which was why I preferred to concentrate on a particular subject whose behavior could be studied and eventually internalized, a method which allowed me to instinctively take the photographs when the proper moment presented itself. Sometimes it worked and sometimes it didn't, but it was the method with which I became comfortable.

It has been nine years since that first trip to the dolphin grounds in the Bahamas, and photography has consumed me every bit as much as spearfishing once did. Crucial to both disciplines is the ability to read the universal language among sea creatures, what humans would call body language. This language can be highly complex and extraordinarily subtle, but once recognizable as communication, it begins to become decipherable.

Even species of fish appear to have their own dialects and in the language of marine animals, it is the verbs that are first understood by the outsider: the twitch of a white sea bass's tail just before it bolts, the yellowtail's slight head movement in the direction it intends to sprint, the grouper's first turn broadside to inspect before moving on, the eye of the pargo (Gulf snapper) shifting quickly when it is ready to run, the tropicals forever fluttering in their dance of sexual exchange and territorial imperative.

The language of the dolphin is far more diverse and complex, and I could not begin to understand the nuances of its dialect. However, there are indications of the dolphin's intent: a dip of a pectoral fin, the lift of the head, movement of the eye or tail, all indicating the intent of its next move or turn or dive or surface. (Dolphins are highly sexual and give clear indications of intent in that regard, turning on their backs and swimming belly to belly, penile erections, and nuzzling of the genitals with the rostrum. Dolphins are one of the few mammals that, like humans, have sex belly to belly.) Initially, it was not difficult to figure out what the dolphins were likely to do in terms of movement, and later through extended observation, what the beginnings of its more rudimentary communication were: recognition, acceptance, affection, indifference and anger.

The dolphins inaugurated my transition from spearfishing to photography, and for that I shall be forever grateful. They, above all others, are my favorite subjects, and I have spent many hundreds of hours over the last nine years photographing them.

In the course of my years in the Bahamas, I came upon Gary Adkison at Walker's Cay. Much of the diving world knows about the sharks of Walker's, but back then Gary had just put his shark dive together. I was privileged to make a couple of dozen dives over a five year period at Walker's, and those hours with the sharks were of immeasurable import, both psychologically as well as instructively, and became the final step in understanding sharks by way of reading their body language, and in general, becoming comfortable with great numbers of them swimming around without feeling the need to keep track of them all. The experience erased the last vestiges of my fear acquired so long ago as a child in Hawaii.

Though the dive at Walker's was relatively shallow—forty feet—scuba was the best tool to use with these sharks because they, like most reef sharks, were somewhat wary and tended to avoid the close contact necessary for photographs. Though there might be as many as eighty to a hundred sharks milling around at any one time, it would have been difficult to get close on a breath-hold dive, and scuba became the practical tool to use. I would hang on the bottom, hold my breath so the bubbles would not spook the sharks, causing them to veer off, and the sharks would swim to within two to three feet of me. (Holding the breath while using scuba can be dangerous if one begins to rise to the surface, which causes the lungs to expand, rupturing blood vessels in the lungs, which can lead to death. To do it safely, one must sustain depth, or sink. At Walkers I was generally standing on the bottom.)

Walker's was my first solid opportunity to study shark behavior over an extended period of time. Sharks have an expressive array of clearly observable undersea language. If, for example, they are irritated, they will drop their pectoral fins down in an exaggerated posture. If the irritation is pronounced, they may arch their back, and twitch and turn their head from side to side. In Walker's I witnessed the lowering of the pectorals in one isolated instance, away from the shark dive, but during the dive itself, no shark exhibited this behavior. However, during the dive there was often a good deal of yawning going on that would often spread from shark to shark, this indicating a sense of well being among them. Gary has observed them rotating their bodies from dorsal fin forward, a signal activating remora to begin cleaning along the gill slits.

235

Sharks, in fact, are quite predictable, almost single-minded in their approach to food. Gary's Shark Rodeo begins when a garbage can-sized ball of frozen fish heads and guts, secured by stainless cable buoyed on the surface and anchored fifteen feet off the bottom, is lowered so it hangs suspended in the water. The sharks circle the chumball in an orderly manner, each taking its turn at the food, priorities appear to be determined by the size of the shark. I could move and have physical contact with the sharks and was basically treated as another predator. Walker's sharks became erratic, raising the portent of danger when a chunk of frozen chumball would break off. The orderly event would turn chaotic as a mad dash then ensued, with sharks fighting over scraps of loose food, essentially creating feeding frenzy conditions. Often in my attempts to get close to the frenzy for a photograph, I was slammed into by the manic sharks (which is similar to being hit with a two-by-four) so as to tear the flesh beneath my wet suit and leave a substantial bruise. Oddly, the chance of being bitten during the melee is slim, though on one occasion my white camera housing was mistaken for a loose scrap of fish and bitten down on at the handle, my hand momentarily disappearing into the shark's mouth. After wrenching it loose I came away without so much as a scratch.

To declare that the sharks of Walker's Cay were not dangerous would be untrue, for one can never speak in generalities with regard to shark behavior. Sharks are different the world over. A six-foot silky shark in the Bahamas is quite passive and scarcely a threat relative to the six-foot silky around Cocos Island in the deep Pacific, which is a terror. However, sharks of the open ocean appear far less wary and more aggressive towards man than reef sharks (the reef sharks of Bikini notwithstanding). This is due in part to their size, which is considerable over the reef shark, and the competition for large prey that makes them more apt to aggressively pursue food. From all I have come to understand of the sharks of San Benedicto, they will pose a far more dangerous threat than any I have ever encountered, for they roam the blue edge, guarding the gates of their final threshold. One cannot enter into the blue edge without passing through these sharks. What awaits me on the other side, I cannot now imagine.

# DAY
# 37

P am flies in with the water pump. Jack replaces it along with belts. While he is going over the engine one last time, Pam and I shop for food. Our small refrigeration unit requires us to give half of our perishables to the *Ambar III*, skippered by Mike McGettigan who will be running a charter down in two weeks. We will depart Cabo San Lucas at noon tomorrow, and it has been far too long a stay.

# PART
# 2
## SAN BENEDICTO

*Sometimes the rare, the beautiful, can only emerge or survive in isolation.*—Loren Eisely

# DAY
# 38

U nder gray skies scarred by bolts of electric
blue on a course of one hundred eighty-four
degrees, we point around Land's End, and with mild
following seas, finally, mercifully depart Cabo San
Lucas. Twenty miles out two humpback whales and
a small school of dolphin greet us. The final leg, a
two hundred and fifty-mile voyage across open
ocean, begins with this meeting of mammals.

All on board have long found the rhythm of the
sea and it becomes their rhythm, the rolling sea
washing away those nine long days in purgatory.
In the open water there is a freshness to the air,
and the sea clings to the face and purges the eyes
of the likes of Cabo San Lucas. The concept of time
quickly fades, and if measured at all, is by the te-
dious arc of light across the sky. The news of the
world cannot reach us and if it did would have lost
all meaning. As Thoreau said, "Blessed are they who
never read a newspaper, for they shall see nature."

Though I have waited months, years really, for
the opportunity to dive San Benedicto, I am somewhat jaded by the prospect. The myth of a great
underwater Eden awaiting is no more, at least in

this hemisphere, save perhaps Cocos Island and the Galapagos, which, as this is written, are being considered for commercial fisheries. We have just spent a month in the Sea of Cortez and not so much as glimpsed a big fish (save for an average-sized wahoo), or a shark, much less a giant manta. Secretly, I harbor doubts about San Benedicto, for nothing is what it once was. In deep longing I seek one last jump into water that will fill me with its magnificence, energy and power, a place that holds animals equal to their domain.

Creatures of the sea rarely attack man by virtue of the fact they do not fear him. I long to be in the presence of the fearless, for it is they who hold my awe, have my respect. It is they who show the way to those of us afraid. Perhaps that is why humans are in such an intractable state of fear; we have systematically destroyed the fearless in both man and beast.

# DAY
# 39

The light winds force us to motor sail. Throughout the day we have seen no other boats or sign of man. I enjoy the fact that there is no other way to reach these islands. Neither car, nor plane, nor most boats are equipped to run two hundred fifty nautical miles, anchor out for a month and then return another two hundred fifty miles without needing fuel, food, or water from an outside source. It is a credit to the resourcefulness of Jack and the sheer will required to prepare the *Nirvana* for such an undertaking.

The Revillagigedo Islands were named after a Spanish Viceroy. There are four islands in the archipelago: Socorro, San Benedicto, Roca Partida and Clarion. Clipperton Island is part of the same fracture zone but not included within the archipelago. The largest of the islands, Socorro, lies thirty miles south of San Benedicto and houses a small naval base. We pray the navy will not see fit to go on patrol while we are anchored up. Both Socorro and San Benedicto are most likely younger than the other two islands and lie roughly along the east-west tending fracture zone that extends some twenty-two hundred nautical miles west of San Benedicto and east to the mainland. Hernando de Grijalva, whose ship was commissioned by Hernan Cortes (for whom the Sea of Cortez is named), first discovered them in 1533. The islands are composed of volcanic ash, lava, basalt, obsidian, trachytes, sand and volcanic byproducts that lend the islands their distinctive brown, red, ochre and sepia colors. During the Cenozoic and Miocene geologic epochs, the first eruptions formed a submerged platform for the future islands. In the struggle between fire and water over millennia, the islands slowly rose from the sea floor some five to ten thousand feet deep and broke the surface of the Pacific. These eruptions indicate that under certain circumstances, a submarine eruption can overpower the pressure of thousands of tons of water, currents and wave action to break the surface, and cool sufficiently to create above water landmasses. The last eruption named Barcena occurred on San Benedicto in 1952, and formed a lava delta one half mile out to sea. This particular eruption is significant because it is the first recorded historic pumice eruption in the eastern Pacific Ocean basin. The eruptions continue to this day, though I rather doubt we will see any evidence for most occur well underwater. But one never knows; an eruption occurred several miles off Socorro on January 28th, 1993, lasting several weeks, spitting smoking pumice and rock, some four feet in diameter, up from a boiling sea.

Discussion among the crew falls to the necessary. We are either on watch, sleeping or eating. I try to pick up a book, but this sea, far beyond the confines of man, appeals to me in ways I don't under-

stand. Content to gaze out over the swell, I contemplate its movement. The ever-moving sea feels
at once permanent and transitory; it has always
been this way, yet never exactly this way. A hundred and fifty miles from land, there is a different,
primal, rhythmic movement, like the blood pumping from an ancient heart that will always pump,
despite man, despite all pollution, despite all calamity; the heart will pump the earth's life blood of
the sea long after man has left the planet and all
evidence of his moments here erased. This idea
brings a certain serenity as the endless water rolls
over itself again and again and again.

# DAY
# 40

I n the pale light of dawn, thirty-nine hours after
our departure from Cabo San Lucas, San Benedicto Island looms dark and primordial from five
miles away, rising out of the black sea, monolithic
and ominous. There is nothing friendly in its appearance.

The rising sun brings common dolphin, their
broad backs the color of soil, the pod scattered for
miles in all directions. A half-dozen spring to our
bow. Pam is exuberant and lays down on the bow
pulpit stretching a hand into the water. A dolphin
allows her to slide her hand the length of its body.
Bringing the hand to her face she looks in wonder
at it, as if it were a strange and beautiful icon. In
the golden light a small yellowfin tuna jumps, a
dolphin in pursuit. We are all on the bow and I begin to holler and whoop in a high falsetto voice as
the dolphin continue to leap high across our prow.
Jack does not partake in such foolishness. Instead,
he asks me why I keep yelling. I tell him the dolphin respond to the attention and will stay with us
for as long as we show appreciation. Everyone loves
a joy-filled whoop. I have come to know dolphin, and

the small gestures of man bring them pleasure. Once, when I had finished body surfing on a crowded beach in San Clemente, California, several dolphins appeared on the surf line and began catching waves as they often do. The crowd on the beach was watching and when one dolphin did a back flip out of a wave the surfers yelled in encouragement. The same dolphin then did a high jump and more people yelled and whistled. More jumps came, higher and higher, and the entire beach came to their feet cheering. The dolphin performed for another ten minutes before the crowd grew bored and their cheers diminished. Only then did the dolphin go its way.

I whoop for another five minutes as the dolphin continue to dance on the bow. Pam is having a great time and is thoroughly captivated. When I stop cheering the dolphin almost immediately break away from the bow. Within minutes the entire pod that had been seen for miles in all directions vanishes to the depths, leaving no sign anywhere.

We approach the island head on, then swing along the west side where, a quarter mile offshore in seemingly safe water, a breaking wave suddenly appears, shedding whitewater down a steep slope. "That must be the boiler," observes Jack. We all are thinking the same thing; this is a ship killer to the uninformed. Continuing down the west side of the island to its southernmost end, we turn into its lee as a humpback whale breaches a half-mile south over the morning sea of glass. What a glorious welcome! Even Jack cannot contain himself and shouts at this uplifting event.

This, the southerly side of the island, is a mass of fissure and volcanic scars, with its bare peak rising eleven hundred feet to the sky, collared by deep gullied erosions like open wounds, splitting the earth from peak to beach. A long welt of molten rock, dark, almost black, indicating where the last flow occurred in 1952, juts out to sea and protects this anchorage from wind and sea that might fetch out of the east. There is little time to ponder the spectacle, as there is much work to do.

The better part of the day is spent anchoring and altering the boat from an ocean-going vessel to a home of sorts for the month-long stay. Solar panels, three feet by six feet, are erected near the bow, to maintain amperage in the batteries without having to fire up the engine every day to feed electrical current into the refrigerator, water maker, radio and lights that will be in constant use. An air compressor is mounted near the mast to refill scuba tanks. The skiff is launched and the outboard mounted on its stern. In the afternoon, after lunch, the dive equipment, camera gear and housings are broken out and the pieces of a very complex puzzle are assembled. Pam has her work cut out in sorting food and determining where and how it should be available. Keeping produce fresh for any length of time is difficult. She must organize its accessibility, bearing in mind the rate of spoilage particular to each product. By the time we have all finished we are watching the sunset.

In the evening schools of bait blanket the cove, only their iridescent yellow tails visible in the low light. Thousands upon thousands ripple the surface as though a great single entity was moving cautiously up from the depths. A white-chested booby with gray wings streaks down from the sky and hits the school hard at perhaps thirty miles an hour, disappearing then re-emerging fifteen feet from where it first plunged; it wings away without ever losing velocity.

# DAY
# 41

J ack and I, anxious to photograph the humpback
breaches, are up before the sun and out in the
skiff awaiting them a half-mile off the island. In
the first hour of light we track a mother and baby
escorted by another female, the nanny. They are
wary of our presence and not wishing to hinder their
passage, we make a guess as to their heading then
motor up a mile and cut the engine to drift in wait.
The whales come close and we manage some rather
uninteresting tail shots. We follow this strategy for
several hours with decreasing success. Jack, restless, is anxious to return to the boat for breakfast
and a dive. I am in agreement but something suggests we remain; I urge we stay for one more surfacing. Within five minutes a large female breaches
completely out of the water not fifty yards away,
but by the time we get our cameras in position it is
over. Knowing she will breach again, I train the
camera where I believe she will come up. She explodes in full frame, rising, as if in slow motion,
her black submarine head sheathed in white water, pushed by a force greater than any other in the
kingdom of living things. Rising higher and higher,

water shedding from the great black body like falls
from a wild river, climbing higher and faster with
such cumulative power that the spectacle defies all
that the eye can absorb—defying the very laws of
time and space and gravity, defying the ocean and
even the sky by its awesome and resolute power.
Climbing fifty feet above us, all but the tail out of
the water, stalling at its peak, water falling from
her body like a monsoon, now slowly twisting to
the left, arching, white pectoral fins flashing in the
sun as the humpback falls and falls and falls, hitting the surface with a tremendous explosion of
white water.

I am awe-struck.

Heart pounding and nearly overcome, I can only
shake my head in wonder, muttering, "The show
was for us. It was intentional. She was giving us a
gift."

Dazed and uplifted by the whale's performance,
we return to the boat where Pam has prepared
breakfast. We dine outside in the cockpit and in the
middle of the meal a large black fin cuts water near
the boat. At first glance it bears a resemblance to
the dorsal fin of a shark. Pam sees it and points,
shouting, "Shark!" But it is the wing tip of the giant pacific manta ray, come to pay a visit. Aban-
doning breakfast, we quickly dress in lightweight
wet suits, for the water temperature is in the mid-
seventies.

As we enter the water, which is a hazy fifty feet,
the manta turns and heads for us. Its markings are
striking—pitch-black save for two wide stripes of
white running horizontal from its horns near the
eyes down to the thick part of its body where the
wings begin. The animal is enormous, sixteen feet

across, nine feet long, weighing close to two thousand pounds. These are mere numbers and do not accurately measure the grandeur of the creature. Jack dives and the manta, seeing him, halts in midflight at a depth of thirty feet. Jack descends gently to the manta's back, stroking the edge of what might be described as the forehead, then takes a grip at the edge of the forehead as the manta moves off. With Jack in tow the spectacle is not one I can relate to any other event above or below the ocean. The gentleness of the manta is in brute contrast to a creature that appears so strikingly formidable. The first thought that occurs to me: would any other wild animal do such a thing? Would an elephant, or a rhino or a cape buffalo permit a man to mount and ride it?

Jack releases his grip and rises for a breath. The manta turns and comes beneath us as we dangle on the surface ten feet above the broad black and white body. It slows and awaits our descent. I dive, but not to its back. My desire is to make eye contact, so I hover within two feet of its eye located on the side of its head near the horn. The eye is blue and covered with a thick membrane, giving it the appearance of being somewhat cloudy. The eye is fixed and must follow me with a turn of its body. Again, I am struck by the gentle nature of the creature. Once called the devil fish, due in large part I should imagine, by what appears to be horns on the top of its head. These horns, when unrolled, serve as a kind of sweeper that ushers in the small plankton upon which it feeds. The pointed and angular shape of its body further supports the myth of the devil fish. As one can plainly see, it is anything but devilish. That this wild animal has chosen to be here with us and seems to anticipate with a certain eagerness our hitchhiking rides upon its broad back is astonishing. Everyone is so moved by this notion that all take special care not to touch any other part of it for fear we might injure it in some way, though I think that would be difficult. In any event, we gently descend to its back then kick slightly so that we are able to reach and cling to its forehead with our fingers. My grip is too gentle and as the manta accelerates my fingers slide away, the leather glove leaving traces of itself against the rasp-like skin down its back. The manta is of the shark family and its rough, abrasive skin is probably one of the few similarities left between the two.

Another manta arrives with three remora attached to its back and wing. The remora are two and a half feet long and must weigh twelve pounds apiece. Remora characteristically will attach themselves to big sharks, leaving the shark when scraps are left floating during a feeding. The manta leaves no such scraps for it eats nothing but microscopic sea life. The remora is getting a free ride but not fulfilling its role as a cleaner. Perhaps it is the size of the creature that holds value for a remora, or perhaps the manta cannot refuse hitchhikers of any species.

The new manta is considerably larger than the first and close to twenty feet across, probably weighing twenty-five hundred pounds. But this manta is more the observer and displays scant interest in the awkward swimmers in its cove. We dance with the first manta in forty to fifty feet of water, and after an hour Pam is exhausted. Jack and I reload our cameras as she keeps the manta interested. She then retires to the boat while we spend another two hours diving to depth before succumbing to exhaustion.

In the late afternoon two whales swing into the deep underwater canyon that rises to within a hundred feet of our anchorage. A mother and a calf blow two hundred feet from the boat before turning. The light breeze carries their breath and its foul sea smell; I have been smudged and purified by the great priestess of the sea.

# DAY
# 42

A bad night's sleep. Ground swells roll out of the northwest and wrap around the island. A half-mile away six to eight-foot breakers curl and tube and crash along the southwest shore. I contemplate the possibilities of body surfing these perfect waves, but there are rocks, unseen and perilous that dissuade me. There is nothing quite so beautiful as a perfectly shaped wave, and I study them at length as they beckon with perfect rights across their glassy face.

It is not the ground swells that directly affect the *Nirvana*, which rolls easily over them. It is the refractory waves that recoil off the high-banked beach in front of us and pitch back as a nagging three-foot chop on our beam. And Jack, ever mindful of our comfort, considers dropping a stern anchor to keep us bow in to the island, but unfamiliarity with our new surroundings dictates that we ride out the swell and see what the day brings.

Just before breakfast a manta circles the boat. We are already jaded after the three-hour dance yesterday, and instead of jumping in we sit down to coffee, ham and eggs, believing the manta will

hang around until we are ready. The manta leaves
during the meal so we decide to make a scuba dive
off a pinnacle in search of a fabled school of hammerhead sharks that have been seen and known to
dwell off the south end of the island. The last time
I saw a school of hammerheads was twenty-five
years ago up in the Mid-Riff on a spearfishing trip.
They were swimming along the south edge of
Partida and I pressed myself against the shear wall
of the island in fear of being seen. Today we go out
in search of them.

We jump a nearby pinnacle that comes up to forty
feet off a sixty-foot plateau that drops to infinity.
We come across strange looking fish, which inhab-
its the plateau. They have the face of a sheepshead,
found in northern waters, with a bulbous head and
heavy lower jaw that enables them to feed on crustaceans and reef bearing shellfish. Their body is
like that of a wrasse, possibly some kind of warm
and cold water aberration indigenous to this area.
Horse-eyed jacks spin their way down, catching
light against silver bodies. Further exploration of
the plateau reveals ensnared fishing nets draping
across reef and rock outcropping like a heavy web
of tropical canopy. Much of this old netting has been
removed by Terry Kennedy and Joyce Clinton, by
permission of the Mexican Fisheries to prevent the
recurring capture of large fish, sharks and mantas—essentially all large creatures that swim. By
all appearances, the damage has already been done,
for only a few fish can be found near the bottom—
several cabrilla, no grouper, very few rock fish at
all. Even the colorful tropicals are scarce. The dive
is disheartening and we return to the surface, our
tanks half full.

Anchored up a scant two days and already Pam has a tight ear and is in pain, Jack has broken blisters on his toes: a bad beginning. The toes can become quite painful as the fins wear deeper and deeper into the knuckle of the toes and never have a chance to dry out and heal. Often these abrasions turn into infections and can become quite serious. Free divers do a great deal of kicking and if care isn't taken problems occur. During a trip to the White Sand Ridge in the Bahamas to photograph the spotted dolphins, Niki Konstantinou wound up in the hospital with blood poisoning due to blisters on his toes from so much kicking. Out here, so far from medical support of any kind, the smallest cut or injury can have serious consequence. Never mind a shark bite.

Jack and I motor east in the late afternoon looking for manta. The water turns cloudy, then milky. A mile later it clears again. Jack speculates every possibility for the change in the water. When he asks my opinion, I shrug, saying nothing. As a product of a culture that operates out of instantaneous information, Jack wants answers to every mystery great and small, nano-second responses to all questions; the computer knows all, reveals all. Our culture confuses information with knowledge, knowledge with wisdom.

One idea, I suggest to Jack, is not to spend all one's time looking for answers, for the questions are endless, and that is all you wind up doing. If I must chart every ocean and sea, I will miss the sunsets. If I must explore every trail in the hills, they will eventually lead back to civilization. If the mind follows every road to its end, every road leads nowhere. To surrender to the mystery is not to promote ignorance of the facts, but to see that one can simply stay with the mystery. With some patience and a little luck, the mystery may well reveal its essence beyond the speculation of the mind. To be forever looking beyond is to remain blind to what is in the moment.

In these calm seas we reach the most northern tip of the island, put on our facemasks and peer over the side of the boat, looking for a good site to make a jump. Below juts a finger reef thirty feet down that falls off the island into depths beyond our vision. In the mid-water swim schooling crevalle jack, blue jacks, horse-eyed jacks and baitfish. A forty-pound wahoo appears, narrow and lean with the hazy markings of a tattooed warrior, built like a spear thrown by the sea god, Poseidon. It drifts up from the deep, surveys us, and wanders off. One has the distinct feeling that anything could materialize out of this startling water. Jack begins to rig up the spear gun. I have brought the small Nikonos camera to take photographs, and dig it out. I take another look over the side before jumping, and spiraling up from the depths are four silvertip sharks, looking to be ten-footers making their way directly to the boat. "Jesus," I say, and Jack drops the spear gun and looks over the side. The sharks are near the surface, circling the boat. Neither one of us speaks, but we are thinking the same thing: Should we make this jump? Already, I am tense with this sighting, and I'm not even wet. Once in the water the sharks would instantly sense my feelings of vulnerability. Through their ability to detect an increased heart rate, they can also sense changes in my bioelectrical field, and with their advanced sensory system, who knows what else. I

do not trust my ability to surpress this anxiety,
which makes me even more anxious. The sharks
continue to circle, and we are reduced to gazing at
them with our heads submerged while leaning over
the boat. I make a splashing with my hand and one
comes instantly to investigate. I quickly pull my
hand and face out of the water. I have lost courage
for the jump, and staring at the circling shapes,
can't believe I will have failed this first test. It's as
if Kamo has suddenly appeared after so many years
of silence, and I am unable to overcome its presence.

Jack throws me a glance; he is both giddy and
edgy over this sighting. I am taken back to the wilderness of the Gulf that I remember thirty years
ago—ancient and primordial, dangerous and beautiful. It's been a long time since I have been kept
out of the water by sharks. We know we will have
to get into the water with these sharks at some
point. Perhaps because of the anxiety I am feeling,
there is a desire to exorcise it here and now. Jack,
unfamiliar with sharks, would follow my lead. But
I have lost confidence and surrender the prospect
of a jump. We turn the skiff south and head back to
the *Nirvana*, silently mulling over these new waters in which we have placed ourselves.

# DAY
# 43

The morning sky is high with wispy clouds blowing south. We jump two mantas in the anchorage, but they move west down the cove without so much as a look in our direction. Perhaps they smell residual fear wafting from yesterday's wet suits. In the afternoon we venture south a half-mile directly out of the anchorage into deeper water. Terry K. had given us bearings on two pinnacles, but in these early jumps we discover two more. It is our hope that eventually one such pinnacle will produce the hammerheads. Though we take bearings off the island, we must search for them visually in the water. There may be times when we can get lucky and drop an anchor on the very heads of these high spots that in some cases are no larger than the average-sized swimming pool, but for the most part Pam is willing to stay in the boat and follow us.

Jack and I are on a bearing but cannot locate the pinnacle so we begin to return to the boat when a large shadow-shape forms beneath us. We both stop and hover to watch. It is a very large shark rising to the surface. It comes to within five feet of the surface about twenty feet away. If the faint vertical stripes down its massive torso are not enough, then certainly its size reveal its species—a tiger shark. Nearing the surface it opens its mouth as if to yawn, gives us a look, then drifts back to the blue abyss and disappears. Jack lifts his head out of the water after it has vanished, pulls his snorkel out, and says, "Tiger." We head for the boat. I neither feel anxious nor afraid at the sighting of the tiger, and at this I am relieved, for I do not need the portent of Kamo hanging in the water every time I make a jump. Though I think it odd that a shark appears to be more of a threat to me when I sit in a boat than when I am in the water with one. Behind Jack, I arrive at the skiff and hand my camera to him and am about to hoist myself in, when ten feet away on the other side of the outboard engine, a nine-foot sailfish appears, dorsal fin flared like a grand mantilla. I call for my camera and Jack is not sure what or why I want it, and is slow to hand it over. He is looking for the tiger and wondering why I have not jumped in the boat. By the time I have the camera the fish has moved off by fifteen feet and the light is wrong, but I knock off a couple of shots anyway. Such a noble creature. I wonder now if the fish would have hung around (as they will do) if I had not rushed about with the camera. Big fish are curious and generally unafraid of slow or non-moving objects.

The evening before the sun sets is the magic hour of the underwater world. I am on the deck watching the dorsal fin of a shark, cutting water a hundred feet away. Up near where the canyon opens up to deep water a manta has jumped clear of the surface, landing with a staggering explosion of white water. A mile off, a pod of dolphin pass through, diving and working the bait. Above them are boobies, circling and diving on the bait ball the dolphin have driven up in explosive boils on the surface, as if the very womb of the planet were giving birth. The activity continues non-stop until the light is so low we are left with silhouettes against the purple sky and reflected sea.

# DAY
# 44

A shift in the wind brings a chill out of the northwest, dark clouds, a portent of weather, and a boat to the cove: a thirty-five-foot ketch *Orea*, single-handed by Dave N. whom Jack had met in Cabo San Lucas, and who has sailed down ahead of Terry Kennedy and Joyce Clinton in their catamaran, *Gladrial*. Dave has anchored well south of us and is content, but later in the morning Terry and Joyce arrive and are visibly upset because they wish to anchor where the *Nirvana* has anchored. It is the primo spot and I rather imagine that Terry, who has been coming down here with Joyce for many years, might be possessive of the anchorage. He demonstrates his displeasure by ignoring Jack when welcomed to the cove. Or perhaps it is with himself, for it was he who laid out the best anchorages for Jack before we left Cabo San Lucas. They eventually anchor between *Orea* and the *Nirvana*, and set up radio communication with the Orea that does not include us. While Jack is baffled by their behavior, I am content with this minor slight, since I am not one to partake in dinner parties for which boaters engage in the name of camaraderie; it often feels forced and uncomfortable to me. Terry and Joyce are excellent sailors and save for this one occasion, are friendly and generous with their knowledge and goodwill.

The water is clear and we are anxious to get in before the visibility is affected by swell and sea. A manta circles the boat and Jack and I work our way into our wet suits while Pam makes a jump without a wet suit to keep the manta occupied. By the time we have suited up and have our cameras ready, she is cold and ready to come aboard. This manta is a willing dancer, and turns upside down exposing its white underside as Jack descends and swims belly to belly with it for a hundred feet. When he rises for a breath, I dive while the manta remains suspended upside down. A foot off its belly, looking directly into its mouth, I see snow-white parasites the size of sow bugs, moving in the corners. The remora shifts and swims off the manta's back and fastens to the right side of its chest where the wing attaches. The shift in weight momentarily throws the manta off balance and I tip to port as the manta does and then re-right in sync with it and continue the swim. When I rise for the surface, the manta twists back to its original swimming position and hesitates in the water like a stalled airplane; it wants to be ridden. Catching a quick breath, I dive again, awkwardly grasping its forehead with one hand while clutching the strobe-laden camera housing. The manta gently glides along, nine-foot wings on either side of me, rising slowly and falling in graceful rhythm. Borne upon a winged creature of the sea with water flowing through my beard, I am in true underwater flight. The sensation is otherworldly. We move together as if in dream, beyond the notion of being underwater. The idea of riding a wild creature this size was last explored in comic books I read as a teenager. Now in surreal fashion I survey the undersea world upon the back of a two thousand-pound flying bird, and at this moment would trade my legs for gills, and travel forever as a rider on the blue edge.

Other mantas come and go through the day and by four o'clock I am in and out of my wet suit on five different occasions. We have not left the cove and we are deliriously exhausted at the end of day. In the low light of dusk three more mantas come to the boat. They seem to know it now, but we are too worked to suit up and watch them circle then drift away, taking the last light to the horizon.

# DAY
## 45

A humpback whale breaches its way down the island at dawn. Sitting in the morning light, we watch its awesome power on display and all wonder why. Jack, ever the pragmatist, believes that by making great leaps and hitting the water with such force, the whale is dislodging sea lice or other such parasites. Pam theorizes that the whale is observing the earth world for a brief moment, perhaps to see us, or to locate other whales. It looks like a lot of fun to me. I submit the whale is playing, remembering as a teenager how we used to endlessly practice our cannonball jumps off the diving board of a friend's swimming pool in an on-going pursuit of the biggest splash. This idea of play rather than purpose is my own projection of the way the world should be. It is certainly revealed in the Atlantic spotted dolphins, which play endlessly for no other reason than to have fun. It appears to me as if the humpback is doing nothing more than getting his splash chops down.

Two mantas come in as we eat breakfast in the cockpit. Off the deep canyon ripples on the water indicate bait moving. Activity comes early and the day feels different from other days. Shortly, Jack observes, "Lots of action this morning."

"It may well last the day," I say. Jack looks at me askance. The observation is unsubstantiated and I can't provide the sort of proof that would satisfy him, so I suggest we get into our wet suits and make a jump. There were days as a spearfisherman when fish activity suddenly went into high gear. It has been speculated by those who spend their lives on the water that accelerated fish activity occurs once every three to five days. I know this to be true in Catalina, Fiji, the Sea of Cortez, in the Bahamas, and anywhere I have been able to spend a significant number of weeks in essentially the same area. That which was sleeping comes awake, alive in play, in feeding, and in general activity. I have no idea why this is so, only that today feels like one of those days.

Pam gets into the water to engage a manta that is cruising a hundred feet off the boat. Moments later she is kicking furiously for the skiff and jumps up on the pontoon in one quick motion. She is breathing hard. "Sharks," she says. "Four, one of them was a big hammerhead. Christ, I think I wet myself. God, they were big!" She is shaken. Having felt safe in the cove, she now has lost that illusion. Thinking she should come in with us, I make light of the sharks, but Jack cuts me off with a look and suggests to Pam that she stay in the boat, but there is no need; she is already in the boat and has no intention of returning to the water.

I point off to where birds are working. "Rig up; there's fish running out there." While Jack might be skeptical of some of my declarations, he rarely discounts interpretations readily observed, and goes for his spear gun.

By the time he has rigged up the gun, the birds have left.

Pam asks, "Big fish, or big shark?"

"Out here you can't have one without the other," I say. Pam stares out into the water, licks and unconsciously nibbles on her lower lip.

In ten minutes the birds are working again and we are shortly on the periphery of the boiling bait. Jack makes the jump. As he is pulling back the three bands of rubber on the spear gun he shouts, "Tuna!" He is not rigged for tuna, having only a hundred feet of line buoyed by a boat bumper, and I do not think he is so foolish as to spear a tuna with this rig. Unless it is a kill shot, which is unlikely, the fish would simply take all the line and spear shaft and be out of sight in seconds.

Free dive spearfishing is as primitive a way to hunt as any that exists. In this deep blue ocean man is extremely vulnerable. This kind of water accentuates his limitations on a breath-hold. It is very difficult to gauge the depth of a dive. There is nothing in the water to measure against: no bottom, no wall or reef or kelp, not even particles that often layer the water nearer shore. It is like diving into space, blue space, and gives the illusion of being always pulled deeper, of sinking into a cobalt abyss.

In addition to these significant psychological obstacles is the Herculean effort of swimming to the surface with a fifty-pound fish at the end of the breath-hold while having to push through two atmospheres of pressure on the journey back.

Jack dives before I can get into the water. When finally I drop in, he is on the surface, the bands of the gun loose; he has speared a fish.

In his journal Jack writes, "A glint of light in the depths, I pump up and drop vertically and level out at fifty feet. Three pelagics moving in to investigate, wahoo! Blue and silver with razor toothed mouths, powerful bodies. I gently leveled off parallel to the lead fish pointing the gun ninety degrees away. The first two swam in but not close enough. I stopped in a standing position, body facing the third fish; he looked me over and finally make a turn to my left about fifteen feet away. The spear dropped a little but caught him above the gut with power. The wahoo exploded away. I stopped the flow of the dragline in about twenty feet but the fish continued to pull me through the water as I headed up. I saw no sharks but called to Carlos to bring the skiff just to be sure. The fish continued to pull me on the surface for another thirty seconds and then I began to pull the dragline in, always checking for sharks. Seeing none, I dive to the fish, checked the shot placement and dragged the five-foot, forty-five-pound wahoo to the surface."

Working the dragline, Jack's roped tendons in forearm and bicep reflect the tension on the line. On the lookout for sharks, I expect to see them at any moment. The strength of the wahoo is astounding. Two thirds of a fish's body is muscle; the rest—head and gut—weigh little. A forty-five-pound fish like the wahoo can, on a short line, drag a man through the water for a hundred yards. Jack works the fish from the surface, then dives to get a hand on it when it is fifteen feet away, still quite alive, but no longer resisting. Wahoo have a vicious set of teeth so as he nears, Jack is careful to avoid the slashing mouth, but it rakes across his forearm drawing blood. Having been bitten by big fish, I can attest to their nasty bite, not as deep as a dog's bite, but enough certainly to easily shred human flesh. Jack gets a hand in the gills and is beaming. This is his first big game fish, a forty-five-pound wahoo. Pam asks how many sharks showed. Amazingly, none appeared.

The wahoo was indeed a gift, for the *Ambar III* has not arrived with our fresh supplies and the fish will be well used, though not by me. Jack cleans the wahoo on the boat, spilling some blood but none of the carcass in the water. Pam is terrified of sharks now and we don't want them sniffing around the boat.

In the afternoon we confine our dives to the mantas in the cove. In the course of three hours, seven make their way to the *Nirvana*. At one point Jack and I are interacting with three at the same time. They seem to be vying for our attention, perhaps even our affection, for they come beneath us as we rest on the surface and hover. On several occasions, near collisions occur when the mantas head straight for one another, their eyes on the far sides of their head, making it impossible to see anything directly in front of them. The wing of one manta has a semi-circular piece taken from the edge of its right wing. A small shark has taken liberties with the docile creature. It is curious that there is not more evidence of shark bites on the mantas as I have seen on dolphins. The mantas, in their slow, almost drifting movements, appear to be easy prey to large sharks.

The novelty of riding the mantas is wearing thin. It is not that they resist being ridden; quite the contrary, they still wait for us to descend and alight upon their backs. Yet somehow it seems an imposition, as if we are taking advantage of their good nature. I am content to brush their bellies and stroke a wing, or to simply make extended eye contact. Often when swimming along eye to eye with them, then rising for a breath, they follow me back up to the surface.

In the course of our dives this afternoon a large dusky moves into the cove, brought on perhaps by the scent of blood washed from the boat three hours ago. The shark hangs on the peripheries and scarcely draws notice as Jack and I continue to photograph the mantas.

Three rolls of film later, I am barely able to climb into the skiff. Jack, with the boundless energy of youth, has been diving non-stop, making two dives for every one of mine, each one considerably deeper. The mantas seem to adore him, and after we are up and showering in the cockpit of the *Nirvana,* they continue to circle the boat.

# DAY
# 46

In the morning we awake to find the *Ambar III* anchored a half-mile off our stern, bringing with it fresh supplies and eager spearfishermen prepared to jump yellowfin tuna. They leave for the west side of the island soon after greetings are exchanged, and will return this evening.

In passing, Mike McGettigan confirms the presence of hammerhead sharks on this southerly, leeward side of the island and provides bearings on a pinnacle. Within an hour we are geared up with scuba. Jack uses the hand-held GPS and without too much difficulty, we find the spot and make the jump. A ridge of volcanic lava fingers out from a bottom of sixty feet and with cameras ready, we follow it. The east side of the ridge falls off into a canyon where bottom cannot be seen at all. We stay high on the ridge and look over into the abyss like overburdened gulls catching a thermocline. Indeed, a thermocline of shimmering waves reflecting a decided temperture change twenty feet below radiates just above a layer of cold water much like heat waves will rise off an asphalt road in the summertime. Surely the hammerheads would prefer the upper warm water to the deep cold. An amberjack breezes by then another, both weighing thirty pounds, both fearlessly inspecting us with that big eye so common to free swimming pelagics. Continuing down the ridge, we come across a strange looking fish with large scales and a rapacious mouth. It moves slowly and disappears into a cave as rock or lingcod are inclined to do. There are some strange and unusual species of fish here on San Benedicto. These archipelagos, hundreds of miles from land, must have attracted all kinds of fish a millennium or two ago, and a certain amount of change had to occur, which rendered them efficient for these waters and perhaps nowhere else.

The tanks are burned without so much as a glimpse of a hammerhead. Perhaps they have simply gone elsewhere and we will never find them. However small this island may be, sitting as it is in this vast ocean, to cover it all in search of an ever-moving school of sharks would be very much like looking for a greased needle in the proverbial haystack.

Later, Jack asks about the large-scaled fish seen earlier on the dive, curious as to its species. I am not particularly interested in the names of things, but he insists that anyone would, out of general curiosity, want to know the names of sea creatures. Actually, I probably have less information regarding the names of species of fish than anyone who has spent an equal amount of time in the ocean. Jack accuses me of laziness. That, I cannot argue, but names of things have never much interested me. My curiosity of the ocean's creatures lies in their connections to the environment and to each other, rather than a name man has given them.

"How do you know what you are connecting to if you don't know their names?" asks Jack.

"I may not know the names of streets with which I am familiar, but I know how to find my way around town," I reply. Things reveal their true nature over time regardless of nomenclature. If I don't label them and therefore limit them by virtue of definition, then the book is always open and eventually I might come to understand something of the creature beyond its alphabetical designation.

In the evening we have dinner aboard the *Ambar* with Mike McGettigan and Sherry Shaffer, along with seven spearfishermen from Hawaii, a group headed by Brian Yoshikawa. They have been cleaning speared tuna, the blood and carcasses bring dusky and galapagos sharks to the swim step. Ten sharks sniff and then hit what is left of a hundred and fifty-pound fish draped over the swimstep. All manner of expression cross the faces of the spearfishermen: respect, fear, anxiety, acceptance. They know precisely what dangers await. An outsider might look upon these ritualistic acts as superstitious, and that would be a presumption of the civilized world. What they are doing, what they are always doing, is connecting to the shark so that they can feel it, sense it from another part of their body. Sharks come from the rear so must be sensed if one is to keep an eye for fish; there is no other way to know sharks are present.

The hunters tell the story of a trip last year on Roca Partida, where, after cleaning the fish and throwing the guts and heads overboard each day for six days, over a hundred sharks gathered around the boat. By the fifth day the hunters could not swim back to the boat. A skiff had to go out and fetch them. On today's hunt we are told that a ten-foot tiger shark came up on the head of one diver, mouth agape, and eyes rolled back (the last act before biting is to protect the eyes). The spearfisherman turned in time to strike it in the nose with the butt of his spear gun, turning the shark in the last moments.

# DAY
## 47

We are transferring supplies from the *Ambar* to our inflatable on a cloudless morning with a stilled sea when one of the spearfishermen hits a tuna. The skiff of the *Ambar*, called a chase boat, is summoned to his aid. This to get both the diver and the fish into the boat as quickly as possible to avoid losing the fish to sharks and putting the hunter in further jeopardy. Shortly, another spearfisherman spears a tuna and with no other support boat at hand, Jack is asked to assist. He goes to the aid of the hunter and in the process of wrestling the fish into the boat, a spear head that has penetrated the fish, slams into the inflatable, ripping a hole in the main chamber on the port side. Jack, ever alert, is able to get back to the *Ambar* before the inflatable sinks. We remove the outboard and winch the boat aboard where it can be repaired.

Most of the day is spent in the repair. When finally, in the late afternoon, we are able to get into the water to photograph a few mantas, my underwater housing floods. What could have been a disaster is avoided when I spot water sloshing around the bottom of the housing early in the dive and am able to keep the camera and lens dry. Careful inspection reveals a hair from my head across a bulkhead seal. The more time we spend in these cramped quarters with hair and particles everywhere, the more chance there will be such mishaps. I am extremely careful with this rather expensive equipment, but as we become tired and worn down from the daily toilings, concentration wilts and sloppy handling of the equipment results. Aside from dropping a camera into a thousand feet of water, a camera flood is an underwater photographer's worst calamity. If seawater finds its way into the batteries, the camera will fry up. If it seeps into a lens, which in many cases is more expensive than the camera itself, the lens is stuffed. I have a back-up housing and camera as well as a mechanical Nikonos camera with a full complement of lenses, so the likelihood of destroying all three systems is remote. Nevertheless, one cannot afford to lose a camera or lens to carelessness. Strobes are another matter; anytime one must rely on electrical current under the water, then problems of one kind or another are sure to closely follow. Strobes, both expensive and temperamental, are always a concern. So far I have been lucky with the Ikelite 200's, but they are a load when rigged with arms and matched with a housed camera on a free dive. The weight is negligible under the water, but the drag of a fully rigged housing and strobe is considerable, and slows me down markedly. Jack is using a small Nikonos with a 15mm lens and a nicely compact digital video camera that is half the size and drag of my Aquatica housing and strobe.

Returning to the *Ambar* in the evening, we float over a dozen sharks milling around the aft end. A large tuna carcass has once again been draped over the swimstep and the sharks are freaking out Pam who, paralyzed with fear, nearly falls in jumping from the bouncing skiff to the swimstep. The sharks are being teased by the divers who are pulling the carcass out of jaws as they clamp down. In this the divers delight, watching in fascination as the sharks gather in their macabre dance. The divers have a mix of bravado and humble respect as the sharks belly up on the swimstep, jaws working, teeth barred.

Nothing is more real in the open ocean than a large shark. A small shark can, to a degree, be ignored or its image repressed nearer the shoreline of a mainland, but out here there is no escape. Out here the shark must be dealt with by each individual on a constant basis, and the ritual that is taking place on the swimstep is part of that process of assimilation. Enraptured, the spearfishermen study the sharks as if looking at death itself. Tomorrow they will go in the water again, and again the day after that. On some level they know that eventually someone will be bitten and quite possibly killed. In that knowledge they are inexorably linked to the sharks. Linked like no other humans have ever been linked to the shark. Like Cerberus guarding the gates of Hades, the shark is the dragon guardian at the entrance to the deep ocean underworld. On the swimstep they can have a close look at the dragon, with its mindless jaw working five feet from where they stand. Their nervous laughter is not directed at the shark or to themselves, but at the situation. There is no way into this water but through Kamo. The last great myth, guarding the final door on the far reaches of the blue edge.

# DAY
# 48

J ack and I are invited to join the spearfishermen
on board the *Ambar*, which runs to the west
side of the island and anchors up in the throes of a
running sea with eleven-foot swells. Jack will attempt to video a hunt and I will take the still camera. Brian Yoshikawa, along with Gerald Lim who
will later become the United States National Spearfishing champion, are the most experienced and
best hunters of this Hawaiian group. Brian, who is
selectively hunting for large tuna, over two hundred pounds, has yet to pull the trigger on a fish.
These Hawaiian divers keep and eat everything
they bring in. They take the responsibility of hunting seriously and treat the big fish as an offering
from the sea. Brian Yoshikawa said that as a child,
his father instilled in him the value of gifts from
the sea; to not eat all that he had brought home
and to turn the life-filled creature he had killed
into garbage was to dishonor the sea and himself.
For some blue water hunters, the landing of a big
fish does nothing but serve a misplaced ego. This
is the worst kind of hunter. They come down, shoot
the fish, and leave, never taking the fish home,

much less eating it, apparently unable or unwilling to understand the gifts being offered. The hunters from Hawaii, to a man, are appalled by those who hunt and do not eat what they kill. In truth, once spearfishing skills are developed and the fear conquered (no easy task), hunting for fish becomes more a matter of spending time in the water than anything else. In the case of these yellowfin tuna, if one is diving in the right place with the right equipment and the fish are running, the chances of landing a moderate-sized fish are quite good. Beyond that it becomes a moral choice. Jack, in his infancy as a blue water hunter, is a good example of one who shows restraint in his choices.

Hunting in this pure form is the last of its kind and these hunters are the last of their kind. To enter an alien domain with primitive weapons to steal a great fish from the dragon's lair is an event of mythical proportions, bringing together the elements and forces of a more ancient time when the world was new and the courage of man was expected. A time when he ventured forth, cloaked in virtue, blessed in the purity inherent in his acts.

Soon, unless something meaningful is done, the commercial fisheries will have their way, and the dragon will be gone. Erased by an unknown and unseen enemy that will never see fit to enter its kingdom. Sharks are massacred every year to fill, for the most part, the need for shark fin soup, so popular in Japan. The numbers of sharks killed is unknown, somewhere from half a million, which is conservative, to three hundred million or more a year. The method used to catch them is standard. A long line is stretched out, sometimes over several miles, baited with large hooks every five feet. Generally the shark is hooked during the night when it feeds, and in the morning, weary from its long struggle against the hook, is brought aboard where its dorsal fin and pectoral fins are sliced away. The animal then is tossed back into the water. Unable to negotiate without its fins, it will often just sink to the bottom and drown, or if strong, will swim off for a while, eventually starving to death.

This is a tragic death for such a noble creature, one whose myth alone sustains the wildness of the oceans and elevates it beyond the forest that no longer holds the grizzly, and the plain where the last lion has been killed, and the deep jungle where the gorilla once reigned. The life force of these animals gives mystery and power to the regions in which they dwell, and without them mankind will be less, for a powerful force within himself that he cannot otherwise conjure up on his own will be gone forever. The inescapable irony of the shark and the blue water hunter is that when the sharks are gone, the last hunt will be over, for the hunters themselves will never again be as they once were. It is the shark that augments the hunter's state of alertness that increases his awareness of all things seen and unseen in the ocean around him. It is the shark that has taught him to sense from another place all that moves. Without the shark the hunter becomes dulled, his eyes uninterested. He will be unable to feel the presence of life in places well beyond his vision.

By all appearances my journey in this ocean runs parallel with the shark. When the seas are barren of the shark, knowledge of the blue water, gained through intuition, will lose its meaning, and so then will the oceans and seas lose their meaning and I will have lost mine.

An hour into the dive Brian Quinn returns to the *Ambar*. He had to fend off a twelve-foot galapagos with the point of his spear gun. The shark charged, pushing the 5/16ths stainless steel, heat-treated, spear shaft back, bending it and finally snapping it off in the trigger mechanism. In the process the shark lifted partially out of the water as the spear lodged in its mouth. It swam off wrenching the gun from Brian's hands. He retrieved the gun but had to return to the boat for a new spear shaft.

A fish is speared and brought to the boat where it is cleaned. Soon there are six galapagos and a couple of duskies milling around the aft end of the boat. Divers who come and go must jump in with the sharks and come back through the sharks. A diver from Guam who has, at great expense, made this trip for the first time, stands with me on the aft end. He is already through for the day, telling me in a clear and rational voice that the sharks are too much. He was not prepared for this and is too anxious out there. "The sharks are always coming up behind so I am constantly looking over my shoulder. I can't concentrate on the tuna." Later he tells me, "I think they can smell me, smell my fear." I nod looking at the cruising shapes circling the swimstep.

Two hours later Quinn has speared a fish. The chase boat trails behind the *Ambar* and is brought forward carefully in the eleven-foot seas. For me to get from the swimstep of the *Ambar*, which is moving vertically eight to ten feet every ten seconds, to the chase boat while holding on to the camera housing and attached strobe, is a major feat. I manage to get into the chase boat, but the swell is like a bucking bull and my feet go out from under me. I hold the camera up so as not to damage it, and take the full effect of the fall on my hip. Luckily it didn't break, but it will be sore for a while.

In the water with Quinn eight minutes after the hit. The fish has run and now he is trying to pull it up. White flashes penetrate from the deep blue fifty feet below. Dark shapes swirl around the tuna, glowing like a lost moon tumbling in vast blue space. The line is jerking. Terrible sounds come from the depths. The sharks have descended on the tuna and are devouring it. My first inclination is to dive down and shoot some pictures. Twenty feet into the dive the sharks can be clearly seen thirty feet away. There are so many around that the tuna can scarcely be seen. The sharks' bodies twitch violently, spinning and jerking at a speed that stops me cold in mid-water. Never before have I witnessed such controlled chaos and brutal fury. At once fascinated and alarmed, I hang in the water, unable to move closer to the sharks or get further away. It is impossible not to watch and project oneself in the middle of the frenzy. The sharks are taking terrible bites out of the tuna, the sound of the torn flesh resonating through the water. They come in, then twist their bodies upside down so they can get more of a bite, their white bellies catching the surface light, twitching like worms whose bodies have been severed. There is only a dim desire to take a photograph. Using the wide-angle 20mm lens would require that I come to within eight feet of the attack, far too close to the violence for my liking. The sharks devour the one hundred and fifty-pound tuna in less than a minute, then all but vanish into the depths. One or two circle the slowly spinning spear shaft as Brian hauls it up. The wild hand of nature is exacting and efficient, reinforcing (if one needed it) the fact that this is indeed dangerous business. Within an hour Quinn spears another fish, and again I am in the water with him. This time though, the sharks, while present as the tuna bleeds considerably, circle from a distance. Brian is able to pull the fish to him. And as the tuna nears the surface the circling sharks back off, allowing him to bring it to his hand, as if they somehow understand that this tuna belongs to the manfisher.

Gathering on board the *Ambar* for dinner, the shark, if not the topic of nearly every conversation, becomes the sidebar of jokes and constant needling among the divers. Quinn's tuna carcass is fed to the sharks as all watch in mesmeric fascination. This particular group, consisting of Brian Yoshikawa, Gerald Lim, Brian Quinn, Vic Baker, Bernard Chan and Pat Agan, are all, save for Lim and Chan, from Hawaii. They are splendid, the way I would like to imagine all blue water hunters being. They possess a true passion for the sea, and exercise high standards (Brian Yoshikawa did not find a fish over two hundred pounds so never pulled the trigger). Their ethics and reverence for the sea and its residents is heartening and so desperately needed in this time of great peril.

The *Ambar* leaves later in the evening for the island of Socorro, thirty miles south. Pam has fallen ill with dizziness, chills and nausea, all signs of heat exhaustion. We go so hard that it is difficult to keep an eye on one another. Something as common as heat exhaustion can be serious. Any injury that would require hospitalization could be fatal. We give her liquids and let her sleep.

# DAY
## 49

I lay in bed well after the sun has risen, still tired with a tight eardrum. Pam is very much in the throes of her illness and Jack, who has no malady other than painful toes that now appear as raw craters on their knuckles, is listless. Common sense would dictate rest for all, but the portent of clear water and two mantas later in the morning drive us into the water.

It is an axiom of all spearfishermen and underwater photographers, or anyone who needs clear water to operate, that immediately upon entering the water it will begin to cloud up, or at best never seem as clear as was perceived from the boat. At any rate the water does cloud up and we never see a manta, so retire to the boat for the remainder of the day.

In the late afternoon, two humpback whales, several miles to the west, begin to breach. They breach in unison and independently, moving south to north as the sun sets and disappears, swallowing their silhouettes. By a loose count they make over a hundred breaches, working their joyous way north.

# DAY
# 50

Dark clouds bruise the sky, sucking the light from the sea and spitting rain. A front is moving in and it remains to be seen what will result. The surface of the water appears oily and shows signs of life not ordinarily seen. Bait moves as if another wind were blowing beneath the surface. A bird dives into the ripple and emerges with a fish, flips it high into the air and catches it lengthwise so it can be swallowed. We have become adept at distinguishing the different ripples on the water and the source of their creation. The bait swirls the water and the mackerel move as if a wind were at play. The manta create a current-like motion that is very subtle when they swim just beneath the surface as they generally do. Often a wing tip might break the surface to confirm the sighting.

The poor light and ruffled seas convince us to make a scuba dive on yet another pinnacle to look for the hammerheads. What a hassle: all the gear, the sheer weight of it, heating us up in our wet suits, dehydrating us before we are able to cool off in the water. When finally we are in the water, I feel like a spectator. All the intuitive perceptions seem to filter through my regulator and seep away with the bubbles. On the bottom, and in defense of scuba, I do see a stonefish for the first and quite likely the last time, for I would probably never see one free diving. I suppose the optimum tool for me under the water would be a re-breather (which is a closed circuit unit that expels no bubbles) reduced to about the size of a decent book.

On the bottom at sixty feet we scarcely see a fish save for the stonefish, a few assorted jacks, and a number of large moray eels; no big fish the likes of grouper, or amberjack, which I would expect to see out here. The nets have done their killing before they were outlawed. We burn half a tank and then return to the surface, wholly disheartened.

Back on board the *Nirvana*, the weather front has brought a strong wind from the north that blows fine grit off the volcanic peak. The grit settles everywhere and forces us to secure our cameras and keep the underwater housings sealed. The sandy grit is in our hair and teeth, and felt in our lungs. We seal up the boat and wait out the storm. In the close quarters we each settle into our own private worlds. Pam, it seems, is often in need of Jack's attentions. Perhaps she believes this journey is more than what it is, and though I am not privy to their conversations, it is clear that there is friction between them. Jack, for his part, handles it well, but her pouting and carrying on take its toll. In the evenings, despite the dramatic machinations, Pam continues to prepare delicious meals cooked from scratch. For all the hardships, we do not want for tasty chow.

# DAY
# 51

Mares' tails linger from the passing front. For most of the morning, we clean the boat and gear of grit and dust. During lunch a humpback breaches a half-mile from the boat. Another makes a dive, tail up and disappears. Pam, resting in the V berth in the bow, hears faint whistles through the hull.

We have a singer.

Humpback whales are the troubadours of the whale clan. Science is unsure why they sing and other species of whales do not (perhaps for the same reason why they breach like no other whale). Their songs are distinctive, beautiful and powerful. My only other experience with a singer was in Hawaii. The sounds of a singing humpback whale thoroughly penetrate the human body when underwater. Within a hundred feet one is more aware of the song's vibrations than the sound itself. It is now believed that the deep notes of a humpback can be heard by another humpback anywhere in the same ocean basin. It is also believed that at one time, before the introduction of combustion engines for powering vessels, a single humpback's song could

be heard around the world. About ten years ago it
was discovered that each whale not only had its
individual song, but that its song changed every
year. The sounds of its song are a cacophonic collection of toots, whistles, barks, grunts, ominous
rumblings, barnyard squeals, coughs and growls.
Fifty million-year-old sounds that rightly depict
their proper age.

We hurry into the skiff.

Pam is at the outboard while Jack and I suit up
and make ready the camera gear. The whale blows
nearly a mile away. Characteristically, a singing
humpback will take two blows and on the third
blow, will lift its tail high in the air on the dive and
settle in forty or fifty feet of water nearly perpendicular to the surface, its head pointed down at a
forty-five-degree angle where it will sing for upwards of twenty minutes before rising for a breath.

The weight of the three of us in the skiff has the
outboard laboring at high RPMs and unable to get
up on a plane; we must plod through wind-chopped
seas. A quarter-mile ahead the whale has made its
third blow and has dived. Arriving at its footprint,
a slick spot created after the whale submerges, we
drop into the water. The sound of the whale's song
greets us and is all pervasive. It penetrates my
chest and stomach, vibrating every fluid-filled or-
gan in my body. The sounds vary from a high-
pitched whistle (almost a shriek) to the deep
throaty roar of a primeval beast.

We see nothing.

The sunlight penetrates far into the depths, rays
dancing to a prismatic point that is indistinguishable. We try to follow the sound, which seems to
radiate from all compass points. The song is at once

glorious and terrifying, generating an otherworldly atmosphere under the water that is as unsettling as it is intriguing. The primordial song rattles the cerebral cortex; the brain doesn't know what to do with this new information and searches for a connection to something familiar but cannot, and the imagination rears its ever-creative muse and suggests danger. Hairs prick and adrenals kick in for fight/flight. But in which direction? The underwater universe is on stand-by.

Jack and I separate, thinking we might have a better chance of finding the humpback. Alone, two miles off the island, in water thousands of feet deep drawn towards a sound that feels like the misty den of one's darkest demons, I plod forward with timid uncertainty. It is the mystical element of the natural world that will never be conquered by man, which beckons me, an element that forever reduces us to impotence when next to superior creatures that have outlived us by forty-five million years.

Onward I swim, lugging the cumbersome camera housing which slows me measurably, following this mystic song like a siren's call to some terrible end.

The sound is everywhere, and the whale is nowhere.

Suddenly it stops. In the utter stillness of the sea I am shot through a worm hole into deep aqua space, where all that is heard is the sound of my breath blowing steadily through the snorkel. Stopping for a moment, I tread water, poking my head up into the air. The whale surfaces fifty yards away, blows once, then vanishes. How could something so large vanish so easily? I find Jack and we shake our heads, smiling behind the snorkels. So easily fooled, so small, following some blind notion to our silly doom. Pam retrieves us in the skiff and we pick up the whale's track, such as it is in this wind-ruffled sea.

Again we find the whale too far away and by the time it has taken its third blow, we are still well behind it, hurrying to its footprint that, by the time we arrive, has all but been erased by the agitated sea. Nevertheless, we make a jump and the song is as strong and rich as before: vibrating, disorienting, ominous. We are no closer than we were a half-hour ago. Still, we swim like lemmings driven by an unknown force toward another abyss.

A pod of five bottlenose dolphin suddenly, magically appears. We had seen no surface sign of them. They are unusually friendly for bottlenose, and I stop and dive. They drift off and I hang motionless at twenty-five feet, and wait. They see me and turn, then come in rather boldly and I am able to knock off a few shots, surface and dive again. They are right on me and are sonaring me, the vibrations palatable in the dense atmosphere as if I have been struck in the chest by tiny bubbles. They know who I am. They know of any illness, my emotional state, and my general disposition. They know me at this moment better than any human could ever know me. Apparently, they have approved and invite me for a swim, turning belly up and gliding by. Accepting, I dive belly up to the surface. One sprints off and comes back with a rush, something I cannot do, but I spin to the surface and the two following me spin likewise. We are communicating in the language common to dolphins. I do not linger on the surface, but take a quick breath and drop down again, turning, spinning slowly, showing my belly.

One comes very close, and we make direct eye contact not three feet away. Then another comes and the three of us swim parallel to the surface at twenty feet for almost a minute. The contact is direct and as sure as if we were lovers fresh from bed. The dolphin stay with me for nearly ten minutes then suddenly, as if called, bolt off. I am alone with the song of the whale. Jack has gone ahead and between swells, I glimpse the skiff two hundred yards away and swim for it.

Five minutes into the swim two big galapagos track slowly up from the depths toward me. Then three more. A couple of ten-footers, a big twelve-footer, and two maybe eleven feet. I continue to swim hoping they'll sniff and move on. The twelve-footer comes to my rear as expected and comes fast; I turn to face it and it breaks away. I turn back and begin to swim towards the skiff, taking a quick look, finding it dancing in the wind chop still several hundred yards away. When returning my head to the water, a shark is at my legs and forces me to stop and face it up. When I turn back to swim, one has come to within two feet of me from the opposite direction and breaks away. They effectively force me to stop swimming and I hover vertically just beneath the surface, kicking evenly to give no sign of weakness or fear. They move with the persistent desire to approach from my backside, wherever it might be. Spinning around, I jab the camera housing out to repel one that has crept up on my back. Another comes from the opposite side and twists away two feet off my shoulder. They are like a pack of dogs, squeezing me, taking away my space. Lifting my head out of the water, I shout towards the skiff, "HERE, OVER HERE!" Then back to the sharks that again force me to spin and turn in defense. Oddly, I am not frightened, though I have every right to be, for I see no immediate way out of this. Perhaps I am afraid to be afraid. It is doubtful Pam has heard me over the noise of the breaking sea. After striking out and hitting a shark I lift my head and shout again, then back into the water. I only hope she will come looking for me, but she will have difficulty seeing me with just my snorkel occasionally revealing itself out of the choppy sea. She has no notion where I am, and will stay with Jack, as has been her habit. The sharks circle closer now and I am spinning clockwise with them. I can't keep this up indefinitely and again try to swim, but it is like a panic now and the sharks sense it and move quicker and tighter, pressing me to turn when one is inches off my fins, its eyes rolled back, its mouth slack, teeth visible, row upon row. Striking it on the head with the housing, it explodes away, stirring up the others who twitch and turn excitedly. The image of the sharks devouring the tuna flashes in my head, and fear wells in my chest and throat. The twelve-footer, the boldest of the five, slips close behind and spinning, I rake the housing against its head. It responds as if the blow was no more than a minor nuisance. They force me to turn with them again. There no longer is a plan to escape. It is all I can do to keep my head and suppress my fear. Suddenly the sharks wheel away and sprint for the depths. A hundred feet behind them race the five bottlenose dolphins. They streak after the sharks that have all but disappeared in the abyss. Into the bottomless water I gaze, waiting for the dolphin to return, but they and the sharks have vanished. In twenty minutes I make it to the skiff and climb wearily in.

The dolphins may well have spared me a grim ending. They are remarkable creatures that I have come to believe are capable of any sort of miracle, great or small. In the nine years I have been out on the White Sand Ridge off Grand Bahama diving with the Atlantic spotted dolphins, there has developed a mutual interest that is difficult to comprehend. Each year for the last four years something wonderfully strange and beautiful has occurred with the spotted dolphins.

On several occasions, while swimming along with other divers, a dolphin will single me out and spin around doing loops and racing by, missing me by inches. She, and it is usually a female, will continue this until I have recognized her from previous years. The recognition takes place in my mind (not in any gesture of body language that I am aware of), and the instant it does, the dolphin will relax and swim with me for a while before wandering off with the rest of the pod. More unusual is the dolphin that approached me three years ago head on, which they rarely do. Usually they like to have a good view and so turn broadside to accommodate the position of their eyes on either side of their head. This dolphin came to within a foot of my face, very close, hanging vertically in the water. I was treading water at the time and so was vertical as well. We were standing in the water just below the surface looking at one another. I rose so my head cleared the surface and the dolphin rose, its head clearing the surface, never breaking eye contact. We were both well clear of the surface and its rostrum only inches from my facemask. Clearly, it seemed to be trying to communicate. I emptied my mind, and opened my heart awaiting a subtle message or indication of its purpose. Taking a breath, I sunk a few feet beneath the surface and the dolphin mirrored my move. We stared, we waited and held our mutual breaths for several minutes. I surfaced and again the dolphin followed, still inches from my face. Reaching out, I touched her chest. She did not move, and I held my hand to her for a long moment as if to somehow feel her language through her skin. She then turned slightly and brushed my hand with her pectoral fin and slid away.

An almost identical exchange happened the following year with a different dolphin. And last year another dolphin swam to me and extended its pectoral fin to rest upon my shoulder. We looked long into each other's eyes and then it too went vertical and we held each other, pectoral fin to hand for several minutes. Many who witnessed these exchanges have asked why they occur. I have no ready answer, only a few theories based on a little knowledge and my overall sense of it.

Through the use of sonar the dolphins can perceive humans in extraordinary ways. They can know, for example, how we measure up physically, having the ability to detect abnormalities within our bodies such as tumors, cancer, disease, bone breaks, and a general knowledge of our health and well-being. These faculties are so refined they can detect menstruation in a woman. Science has no idea how they are able to do this. Some believe that they use their ultrasound to scan the lining of the womb in order to recognize the menstrual cycle. There is another theory that relates to the dolphin's ability to pick up subtle changes in our bioelectrical or electrodynamic L field. This ability to sense changes in the L field would explain how they can detect illness, both emotionally and physically, as well as determine when we are in good health. Or, as researcher Dr. John Lilly observed after studying them for over twenty years, dolphins are telepathic and appear to operate more out of the intuitive right hemisphere of the brain. Lilly also suggests the dolphin's brain waves equate with alpha and theta waves, the same brain waves in humans that accompany meditative states.

My first inclination is to acknowledge that the dolphins do know my general well-being, both physical and emotional, through sonar. My training as a spearfisherman may well come into play as I seem to automatically slip into the right hemisphere of my brain whenever I enter the water, falling into what would be termed a meditative state. If I am nothing else in the water, I am relaxed. So thoroughly relaxed that I may well emit alpha or theta waves as if in meditation. Or, if the dolphins are telepathic, they know my thoughts, and if they know my thoughts then they know me to be a friend. Perhaps all these elements play a role in this ongoing relationship of man with dolphins.

Dolphins are intelligent and the sensory system through which they explore, define and interact with one another has been refined and shaped within the unsullied confines of the natural world of the seas. In almost direct contrast my intellect and its accompanying sensory system is a product not so much of nature but of the aftermath and continuing carnage of the Industrial Revolution. This influence, to a large degree, has arrested and ultimately diminished my capacity to utilize what was once a highly sensitive sensory system. As products of this environmental overload, we are unable to feel nature as we once could, or see its subtle beauty, or hear its whispered voice. In effect, we enter the natural world dulled to the point of numbness, ignorant of the capacity we once possessed and no doubt used quite freely when in the environment the dolphins now inhabit. Our intellect has been warped by technological abstractions that give more attention to the virtual reality of a rose than the rose itself. The intuitive right hemisphere of our brain, the pathway to the natural world, has been declared null and void by way of our culture's fixation on the linear. It is not the dolphin who must somehow make the adjustment to understand us. If communication will ever occur, it is we who must return to the highly sensitive creature we once were and were born to be.

# DAY
## 52

Winds continue to erupt out of the north, whipping plumes of volcanic dust off uppermost peaks, and inducing the Pacific to wrap its swell around the island and batter the lee shoreline, bringing silt and debris that renders the water unfit for diving. We decide to run east and venture up the southeast side. Two-and-a-half miles into our trek, we come across a coral-studded finger of lava that extends out from the island for a hundred yards. The layout looks ideal for lobster, and being always in need of fresh food, we anchor.

Much of free diving is, or at least becomes, hard work—diving for lobster in shallow water is similar to an Easter egg hunt; far more fun than work.

It is all in the eye.

One must be able to ferret out the hidden and well-camouflaged lobster while twenty or more feet away on the surface. There are no straight lines in the busy topography of a reef system or coral garden, and it is the straight line of the lobster's antenna, if only visible for an inch or two, that gives away its hiding place. If no straight lines can be found then one must selectively choose which caves and crevices to dive. This choice is based on a number of variables: surge direction, availability of food (lobsters are primarily scavengers), tide, and current that might bring in food. The intuitive choice, as examined earlier, is based on something less tangible than those variables. By any method this place, with all its nooks and crannies, and proximity to current and surge has all the earmarks of being chock full of lobster.

In the first hour we are unable to locate a single lobster. There is no explanation other than they have been trapped out, not uncommon these days. A properly equipped boat with enough traps and pangas could wipe the island clean in a month, a staggeringly brief period of time when one considers that it takes a lobster approximately two years to reach maturity, at a pound and a half. The very large lobsters, over twenty pounds, which are all but extinct, had been known to reach an age of over sixty years. Wild lobster could well be trapped out of existence in my lifetime.

Eventually, we find two small pockets hiding a dozen each, and take five four-pounders in thirty feet of water. Taking lobster by hand on a free dive can be a simple matter or difficult in the extreme. In either case, despite wearing gloves, it is usually at a cost of a few puncture wounds in the hands. For the first lobster I merely reach into a hole whose entrance is the size of a large salad bowl and make a quick, sure-handed grab, pinning the lobster to the floor or wall to ensure a firm grip, then pull it out. If the lobster is large, two hands are needed for they are strong in the tail and a hard whip will jerk it free from a weak handhold. Subsequent dives become increasingly difficult, for the remaining lobster will retreat to the corners of their cave and a deep reach to the shoulder is needed to pin them before dragging them out amongst others scattering deeper into the coral labyrinth. Actually, we pull out six, but two are females and we put them back so that they might restock such a lovely homesite.

I, of course, am unable to eat lobster, but will barter off my catch to Pam for the last of the steaks.

In the afternoon, we haul out the scuba rigs and devote the remainder of the day to searching out high spots south of the anchorage for hammerheads. We have attempted to locate one particular spot whenever our travels take us over the area, but it is deep and impossible to explore on a breath-hold.

Taking land bearings has never been one of my strengths, and apparently Jack is not much better. Pam, however, has a keen eye and after an hour we locate the spot, lose it to current and relocate it again, managing to anchor on the pinnacle itself, which is a stroke of luck.

Diving to the top of the seamount, we settle into large schools of orange and neon blue humuhumunukunukuapuwaa (as the Hawaiians would call them), more commonly referred to as triggerfish, who hula about the ocean floor in greeting. We follow a ridge out into deeper water and as we proceed gradually to depth, the surface light dims, as if to match the darkness of the water with the increasing pressure on our bodies. The technology of scuba masks my ocean sense, and without a depth gauge, I have no idea how deep we are. At this point I am curious enough to ask Jack our depth, so turn and find him pointing his video camera out into the cyanide blue of a deep canyon. Six ghostly pale hammerheads, the dull light glinting off silvered bodies, move like apparitions, aware of us. They are deeper than we, rising slowly from the fathomless canyon.

Dropping into the canyon, I descend to their level, a ten footer turning towards me, but still too far away for a shot. The 20mm lens and strobe require a tight shot and I hold my breath, for the bubbles unsettle hammers who will move off with little provocation. Able to ease to within seven feet of one as it begins to turn, I knock off a couple of shots before it slips away into dark water. I drop down a bit further into the canyon for another shot of two trailing behind, but am unable to hold my breath any longer, and upon my exhale, they immediately break away from the disturbance. Hovering in the emptiness of mid-abyss, I eventually look up to where Jack is waving frantically on the edge of the canyon. It occurs to me that I must be fairly deep so begin to rise. Once I reach him, we immediately begin to ascend. He issues hand signals that I nod yes to, without understanding. Later I learn that he was not guessing my weight at one-six-five, but alluding to our depth. Returning to the anchor line, we make a decompression stop at twenty feet, still a thousand pounds of air in the tank.

It distresses me to learn how deep I have been. When Bob D. became severely bent in Hawaii at a hundred and twenty feet, I vowed never to go below a hundred. It is my belief that free divers are more susceptible to the bends than are frequent scuba divers, the theory being that a free diver's body is accustomed to carrying a certain amount of nitrogen that is forced by virtue of rapid ascents to remain for long periods in the blood stream. When that same diver puts on a scuba unit and goes to depth for any length of time it produces a nitrogen saturation that his body is unfamiliar with, and he is unable to expel in a manner consistent with a veteran scuba diver. I know that deep diving with scuba (over a hundred feet for me) is a walk in the park for most, and is often done twice a day. But scuba diving is very much a black and white world in terms of the laws and rules one must abide by. It comes down to clear-cut physics. If the laws are broken, severe penalties are exacted, including paralysis or even death. The world of free diving is much grayer, an instinctive world that divers must feel their way through, with a bit of room to expand and contract. Diving with scuba, which I rarely do, requires a different mindset. It is becoming apparent that there will be deeper scuba diving here at San Benedicto than anticipated. Without a computer or depth gauge (I do buy a computer upon my return), I must rely solely on Jack's judgment, which is not something I am altogether comfortable with, having relied on myself for nearly fifty years. The adjustment is difficult but necessary. Fortunately for me, Jack is most astute in these matters, and I am grateful for his knowledge and diligence in adhering to the laws of scuba.

The laws of scuba diving, as done by the experts, can be bent at times (pun intended), but few are able to enter this territory. Some years ago I was privileged to introduce Sheck Exley to an Aqua Tek conference put on by Michael Menduno. Sheck was the best scuba diver in the world; no one was better. I met with him and we chatted for almost an hour. He was humble, introspective, and had none of that self-congratulatory nonsense so many in this and other areas of our culture indulge in these days.

Shortly after he appeared at the Tek conference, he died attempting a very deep dive to nearly a thousand feet, I am told. Personally, I would rather take my chances riding the back of a great white shark than dive to three hundred feet. Sheck taught math in high school. He understood the laws of scuba and respected them, but to even consider a dive to that depth, he had to have some gray in him somewhere.

# DAY
# 53

The wind has lessened but still drives popcorn clouds across the sky with considerable force. A manta comes alongside the boat and Pam jumps in to keep it company while Jack and I suit up. When we make our jump, five mantas have converged about the boat. They are all on the surface feeding on what appears to be tiny red eggs the size of poppy seeds. The manta's body hunches and expands as its mouth opens and its horns unfurl and, in the manner of a rudder, funnels the eggs into its mouth as it swims along. How incongruous for something so large to be feeding on something so small. None of the mantas are interested in us and want no part of playing. The five in the cove are coming and going in every direction, scooping up the red eggs that may well be their primary reason for residing at San Benedicto.

Near noon I am over in the far northeast end of the cove and the manta with the shark bite in its wing takes an interest in me. Diving to its depth, I engage it with eye contact and brush my hand lightly down its back, generating quivers in its skin. Swimming with these creatures is very much like diving with dolphins. Usually, eye contact is made and then some form of interacting play ensues.

This manta and I have connected; we are in the rhythm.

It waits for me and when I join it, we spin down three hundred sixty degrees together doing a complete barrel roll. Moving to its white belly, I rub the area beneath its mouth. It responds like a cat being petted and quivers, holding still in mid-water while I scratch its itch. Every so often I shoot a picture then return to the play. It dives to the bottom at fifty feet and I follow. We are on the sand. Sprinting in front of the manta, I lay down on my back, attempting to get a shot of it going over me. When it is over me it stops, presumably to be stroked again, inches from my body, blocking out all the light and preventing me from surfacing. If it should decide to settle, I would be easily crushed. Letting go of the camera and leaving it on the bottom, I reach up and gently stroke its belly with one hand and push with the other. It does not move; it is like pushing against a building. Out of air fifty feet from the surface, I reach up and place my hands across its mouth and see if I can pull myself out. As I put my hands over the lower jaw and apply pressure, the manta begins to move. I don't know whether to hold on now or let go. If I let go and it stops again, I am in trouble. If I hold on and it doesn't gain altitude, then I cannot free myself to escape. I let go and try not to encourage another stop by avoiding all contact. It continues to move forward inches off my body and once past, I am able to push off the bottom and dash for the surface. There I catch my breath, then dive to retrieve the camera. Meanwhile, the manta circles back and is waiting for me.

We continue to dance until I am out of film.

Diving down, I give it a stroke on the edge of its wing in gratitude for time spent, then turn away and begin the swim back to the boat some three hundred feet west.

The manta follows me.

Reaching the boat, I climb aboard to reload as the manta circles the boat. After a good ten minutes I re-enter the water and the manta is there waiting. Rather than play by the boat as I begin to do, it swims off, turns around and comes back then swims off again. This time I follow and it leads me back to the precise place we had been playing on the far side of the cove. Once there, we resume the same dance as before, and continue for another forty minutes before it wearies of my limitations and drifts off.

In the rhythm.

I cannot find this rhythm anywhere but beneath the surface of the sea. In the forest I have camped among great trees, and nature's song has whispered to me in soft tones and gentle hushes and sighs of wind. In comparison, the pulse of the natural world under the water shouts and shakes its tangible presence. Perhaps because the density of the water carries this message so much more effectively. And underwater, we humans are more susceptible to such messages. Our skulls, organs, eyes, and our mind-body can more readily feel the language of nature when beneath the water.

It should be remembered that we began our lives in a liquid world. Like the planet, humans are two thirds liquid. Our blood is similar to seawater. Human babies are able to navigate underwater from the moment of birth. They seem to be quite happy with their heads and bodies completely submerged, making no effort to breathe, while calmly gazing about wide-eyed and unafraid, appearing to enjoy the weightlessness of their underwater experience. Allied to our instinctive ability to move about underwater is the reflex that comes into play as soon as we put our heads beneath the surface; our heartbeat reduces involuntarily as does the rate at which our bodies use oxygen. This "dive" reflex cuts the normal pulse rate from seventy to thirty beats a minute, something we share with whales and seals; it is not known to exist in any other land animal. Theories abound to our ancestral backgrounds with regard to the sea. Sir Alister Hardy, a British zoologist who served his apprenticeship as a marine biologist, drew a direct connection between man and the sea. "I see our ancient ancestors becoming more and more of an aquatic animal, going further out from shore; I see him diving for shellfish, prizing out worms, burrowing for crabs and bivalves from the sands on the bottom of shallow seas, and breaking open sea urchins, and then with increasing skill, capturing fish with his hands."

In the rhythm.

# DAY
## 54

This morning I wake up sore and tired with legs tight from kicking. Shoulders, arms, legs and torso are filled with bruises and abrasions from accumulated bumps and scrapes that daily life at sea in a small boat produce. My body is slowly being ground down to exhaustion. Lately, whenever it's time to suit up, I find reasons for staying on board. Here we are in one of the last of the truly wild places left in the Western Hemisphere, and I must talk myself into jumps. Jack is tired as well, and his sore toes look awful. He fairly screams every time he puts on his fins, but never complains outright. Pam has not fully recovered from her bout with heat exhaustion, yet still spends hours in the heat of day manning the skiff while we are diving. It is the sharks that keep her out of the water. Her fear runs deep and now she is fearful for both Jack and me every time they come around. She is determined to keep an eye on both of us, particularly after the incident when the galapagos had me cornered. This is not an easy task for her as Jack and I tend to go our separate ways. To keep an eye on both of us in choppy water is next to impossible.

All she really sees is the descent when the swim fins break water and slide beneath the surface. That she might fail to pick someone up in trouble is beginning to take its stressful toll. It is for that reason, I think, that she remains in the *Nirvana*, while Jack and I go out to investigate ripples on the water a mile offshore. No doubt it is the school of skipjack we have seen on occasion, but we are curious as to what brings them up.

We float directly above the school and by way of a silver explosion of scale and light, discover a nine-foot dusky working its perimeter. Jack dives directly on the chromed school of skipjack, sixty feet deep and forty feet wide. Glint and shadow part, creating a perfect tunnel of fish for him to dive through. He is down seventy feet and looks up through the rotating tunnel of fish at me on the surface; as he does, a manta swims through filling the empty sphere. Later, he says the vision was spectacular with the overhead sun. More manta come; they seem to find us now wherever we are diving. The school of skipjack sound, leaving us with the manta. The pink fish eggs are still in abundance and suspend everywhere in the water. It appears the mantas that have been feeding on them day and night have themselves swelled in size. One becomes playful and flips over exposing its white undersides, whirling wings wrapping me like a cocoon, then allowing me to swim out. While I hover just above it, a wing curls and then whips in, striking me on the side of the head, stunning me for several seconds. Jack, having picked up his video camera, catches it on tape. It is a solid blow, and initially he believes I have been knocked unconscious and begins to come after me, but I recover and swim to the surface without assistance.

In the afternoon, we are out searching for pinnacles and in the depths, I catch a flicker of light, which is about all one sees in this kind of diving. Any indication of light, no matter how insignificant, has meaning and I drop to investigate. Tuna, yellowfin, eighty to one hundred pounds. The school of maybe thirty is breezing and scattered. Several draw close to within fifteen feet. Muscled power, built like kegs of beer, in search of food. The spearfisherman in me gazes out, the shot is there on a big one. I have never speared a tuna. If Al hadn't been killed by the great white while hunting tuna, the tribe of hunters would have probably been doing it ten years earlier, and I might have had an opportunity. I draw a bead down the stock of an imaginary spear gun and knock off a shot. It is all I can do for the 15mm lens of the Nikonos is far too wide for the distance and reduces the fish to the size of a guppy. It is enough to see the yellowfin roaming the blue prairie through which they graze and though it does give me pause, there is no pull on the line in my future.

Another subtle glimmer of light in the depths and it becomes a wahoo of forty pounds come to investigate the intruder. Jack sees the fish as well and returns to the skiff for the spear gun. We are in need of food. By the time he rigs up, the fish has gone, but soon he comes upon a school of fifteen that he dives and though circling him, they are small and he doesn't pull off.

We are a mile offshore and the diving is deep. I can punch out a dive to sixty with some regularity, but Jack can go to seventy-five feet continually. He is two minutes down and a minute up. By mid-afternoon my legs are worked and I can scarcely swim to the boat. Jack and I track our way back to the boat and a ten-foot dusky picks us up and continues to make passes, forcing us to stop every twenty feet to turn around. We take turns diving on the shark to scare it off, but it must be a rogue for it remains undeterred and shadows us all the way to the boat. Resting in the skiff as the shark circles, we watch until it drifts back to the depths.

# DAY 55

S wells are up and the water on the south end of San Benedicto has clouded and is undivable. Our supply of food has begun to run low, and today there is talk of our return to Cabo San Lucas. Pam estimates that we have another week of food, discounting anything Jack might spear. I think Pam is ready to go now, but just raising the specter of leaving rejuvenates me for the clock that has become the food supply is now ticking.

It is decided to try the west side, maybe go up to the Boiler see if we can find some clear water. Pam is on the outboard as we round the southwest corner and face towering swells of ten to twelve feet. After a slug of blue water cascades over the bow, she comments, "I think it is too rough." Neither Jack nor I respond. Indeed we don't even acknowledge her concern as our little boat labors up the next swell and down the other side. She has not been in seas like this in such a small boat and argues that if something were to happen to the boat barring any currents, which is unlikely, we would have a difficult, if not impossible, time getting back to the *Nirvana*. She has a point, but instead of responding, Jack simply points in the direction we wish to go, and Pam shakes her head, eyeing me for support, a skein of common sense. But nary a whiff of reason blows between the two of us.

The Boiler is one of those "must" stops for the charter operations out of Cabo San Lucas. The *Ambar III* and the one hundred ten-foot liveaboard, the *Solamar*, are the only two boats that have permits at this time. Turning up sea on the tip of a swell we spot the *Solamar* anchored off the Boiler. It takes nearly forty minutes to reach them. We make our first jump a hundred and fifty feet north of the Boiler, and on this day it is a good place to begin as ten-foot swells curl over the rock in huge white water breakers that give the place its name. The *Solamar* has dropped in fifteen scuba divers who are now on the bottom in seventy-five feet watching the mantas swing by them. One fellow tries to mount a manta but is tentative and the manta twists away, enough to give the fellow misgivings. He hovers ten feet above the bottom, trying to decide if he should give it another try. We are above them on the surface and Jack drops down on the deep manta. The lone tank diver sees Jack parallel to the manta sixty-five feet down shooting his video. He looks around, glances back to the other divers strung out in the protection of a reef, seeking some kind of verification; is there really a diver down here without scuba, swimming around nonplussed with a manta? He looks at his depth gauge then back at Jack, then back to the group who doesn't appear to see Jack. He is trying to reason out this scene playing before him. He looks back to the group and points behind him to where Jack was, but Jack is ascending. Finally he is able to get another diver's attention and points to the manta and open water—no Jack. He looks around, never looks up, and finds nothing. Vanished, a tale to tell later. We move on.

The mantas on this side of the island are all at depth and when we near, they wander off uninterested; perhaps they are used to scuba divers. We continue toward the north end of the island, deeper into the swells, out into no man's land. Pam is caught talking to herself. She says she is praying. We don't pursue the question, and by our silence she assumes we may be weakening and will turn around. She tries to talk us out of our pursuit. We have no pursuit other than wanting to see what's over here. She returns to her whispered prayers.

Having made our way to a point just outside the north end of what should be a transition zone of sorts, we jump a pod of dolphins, but are too late into the water. Directly beneath us, however, is a school of yellowfin, then a manta passes through, and a couple of large galapagos weave in the depths, just sniffing.

Suddenly the water is empty—no bait, no tuna, no manta, just the sharks.

When I used to spearfish out in the blue water waiting for yellowtail and the bait was all over the place, I took comfort in their presence. When suddenly the bait disappeared, I felt naked and vulnerable and in a state of suspended anxiety. Immediately, I began to search for the source of the bait's departure, for in the back of my mind the great white swam as the ultimate source of the bait spook.

In this barren water it is not difficult to locate the source of the exodus: galapagos sharks. I count nine, but it seems like more. They methodically zig-

zag their way to the surface. We have entered their
territory. Jack flashes five fingers on his hand twice.
He counts ten. We have seen enough sharks now to
feel we can hold our ground, but not this many. They
circle beneath continuing to rise all the way to the
surface and immediately test our backs. We have
gone back to back, treading water vertically on the
surface. Pam is standing in the inflatable fifty feet
away, and has seen the sharks and begins to shout
at us to get in the boat. Though the boat is only
fifty feet away, there is no way we can swim to it.
The sharks are squeezing us, making passes, seeking areas of vulnerability. Later she said it seemed
like there were twenty sharks on the surface and
we had no chance for survival. Finally realizing that
we can't move, Pam fires up the boat and comes to
us. With the boat now at our backs and feeling somewhat comfortable having it within scrambling distance, I feel confident enough to drop down and test
the resolve of these sharks. They break away as I
approach. Gaining confidence by the moment, I look
up to Jack and give him a thumbs-up. He frantically points in a direction behind me. I turn and
the largest of the sharks is bearing down on me,
huge in the chest, teeth visible in its gruesome grin.
It doesn't break off and keeps coming. A twelve-
footer, and now we are nose to nose at arm's length.
It has stopped and we hover. Down a while and in
need of a breath, I cannot begin to ascend at this
point; kicking legs might be all this shark needs
for encouragement.

Out of breath.

Left with no choice but to swim toward it, hoping it will spook and turn. I make the move, but
the shark does not flinch an inch. Other sharks

twitch and jerk around me, perhaps sensing my anxiety. Left with no alternative, I begin to drift up slowly. Ten feet into the ascent I nearly hit one above me in the belly, which forces me to stop. The big galapagos is still with me, and figuring what the hell, I take its picture. When the strobe goes off the startled shark bolts off and in the flurry scatters the other sharks, allowing me to kick my way to the surface.

On the surface Pam is frantic. She is begging Jack to get into the boat. She doesn't beg me, no doubt believing she has pinpointed the source of this madness, and has given up all pretense of reasoning. But alas, I have infected Jack. "Is this cool or what?" he says, and dives down into the sharks. Pam is swearing at me from the boat. Jack ascends for a breath and I make a dive. The sharks don't know what to do with us. They circle, but they are not nearly so bold. The current here is strong and shortly we find ourselves drifting south on it. In a few minutes we have moved out of the shark's territory and they seem content to stay within those boundaries and settle back down to the depths.

In the boat we try to analyze the shark's behavior. With the numbers in their favor, why wouldn't they be in our face? Pam comments dryly in the stern, "Nobody wants to screw around with crazy people." To which I reply, "How do you explain your presence in the boat?"

"It's a question I keep asking myself."

We turn, and with the flow, slide down the big swells south along the west side of the island en route to the *Nirvana*. The engine winds hard and Pam's face is frozen in determination as she steers a serpentine course home.

# DAY
# 56

The wind has finally let up and the morning sky is cloudless. The manta with the bite mark in its right wing circles the boat twice. On its third tour around the boat it lifts a single wing out of the water and waves. Pam cannot resist the invitation and is in the water. It swims around the cove with her on its back and stays close enough to the surface so she doesn't have to hold her breath, just breathes through the snorkel and rides.

There is almost always one or more big remora attached to a manta, but never more than three. They scuttle about, always shifting away when a diver comes close. I wonder what they eat; they are not plankton feeders. Are the seven- to fifteen-pound hitchhikers in for the ride alone? The largest remora I've seen was riding along on that tiger shark in Fiji. More is known about remoras than mantas. The mantas seem to have slipped through the marine biological cracks. Only now are studies in progress.

In the late morning the three of us head out into blue water several miles south of the island looking for whales. Coming across a friendly manta, we stop and play. We have become so familiar with these incredible creatures that I tend to forget they weigh over a ton and are enormously powerful. At one point while riding its back, I impulsively attempt to pull myself over its mouth so I might ride upside down on its belly. Halfway through the maneuver, draped over its mouth, the manta panics, for it can't see me as its eyes are on the outside of its head, and turning down, it accelerates for the bottom. The power of its flight is such that I am pinned perpendicular across its mouth. Jack, who is in perfect position for a photograph, takes one as I fly past him. The manta does not stop until we are five feet off the bottom at sixty feet. When it arches up to avoid hitting the bottom I am able to break free from the force that holds me. Had this occurred ten minutes earlier in several hundred feet of water the consequences might well have been different. And deservedly so, for the entire episode was one of utter foolishness. It is a reminder that regardless of how comfortable I am in the water with the mantas or the sharks or any of these creatures, they are still wild, powerful and quite capable of doing harm.

In the early afternoon Jack is ready for another dive, but I am giving in to profound fatigue and cannot pull myself from my bunk. He and Pam leave without me, and as they pull away from the *Nirvana*, I feel I have made a mistake. It has taken years, my entire life actually, to reach this blue edge. One cannot shirk the opportunities that the experience offers.

Returning to my bunk, I fall asleep. Several hours later I am awakened by the return of Jack and Pam, and ask before they have come aboard if they had seen anything interesting. "Not much," comes the reply I was hoping to hear. In the evening, as is our nightly custom, Jack plugs in the video and reviews footage of the day on the monitor. There are a few sharks and the obligatory mantas, nothing special, until the camera is suddenly in rich blue water, and a humpback whale and calf come swimming through at a depth of fifty feet. The calf sees Jack, stops and turns to its side and looks up at him for a moment and then turns and goes its way. The footage is beautiful, and Jack is ecstatic. The well-kept secret has made its point, and I resolve to not let the moments slip from me again.

# DAY
# 57

During the night a wind comes out of the north. Stronger than we've seen. We are up and down all night, checking lines, securing loose gear and tying down halyards. The blow continues into day, and in our little protected cove we are getting twenty-two knots of wind. The west side of the island is swell and foaming seas. The conditions drive a commercial Mexican fishing boat into the cove. Such fishing vessels have been restricted to within twelve miles of the islands. This restriction has been in force for a year and was placed as a direct result of a single incident that occurred on February 14, 1994, which has come to be known as the St. Valentine's Day Massacre at San Benedicto Island.

Terry Kennedy and Joyce Clinton who were there recorded the incident on video and reported it as follows:

At dawn on the 14th of February 1994, while anchored at the south end of San Benedicto Island, we were awakened by two Mexican fishing boats laying long lines and inshore gill nets on the reefs, just 200 yards off the beach. At about 9:00 A.M. the *Unicap III*, a Mexican government boat, started pulling in their nets and, as Joyce and I watched helplessly, our worst fears came true.

Two of the mantas we had been riding the day before were helplessly tangled in the nets. These gentle giants had fought the nets and had been torn to pieces. Because of the damage to the nets and to the mantas, the fishing boat, a Mexican Department of Fisheries boat, decided it would be easier to cut their nets loose and throw them back in the water—entangled mantas, nets and all. When they left, there were thousands of feet of thin monofilament net all over the reef, still killing. When they pulled in their long lines there were nothing but reef sharks on the hooks. As these dead or dying sharks came up over the back of the boat, the lines were cut above the hook, and the hook and shark were dropped back into the water where they immediately sank to the bottom. The underwater reef was littered with dozens of dead sharks.

In all this killing, not one usable fish was caught.

In the meantime, the other fishing boat, *Mero VII*, was busy harpooning the first manta that passed by their boat. The twenty-foot, one ton manta was then gaffed with large hooks and lifted out of the water, still very much alive, alongside the boat. Then, the men got out in a small boat and proceeded to use axes to cut the wings off the still-living manta.

In just a few hours over five tons of fish were

killed near this pristine volcanic island, and
many more were going to die in the discarded
net. The two boats had nothing to show for all
that carnage, except two, almost useless manta
wings.

The video by Joyce and Terry was forwarded to
Mike McGettigan, who, in addition to skippering
the *Ambar III*, heads Sea Watch, an American non-
profit organization dedicated to a healthy Sea of
Cortez. Mike was able to pass it on to newsman
Armando Figaredo who had it aired on Mexico's
largest television station, Televisa. The Mexican
Government was duly embarrassed and took immediate action, fining the boats and their owners,
creating a twelve-mile limit for commercial fishing
on the Revillagigedos Islands, and placing the mantas on their species protected list.

The problem is policing the restrictions, a dilemma Third World countries must contend with
and find difficult if not impossible. Simply put, they
do not have the finances to protect their natural
resources. Plus, the level of corruption is high and
the long-term vision is low. However, dive tourism
is beginning to play a stronger role as these countries are discovering that a live shark is far more
valuable than a dead one. Divers will pay good tourist dollars to see wild life under the sea.

I rather doubt this commercial vessel will undertake any shark fishing in our presence. Word
had gotten out that Americans are a bunch of
whistle blowers. However, in reality the fines lev-
ied on the *Unicap III* and the *Mero VII*, while heavy
and unique, probably did not make much of an impression; most commercial fisheries in Mexico and

elsewhere accept fines as a part of doing business. Fines notwithstanding, unless the Mexican Government can find a way to police its fisheries outside of American watchdogging, it will only be a matter of time before the fishing boats return and renew their slaughter of the giant pacific manta ray and shark.

Rations are beginning to become a problem. Pam is scratching about for remnants of the food supply, her resourcefulness tested daily. I am dining on soy burgers this day, bought by Margaret on a whim in La Paz. At the time I argued it was a waste of money, that they would never be used; now the purchase looks better by the minute.

Boat-bound and bored, I suit up in the afternoon and swim off, despite rough water and poor visibility, to find lobster I spotted on a pinnacle a couple of weeks ago. Jack comes along and brings his spear gun, but in these less than ideal conditions it would be a stroke of supreme luck for him to come across a decent fish.

Locating the lobster hole on a pinnacle, I pull two out. Jack has seen no fish and drags the spear gun back to the boat. Having begun this trip nearly two months ago as a spearfisherman, he has made a decided leap towards videography. There were grand expectations of spearing big fish down here, but after the first wahoo and with no grouper to be found, he seems to have lost interest in the stalk. Which is a pity, for the sea reveals itself in many ways through the stalk alone and Jack has the heart of a hunter. Now, however, it appears the photography and its more linear appeal has his interest rather than the intuitive inclinations demanded in

the hunt. Perhaps the explanation is not so complicated. He knows he can spear fish, and though the
challenge is great, it is far more difficult to secure
a fine photograph, and equally as difficult to obtain good footage on the video. Like everyone else,
Jack is searching for a sturdy challenge to push
against, something that will reveal more of who he
is, and underwater photography presents all the
challenges one would ever require in that pursuit.

After returning to the boat, the winds keep us
hunkered down for the rest of the day. Eating (very
little of that) and reading are the only pleasures
available in this confined space. It is an ill wind
that blows from the north, for I make a comment
about the lumpy anchorage and Jack gives me a
patronizing smile of feigned tolerance, one I normally dismiss. But on this day I can't recall a smile
so annoying, and I tell him so.

He responds in anger and heated words are exchanged between us for really the first time in two
months, which in itself is extraordinary. The weather, I think, has put us all on edge. With supplies
running short, Jack feels an obligation to hunt up
some food, and failing that, has become frustrated.
He assumes responsibility for everyone's well-being and takes that responsibility quite seriously. I,
on the other hand, am responsible for the dishes,
my cameras, and little else. This self-indulgence no
doubt wears thin over time. We all need to be out
in the water, but the wind and high seas have seen
to that. So we are stuck together in this tiny cabin
that is seven feet wide at the galley and long enough
in livable space for two people to sleep lengthwise.
Not much room. Confined to our separate worlds,
Pam goes forward into the V berth and closes the

door; I catch up on my notes, and Jack, perhaps the cheeriest of the lot, does what he does best—tinker. There is plenty to tinker with on this boat. Aside from his endless search for the extra amp or two, running a small boat that is completely self-contained is a tinkerer's delight. There is the water maker that needs constant attention, the engine that is old and will break under the slightest provocation, all the hydraulics and electronics; it is endless.

A tinkerer, I am not. Make minor repairs on the camera gear, maybe. I have fixed a few things when hard pressed. Once when out on the *Low Now* off the Coronados and the outboard stopped running ten miles out in a light fog, my partner on board knew less than I, which I didn't think was possible. At any rate, with minimal tools, I had no choice but to repair the outboard and surprised myself by doing so. On the whole, the machine has always been, and will remain a mystery to me. One would think that with all the time spent on boats that some grease would have rubbed off, but after all these years I remain squeaky clean.

So we sit and we tinker—Jack with gears, Pam with her emotions, and I with words. Meanwhile, time is running out, food is running low, and we have yet to find the schooling hammerhead sharks.

# DAY 58

The winds died during the night, and blue water has blown in from the west, bringing with it a single humpback who is swimming off the canyon. By the time we have suited up and prepared the cameras, the whale has moved southeasterly by several miles. The Marine Mammal Act is in place to prevent man from harassing the animals as would be the case if we ran down the whale and made a jump on it. Actually, that wouldn't work well anyway, for the decision is always with the whale. If they do not wish to interact, they will swim off and in general, make themselves unavailable. The best we can do to encourage interaction is to place ourselves in its path by a quarter mile or so and hope the whales will be interested enough to stop when they pass by.

The whale bears down on us, and from the skiff, we see there are two blows: a baby and its mother, no doubt the same mother and baby so frequently seen on this side of the island. The very same that Jack encountered last week. We station ourselves in their path and wait. They surface and blow a hundred yards in front of us. Jack and I enter the water and dive to thirty feet where we wait. Within moments the two whales pass far beneath us. Diving to fifty feet we stop and hover. The baby has seen us and turns sideways coming to a halt while the mother continues on. The baby is down in ninety feet of water slightly in front of us, sixty feet away. Its long, white pectoral fin raises and it turns to its side so that it might view us better. Both Jack and I move slowly toward the baby and by the time we are above it by forty feet, I am out of breath and must rise to the surface. Jack, able to stay down, continues to run the video. On the surface catching my breath, Jack begins to ascend as the baby, unmoved continues to hang and observe us. Taking a deep breath, I turn down and drop slowly. Twenty feet into the dive the mother appears to my left close to the surface, gliding past me forty feet away and turning gracefully to view me. Halting in midwater, I take in the whale. The details of its description are lost on me, for to see a whale under the same water while on a free dive is to suddenly find oneself in an area of ocean previously untraveled—in another arena gazing upon a living organism that dwarfs all that I am or represent. The whale emits a power and a presence that transcends earthly experience, and through the conduit of water this power is readily transmitted. The whale appears to occupy more space than is represented in its mass. The water feels denser, as if it was a part of the whale, and I can feel its presence as though it were next to me.

In the briefest of moments our eyes meet, and then she slowly turns and dives to the baby, which rolls to her back as she goes by. In another instant they are gone, absorbed into the blue.

Floating back on the surface, I am left with a sense of the expansive intelligence of this whale. Its countenance was that of a wisdom beyond my grasp. Feelings of profound insignificance and shame pass through me, as if suddenly I had been granted a brief audience and had not brought an offering or at the very least, an apology for all the cruelties inflicted by my species on such a superior life form.

Back in the boat, Jack, exuberant, speaks of the whale in glowing terms. I am struck dumb and stare out into the blue waiting for it to appear again, awaiting something to latch on to that would further entrench the experience, or close it; I am not sure which. The mother and baby surface and blow a hundred yards away and only then do I realize I have been holding my breath, and I let it out in an audible sigh. In that release my heart fills with the whale and I am smiling, laughing, shaking my head in wonder.

We motor back toward the island where the mantas breeze in numbers at a depth of forty to sixty feet. Deep dives are required to reach them. As the hours drift towards noon both Jack and I have found our pace. There is a distinct rhythm to free diving to depth: the steady, deep breaths on the surface, then filling the lungs for the last breath, the descent, leveling off into a glide down, down, down, then glide, drift/swimming until the body, which maintains priority over the mind, softly suggests it is time to breathe again. Then there is the difficult trek to the surface, heavy muscled thighs pushing long bladed fins through the dense atmosphere in sweeping, unrelenting strokes, feeling the pressure ease closer to the surface, then greeting the surface with an exhale and inhale, never looking up out of the water, never losing contact with the depths. The body knows precisely how long it can go without oxygen; it does not need nor require the mind to interfere with what has become routine. My body is without tension, my mind without thought. In the nether world of the breath-hold I am more alive and alert than when I draw breaths.

In the rhythm.

Matching the manta's speed, I spin as it spins and rise as it rises. In turn, if I rise it will rise, and if I fall to the depths, it will follow. It rolls to its back and I roll with it going forward. When I come to it head on, it meets me and comes to a halt, then follows wherever I swim. These are the steps, but like all dances there are steps within steps that direct with a simple touch, playful, intimate and loving. And so the dance goes, the rhythm unbroken until four hours have passed and I am weary and must leave my partner who, in my leaving, turns her white belly to the ceiling and falls away into indigo until she is a dot of light in the depths.

# DAY
# 59

Terry and Joyce spotted hammerheads off the west side of the island while on scuba yesterday. The sharks, they said, ran deep and scattered. We have not looked in that area, chiefly because the wind and weather that come out of the north rips through that exposed area on the west leaving it stirred with poor visibility. However, the wind has shifted and blows mildly from the south, the only direction from which we are exposed and vulnerable in the anchorage. Though the small swell barely disturbs the boat, it has drawn silt from the beach and wiped out the visibility. Such reversals create new possibilities and we elect to try the west side for the hammerheads, as such rumors will take us just about anywhere.

Terry and Joyce had seen the hammers near a hundred feet so we have taken scuba. The west side of the island drops steeply off in incremental ledges, like great stairs, to several hundred feet. The water is reasonably clear, a hazy sixty feet. Over one ledge and in the blink of a bubble, one is down a hundred feet. At that depth we settle on a ledge and almost instantly six hammerheads roam out of the gloom toward us. They disappear almost as quickly, the sound of the scuba and its accompanying bubbles causing them to retreat. Knowing this we still search the area, which, to our delight, is filled with all manner of wild life: schooling skipjack, dusky and galapagos sharks, breezing yellowfin tuna. Three bottlenose dolphins come to inspect, along with two mantas. We burn the tanks in search of the hammerheads but to no avail. We have, however, seen enough to know that while the swell is down on the west side, this area is alive with possibilities.

In the late afternoon we return with scuba, this, my second tank dive into deep water in a single day. I cannot remember ever having made two such dives. The water is somewhat cloudy due to a northeasterly current, but the visibility holds near sixty feet. Near the same location as this morning we find the mid-water column overflowing with sea life. The late hour has aroused the sharks. We have not seen this many in one place save for the north end. Yellowfin tuna streak in out of the wild blue, slowing to observe us, then wander off again. There are schools of mackerel and horse-eyed jacks, schooling wahoo, rainbow runners, and big amberjack. There is more life here than we have seen anywhere on the island at any time. A transition zone. Obviously current, rather than bait, is drawing these fish. Bait is a relative term, for these mackerel and even the jacks serve the big pelagics. Recollections of virgin water discovered decades ago emerge. There is electricity in the water, goose bumps rise on my forearms. It feels like the center of the ocean universe. If there is such a place, it would look and feel like this.

We are in the water no more than five minutes
on the same ledge at a hundred feet when the hammerheads show again. This time it's a school of
twenty, silver glinting dully in the deep water, moving ghostly in a drift. Some are well over ten feet;
they cruise on the outside fifty feet off the ledge. I
move closer for a possible shot, but the sound of
the scuba alerts them and causes them to veer away
en masse. Impatient, I take off after them. The
chase is futile. They quickly disappear into hazy
depths. Giving up the pursuit, I settle on an outcropping off a ledge at eighty feet. Two amberjack
over sixty pounds, the biggest I have seen here,
move right into me in the way of amberjack, fearless, curious, big eye surveying at three feet away,
forked tail scarcely moving as they cruise off towards the schooling skipjacks fifty feet above. Big
yellowfin tuna blow in, turn on a dime then race
off to hit the same school of skipjack. They strike
quickly, bolts of light hitting flickers of light; a
wounded skipjack, like a candle in a wind, is
abruptly snuffed out. The hunt of the tuna and the
twitching dead fish has brought in a single hammerhead that warily peers at me on the rock outcropping. Holding my breath, I wait for it to circle
close. Suspicious, it hesitates twenty feet away,
making a slow turn, eyeing me. I wiggle the white
camera housing as though it were a wounded fish.
The dome port catches strange light and the shark
moves toward me. Still holding my breath and wiggling the camera, the hammerhead works its way
to within ten feet of me. Barely within range for
the 20mm lens, and two feet further away for the
light of the strobe to be effective. Finally needing a
breath, I take a shot and the shark jumps out of its

skin at the sudden presence of a flash, and vanishes to the dimming depths in a wink.

These hammerheads are seductive in their photogenic appearance. I recall the efforts of cinema-
tographer Howard Hall free diving his 16mm movie
camera up and down the depth scale to secure footage of schooling hammerheads. It was a Herculean
effort and though he did manage some good footage, he was not happy with the results and returned
with rebreathers that don't emit bubbles nor make
noise. Rebreathers are the way to go with hammerheads, but we are a long way from such technology,
and I now contemplate the obvious. Despite the
depth, these sharks will have to be free dived; there
is no other way.

It occurs to me while Jack and I hang for a decompression stop that I have taken far greater risks
in the water as a photographer than as a spearfisherman. The desire to get a shot begins as a mild
sort of vision that slowly develops into an obses-
sion that will not release me to common sense. It
appears to blossom most with sharks, though I have
long had the desire to spend time in the water with
orcas who are far more wary than the hammerheads. It seems the more time one spends with
sharks, the greater appreciation one has for their
beauty and grace. But there is a deeper fascination
that is difficult to describe. Nick Caloyianis, the
highly respected documentary filmmaker, has been
filming sharks for thirty years and though attacked
and severely bitten by a bull shark, is undaunted
in his fascination of sharks as he continues to film
them at every opportunity throughout the world.
"The sea is filled with stunning creatures," he once
remarked to me, "but none are so intriguing as the

shark." Who can argue? They remain the object of myth and fear throughout the cultures of the world, and hold the attention of humans in physical and symbolic presence like no other animal. I have no doubt that unless man kills off every shark in all the oceans and seas of the world (which is a very real possibility) that the shark will still be swimming long after humans have erased themselves as a life force on the planet. Having lived for three hundred and fifty million years, give or take a millennium, they have established themselves as the ultimate survivor on this rotating sphere in a vast and uncertain universe. I find solace in their presence and cannot help but regard them in the privileged light they have earned.

# DAY
# 60

The morning is without breath, the sky without cloud, the light without peer, igniting all it touches, catching the slight ripples of the schooling skipjack as they pool their way across the outside edge of the cove.

Jack and I jump the school of skipjack. The tuna-like fish, weighing from one to five pounds, spin counter-clockwise when we dive in their midst, swirling blue and silver shards of light in the cobalt galaxy of the sea; they circle far into the depths and I am the atom in their moving nucleus. The fish maintain the same distance from me—eight feet—no matter where I swim.

The galaxy explodes in a shower of light. A dusky shark has hit the school. Big in the shoulder and deep in the chest, it slashes into the school again, and like a single entity, the school parts in an instant, then slowly recloses as reflecting light shimmers in the sunless sea. The blind speed of the shark is unnerving and I consider the possibility of being hit by accident.

Ascending to the surface, I catch my breath. The shark is working deep, and difficult to see. Pumping up, I drop down, but cannot find the shark. Jack is on the other side of the skipjack, out of sight as well. Drifting into the school, I knock off a few shots, though it is enough to hang in the eye of a fish-filled hurricane of spinning light, observing the whirling energy created out of so many fish—thousands—that become a single organism. Out of breath I begin to rise for the surface. In an involuntary move that has no apparent justification, I turn my head quickly to the right. The dusky is barreling toward me. In the time it takes to complete the turn of my head, the shark has traveled twenty feet and is now two feet off my shoulder, mouth slack, teeth visible. At the completion of my head turn it veers away, almost doubling back on itself in the blink of an eye. The entire episode takes less than two seconds and leaves me shaken. Not so much by the fact that had I not turned my head I might well have been bitten, but by the speed and agility of the animal. It occurs to me that I dive in this water because I have convinced myself into believing that, through awareness, I shall always be able to anticipate an attack and protect myself from serious injury. In truth, if that dusky or any shark really wants to attack, it can without troubling itself very much. All that I have is my awareness, and that is all I ever will have, and try though I may to convince myself that it will be enough, I know that it will never be so.

In mid-morning Terry and Joyce in the *Gladrial*, and Dave in the *Orea* pull anchor and head south for Socorro Island, thirty miles away, leaving us to ourselves in the anchorage. We say our good-byes and wish safe passage. They will spend another three weeks in the Revillagigedo before returning to Cabo San Lucas.

In the late afternoon near 5 P.M., after the northeast current has abated, Jack and I prepare to free dive the transition zone for the hammerheads. I am far from convinced that I am capable of cutting seventy-five-foot dives carrying the big housing and strobe required in these low light conditions. He suggests I take the small Nikonos, which I am hesitant to do for then I have nothing with which to bump away the duskies and galapagos.

"We probably won't see the hammerheads, but it might be an opportunity to shoot some tuna," he counters. This logic makes sense to me as we climb into the skiff at this late hour.

Heading directly to the southwest corner three hundred yards off the island, we drop in at the edge of a shallow forty-foot ledge near the transition zone. Over the ledge is a shear drop-off, and via more volcanic ledges is blue oblivion. It is the outside edge of these ledges we intend to follow north.

The dimly lit water becomes a shadow of itself losing its dimension of depth. Two duskies circle up from the bottom, one large, around ten feet. We turn on them once and they veer off, slipping away to the depths. Moving northward we encounter four more sharks which, much like the first two, approach from the rear and come within a foot of our fins until we turn around. Despite the drag, I should have brought the big housing; this Nikonos is about as big as my hand and offers no security. We continue north leaving the territory of one pack of sharks to be picked up by another as we enter their territory. We are never without duskies or galapagos wheeling beneath us or behind us. Despite the sharks, in the dim light of late afternoon, I am relaxed, feeling them come and go behind me, focusing on the outside in search of the hammerheads.

We have been in the water forty minutes. Jack is down, lying on a ledge at sixty-five feet, looking out over the abyss. I am on the surface recapturing my breath. He is looking south, and from the north, slightly above him, drifts several hammerheads. He doesn't see them. More follow behind the three. They are swimming at eye level to him. Still he doesn't see them. Silver bodies are beginning to pour out of the blue gloom. When he rises and sees them for the first time they seem to fill the ocean around him, more than could be imagined, impossible to count—at least sixty, probably more. The school is loose knit and spreads twenty feet deep, fifty feet across and a hundred feet long. Momentarily mesmerized, I regain my senses, pump up and dive. Once down twenty feet my view clears and broadens, and the breadth of the school stretches out over the abyss with sharks of all sizes fading into the haze seventy feet away. Dropping to sixty feet and nearing the edge of the school, I hover and take a few shots. The hammerheads have not flinched, and I am drawn deeper toward them. Photographs are forgotten as they are now very close, not ten feet away, and I expect them to veer away en masse at any moment.

I drift/swim alongside, then on impulse, slowly bank into the school. Sharks are above me, below me, on either side, in front and in the rear, within a few feet in all directions.

Drifting in the vortex of the school. Pulling me along, barely kicking, floating as on a current. The sharks, sometimes inches away, are aware of me, tilting their prehistoric heads in my direction, eyes on the end of their hammerheads, offering a strange perspective.

Time has stopped. Breath-hold forgotten.

I am of the school.

We move as one, the school and I connected.

Wholly alive, unafraid.

Moving in the suspended world of the unimagined, as if in a dream, slow and clear, a part of some mysterious whole that has included me into its tribe. Running with wolves beneath the sea.

Not a single animal has flinched. I do not know how long I have been down, but a gentle nudge informs me it is time to breathe again.

Gently so as not to hit and disturb any hammerheads with my fins, I bend up and away, then make the long trek to the surface. Now, as if coming out of a trance, I realize it is very deep, seventy-five feet. Though beyond my limit, I am relaxed and incredibly energized. There is ample strength in my legs on the ascent. Jack, who ascended then dove again, is also rising and we see each other from a distance and shake our heads, the absolute wonder of it all. By the time we reach the surface, the school has moved on and we must swim hard to catch up.

It is a long, difficult swim. If we do not place ourselves well in front of the school they will move beyond us by the time we dive to their depth.

The focus is unwavering; there is only the hammerheads. All else falls away. The duskies make their passes, but I do not turn on them for fear of losing sight of the hammerheads. When finally I make my drop, four duskies are off my fin tips.

The school has drifted into deeper water. Diving to seventy feet, I again drift into the school. The dream state of the last dive has diminished and details of the sharks emerge: silver sides glow, their backs are shades of gray/brown. Their hammer heads are scalloped in front and their eyes follow me with a tilt of the head, which like a rudder, changes the angle of their bodies, so when they look up or down at me their entire body turns in that direction. Within the school is a slipstream, where scarcely any tail movement pushes them along, and thus with very little kicking I am able to keep pace.

Running with wild animals, with predators, being accepted as a member of the pack is unlike anything I have ever experienced. While the dolphins and even the mantas and sea lions included me into their realm, they did not seem nearly so wild, so primordial. These sharks are an intelligence from another millennia altogether, operating in ways deeply mysterious.

The hammerheads slide up to view me again, moving close. Scratches and scars around the heads and torsos underscore the rigors of their journey. There is a sense of safety within the school, of solitude and fearlessness among the hammerheads. No other sharks venture close to the school.

Again, time has ceased to exist in its familiar way, and I am unaware of minutes and seconds until my body rings up for air.

The water is dark and I am very deep, the surface a light year away. As before, I gently break away from the school and once cleared, begin my ascent in earnest. As it is bad practice to look down from a high place when climbing, so it is to look up towards the surface when deep and short of air. The jolt of seeing just how far one must travel is enough to steal the strength required to sustain a smooth and relaxed ascent.

Just keep kicking. My legs have not left me and respond well. Once on the surface, I have no opportunity to rest as the school continues to move. If I lose visual contact, it is unlikely, in this low light, they will be found again.

Swimming hard for a hundred yards, my legs begin to tighten and heat up. In the distance the school appears to have broken up into two groups, with only the glint of their bodies visible. They are sinking into the abyss, and in a flicker of lost light, the great school vanishes altogether.

Floating on the surface, I attempt to absorb all that had occurred, but cannot begin to. There is a sense of exhilaration, mixed with a strange calm, as if the experience had been awaiting me.

A lone hammerhead wanders below me and I dive to it, but it is wary without the comfort of the school, senses me early and swims off. The deep dives take a strange toll. I do not get suddenly tired, or even increasingly tired, and feel no fatigue whatsoever, until I turn to make the ascent and discover my legs to be as dead as stones. Pushing through the tonnage of water to reach the top, I can scarcely drag myself into the skiff.

Jack soon joins us in the skiff. He too is exhausted. Pam asks if we saw any hammerheads. Jack nods. "We found the school," is all he says.

In the evening during dinner, Jack barely manages a word. His silence speaks volumes as our eyes catch, hold for a moment, and then fall to our plates. Pam, nervous in the hush, jabbers on about the sharks. The experience has separated her from us and no amount of talk can close the gap. After dishes I crawl into my bunk and fall directly to sleep.

# DAY
# 61

It is well after sunrise when I awake with legs heavy and stiff in the thigh. I should rest this day, but the good water is here and we must take what advantage we can of the favorable conditions. As it stands, I need rest after two days of hard free diving.

We lay around until late afternoon. There is more talk of leaving. Pam is steadfast in her desire to weigh anchor and return to Cabo San Lucas. We are virtually out of food. A part of me is ready to leave, and would have left at any moment had we not located the hammerheads. But now I vacillate; we could catch our food. Jack reminds me that if I could eat seafood; we could stay another week. It is decided that we shall leave in two days.

Early in the evening, around five, we jump the southwest corner again. We are not in the water long, and two wahoo appear as if materializing out of the blue void as they do. The two become four and then ten. They are all big, around sixty pounds. They hover off the abyss and observe as we swim north. At every outcropping that more or less defines a lava formed canyon, swim the duskies and galapagos. They are the same sharks we encounter each time in the same places. They make their obligatory passes until we turn on them and they wander off satisfied that we are still breathing. Another canyon, another pack of sharks. They circle below as if anxious, waiting for me to enter their territory. When I do, they sneak in behind; we do our dance.

Yellowfin tuna weave below, the low light catching their skin like freshly minted gold. Dropping down into the golden light of the tuna, I find most are small, around fifteen pounds. More arrive, and more after them—larger, streaming golden bullets out of the deep blue. They are all about me, some weighing as much as a hundred and fifty pounds. Among the tuna are rainbow runners, beautiful pelagic fish that appear very much like a common yellowtail, save for its neon blue colored stripes. More tuna come; the sea is filled with fish. They circle me at high speed at forty feet, while above me near the surface skate the wahoo, and on the peripheries, the ever-present duskies.

In this moment the realization comes that this is the deep ocean as it once was everywhere on the planet, and will never be again.

When I was the child in Hawaii, and was given the sea and its attendant mystery and magic, there was never any reason to doubt that the sea would not always be there as I first experienced it. Even as I grew into the sea and it grew into me, and I taught my young son all that I knew, I still believed the sea would always be as it was.

But that did not come to pass.

Diving the blue edge, I feel the sea in places that man has just begun to discover. The language of its

creatures—the dolphin, the manta, the shark—is
known to me in ways I cannot assemble into full
understanding or complete perception. I know only
enough to realize that with time, perhaps more of
the sea's language could be understood. It was my
dream to pass on all that I knew of this lifetime
journey so that my son or another man's son would
take this knowledge and from it, pursue the language and explore the mysteries. Perhaps in ten
generations man would know the language and in
the knowing would finally come to understand and,
more importantly, come to respect the dwellers of
the sea. For then man could make a spiritual connection with the sea in the way that the Native
Americans connected to the land, and the Inuit to
the ice, and the Masai to the plain. I dreamed that
eventually man would not have merely brushed the
face of the Spirit of the Sea, but come to know the
face as he knows the face of his mother. In this
knowing he would come to be truly connected to
the planet, and through nature come to know himself as an aspect of it, no less nor greater than all
its creatures. Here, he could again know the magic
and embrace the mystery, and retrieve what was
lost, given up and destroyed.

But that will not come to pass.

There can be no blue edge without the fish, the
manta, the dolphin, the whale, or the shark. It is
the abundance of wildlife and the freedom of their
movement that gives the ocean its energy, and
brings meaning to its presence here on the planet.
With the absence of wildlife, mankind will have
missed its last chance to know itself in relation to
nature, for without their life force the oceans will
become a barren and empty wasteland and the soul

and spirit of mankind will have lost its final opportunity for redemption.

The tuna vanish leaving me alone on the great blue veld, suspended in wonder of the spectacle that has played before me. How magnificent the performance, how grateful I am to be another strand in the web of this liquid universe, to be carried off from the self in these moments and truly know the miracle of being alive with all of life.

We work the transition zone until the light fails altogether without ever seeing the hammerheads.

# DAY
# 62

The motivation to push ourselves beyond fatigue seems to have been lost. The weariness is endemic, and each of us labors about the boat in deep lethargy. Even Jack shows his fatigue after adjusting the solar panels by sitting on the deck and staring out to sea one moment, then laying atop the cabin asleep the next.

Staying with the plan, we shall be leaving the island tomorrow. By the looks of the weather we may have to motor the entire way, going as we will against the northerly flow. Jack believes if that is the case, we may not have enough fuel. He takes the skiff over to an American sportfishing boat that has run down here from San Diego to fish the tuna, and buys five gallons of diesel fuel. Their luck is poor fishing the pinnacles south of our anchorage, and Jack suggests the west side where we have seen so many tuna. The skipper says there are too many sharks and almost every time they hook up, they lose the fish.

I have mixed feelings about our departure. I am exhausted to my bones. This life is demanding by any standard. Never mind the diving and hauling ourselves in and out of the skiff all day, but even the daily close quarters where every time we need something, a major move must occur, exhausts us. Clothes and bedding reek, and the smell of a month's accumulated garbage, though stowed neatly in white plastic bags aft in the cockpit, nevertheless makes its daily presence known. Sleep is always at a premium, and I fantasize of stretching out in a full-sized bed with clean sheets, eating a bowl of ice cream.

Beyond the shark and manta and whale encounters that highlight our moments here at San Benedicto, it is the small events occurring daily that I shall miss: the schooling fish that have taken residence beneath the *Nirvana*, who keep the ocean free of our scat, and who welcome us back after a day on the water. I will miss the stark, volcanic rock island that stands almost in defiance of its isolation; the night sky filled with stars, illuminating the cove in star-shine; the phases of the moon. We have seen them all and they reveal themselves more on the ocean then anywhere on land. The water, both dangerous and seductive, is still somehow detached—an entity that moves and sighs, rages and dances, sings and cries, beckons and rejects, at once humbling and elevating, always lifting the soul. These elements bring a certain edge to the life of a body of water as it does to a mountain, a forest, a jungle and a fertile plain. To be here is to be fully alive and in sync. To be immersed so as to be unable to distinguish between the self and the other, if even for the briefest of moments, is to be awake and mindful of how important it is to live a life of risk.

Take the duskies out of the ocean and the wind

out of the sky and we all shall soon become dulled and unseeing. The wind and shark have delivered me to a place I cannot conjure on my own. They invite me to see beyond the obvious, into the subtle mystery of things, both in myself and in the glint of sun reflecting off a gull's wing or in the footprint of a humpback whale, in the grace of the dusky, the unaccountable friendliness of a manta, the stealth of the wahoo, and the lightning speed of the tuna. Let me fly to the dark water on a breath-hold dive and drift with magical creatures on a cerulean wind, then push hard toward the light and be re-born just a little bit on my return to the surface.

We make one last dive on the southwest corner in a final attempt to relocate the hammerheads. The duskies are in numbers this day, and are aggressive in their dusky way, pretending to ignore us then slipping up from behind. I let a big one track me just to see how close it will come, and eventually it bumps the tips of my fins. I hold them there for a moment, but when it nudges again, I turn and it falls away, but not by much, just a few feet below me. Reaching out, I could grab its dorsal fin and contemplate doing just that. We swim together for twenty feet then the shark drifts off and I rise for a breath.

In the rhythm.

The yellowfin move in and the baitfish explode away.

A single wahoo glides near the surface.

The rainbow runner skips near the peripheries of the bait looking for easy tidbits.

In the rhythm.

The swells and accompanying surge of the sea is its heartbeat. The ebb and flow of tide is its metabolism, the currents its vessels, and in these blue veins of the sea pulse the creatures who feel and know this rhythm. It is their rhythm; it is our rhythm. It is the rhythm of the water planet. It is the rhythm of creation.

Within this rhythm weaves the melody of creation's song. It is this song to which all life dances in the stalk of the tuna or the pass of the dusky. All in the present moment know the steps to the dance, all in rhythm of the hunt, and in the comings and goings of the cycles of the moon, the tide, and the currents.

A whispered voice beckons and I follow the sound wandering off in an odd direction toward the shallows of the island, a sandy area with a sixty-foot bottom. There, the hammerheads drift near the bottom. Slowly bending into a dive, I gently descend on the school that has perhaps fifteen sharks. They turn in that awkward movement so they might see me better, and allow me to enter the school.

Drifting with the hammerheads, I have forgotten my name.

In the rhythm of the school, gliding with the pack, running with the wolves, accepted.

In the rhythm on the blue edge.

# PART

# 3

# HOMEWARD BOUND

*For all at last returns to the sea—to Oceanus, the ocean river, like the everflowing stream of time, the beginning and the end.*—Rachel Louise Carson

# DAY
# 63

After a breakfast of aged cereal further softened with water and garnished with dried fruit from an old bag of trail mix, we begin to make ready the *Nirvana* for the two hundred and fifty-mile journey to Cabo San Lucas.

It takes several hours to break down the underwater camera gear and stow it properly. Jack is methodical in his approach to stowing gear, and wants no part of heavy gear flying around the inside of the boat in the event seas become big, headed as we are directly into the northerly flow. Air compressor, solar panels, scuba tanks and dive gear are also broken down and stowed. Then the outboard is hauled, followed by the skiff. Sail rigging is inspected and tightened, as are all engine belts, filters and fuel lines. When all is done, we wash down the boat.

Pam surprises and pulls out a whole canned chicken she had been saving, and fixes up a fine lunch of baked chicken and pasta salad, our last good meal until we reach Cabo San Lucas. We clear the cove at 12:30 P.M. with a clear sky and calm water. Visibility in the blue water appears endless.

There is talk of returning and staying another few days, but we press on. Jack clearly doesn't want to leave and I am ambivalent, as usual, though I have become deeply attached to this wild place and will miss it terribly.

We motor directly into the northerly flow, but by mid-afternoon an unexpected wind out of the west places us on a beam reach, and we cut the engine and sail, averaging five-and-a-half knots. As with the journey to San Benedicto, once underway, everyone retires to themselves. I have the eight to midnight watch and the eight to noon watch. Jack and Pam again sleep on both watches and I am alone for most of the time. The lapis sea rolls upon itself leaving foam trails that melt away to blue again. I have been to the edge of this blue and the journey has taken a lifetime. Even now, for all I have witnessed in all the years, in all the seas especially this one, I feel as if I have only managed to touch the shallows with my fingertips. That I have seen and felt and understood so little as to know nothing at all, yet it has filled me with that which I cannot fill myself.

The sea drips from my pores and falls from my eyes as the old one in Hawaii, so long ago, said that it would, and it has been quite a journey.

# DAY
# 64

The wind rises and the swell follows. We are entering a major squall.

To sail at night is to sail on a dark wind in the hollow of a black and forbidding cavern. The monstrous noise of the wind and sea dull the senses and convince the mind to retreat. But there is no place to run, no sanctuary on this small boat. The *Nirvana* rises and falls, twists like a bull with a man on its back. In the cockpit, my back to the bulkhead, looking into the night off the stern, water sprays over my head and I hunker down, feeling queasy. Every twenty minutes I go below and check the radar for vessels in the area. One has appeared on the screen for the last forty minutes. Unsure of its direction, I go topside and make visual contact, but the raging seas prevent my locating the running lights with binoculars. Eventually the vessel, a large freighter, passes off our bow by three miles.

At midnight Pam relieves me and immediately accesses the GPS to see where we are. We are in a storm at sea, I say to myself, finding little solace in the wonders of GPS in these moments. I sleep off and on as the storm blows us into the following day.

# DAY
## 65

J ust before dawn the wind suddenly dies and though the swell continues, the wind-blown surface chop soon settles. Without wind we fire up the engine and motor/sail our way north.

I am changing worlds.

I am leaving a world whose time was once measured in epochs and now is measured by years, months, perhaps weeks.

How long before the treasured waters of San Benedicto become barren, like its sister, the Sea of Cortez.

Such places are now few and so very precious.

Such places create their own breaths. And from that breath breathes the whale and the dolphin. It is the breath of the wind, the breath of creation, of balance and of harmony.

To breathe that breath is to be washed clean of my civilization.

Mankind needs such places as much as the shark and the manta need them, before he neglects entirely his threads of connection to the natural world.

We make landfall near two in the afternoon. As we round Land's End the grind of civilization can be heard. Whirring away, deep throated, chewing up the tourists in their oversized hats, and butterflies in lawnmower blades. I know my return will be complete when I can no longer hear the grind, yet I am changed. I have been profoundly touched and find a comfort in myself I have not known for a long time, solid as the rock island I have left behind. Like that island which defies the very water that birthed it, I will, in some measure defy the civilization that bore me, knowing that the gossamer threads which link me to this ocean world will hold fast and sustain me for the rest of my days.

# EPILOGUE

Shortly before this book was going to press in 2000, I received an E-mail from Mike McGettigan of SeaWatch, which read as follows:

On about April 29th a fleet of seven 70- to 90-ton drift gillnet boats, carrying 2 miles of net each surrounded San Benedicto Island, which is the home of the worlds largest Giant Pacific Mantas and for 4 to 5 days decimated the sea life in this famous Mexican Marine Park. Even after 4 days of fishing, their nets were still getting from 100 to 200 sharks per boat per day. Based on counts from several nets it is estimated that they killed between 2000 and 4000 sharks, plus mantas, turtles, tuna and other marine animals. In two days of diving at Benedicto after the gillnet boats were gone we didn't see one live shark, whereas before we would have seen hundreds.

# OTHER BOOKS BY CARLOS EYLES

*Diving Free*

*Sea Shadows*

*The Last of the Blue Water Hunters*

*Secret Seas*

*Dolphin Borne*

---

## AVAILABLE TITLES BY CARLOS EYLES

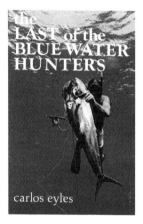

### THE LAST OF THE BLUE WATER HUNTERS

This is the extraordinary account of a handful of men who made their way into the last wilderness, armed with only their courage and driven by an insatiable curiosity.

From his early beginnings on the island of Hawaii, the author progresses to his apprenticeship with the "blue water tribe" in the Sea Of Cortez, Mexico during the 1960's. There he learns to stalk the powerful game fish that inhabit the deep waters.

After 20 years of blue water hunting, he returns to the island of Catalina where he fulfills his dream of living off the sea using only a speargun to sustain himself.

The climax of this book is an incredible expedition to the far reaches of the vast Pacific in search of the giant blue fin tuna. *The Last of the Blue Water Hunters* is also about the sea, as viewed not by the scientist, but by the hunter, who sees it with a sharp, all-encompassing eye, exposing the reader to an ocean world never seen by the majority of divers.

**184 pages, 5-1/2x8-1/2, paper, 26 B&W photos............ $14.95**
ISBN 0-922769-15-X

## SECRET SEAS

In this rich collection of 16 short stories and essays Eyles takes the reader to the far corners of the heart and mind, as well as the ocean's realm in Micronesia, California, the Sea of Cortez and the Bahamas. These stories of the sea and man's interaction with its creatures represent the search for meaning and spirituality in the alien enrivonment from which we came.

*"Eyles writes about a wilderness—the wilderness within each of us—as it is reflected back through the environment. He takes us beyond the safe confines of the unknown, like the free diver, unencumbered, vulnerable, operating in an alien environment with uncommon ease."*—**Michael Menduno from the Foreword**

**160 pages, 5-3/8x8-1/2, paper** ....................................... **$12.95**
ISBN 0-922769-23-0

---

## DOLPHIN BORNE

*Dolphin Borne* is a sea survival story that develops into a message of the sea's creatures to mankind. When a veteran and a novice blue water hunter are stalking prey off an island in the Sea of Cortez, the novice spears a large amberjack that proves more than he can handle. The fish bolts for the open sea pulling the novice with it. When it finally tires, the hunter is caught in strong currents heading down the channel. The veteran comes to his assistance, and the two must survive by their skills and what little they have with them. Eyles weaves a masterly tale that twists and turns with the unexpected, where the impossible becomes possible and the real becomes surreal. It is a breathtaking adventure that ends with a series of phantasmagoric experiences that become only too real. Though a novel, this is a classic Carlos Eyles adventure you won't want to miss.

**160 pages, 5-1/2x8-1/2, paper** ....................................... **$12.95**
ISBN 0-922769-25-7

## DIVING FREE HAWAII

Carlos has established a free diving school in Kona, Hawaii called Diving Free Hawaii. It closely follows his philosophy of infusing the human elements of mind, body, and spirit with the ocean world thus allowing the diver to intimately interact with the environment. He offers three distinct levels of development: beginner, intermediate and advanced diver. Each level is designed to enable the free diver to reach his full potential in the water. More information is available through his website:

**www.divingfreehawaii.com**

# ABOUT THE AUTHOR

CARLOS EYLES became deeply connected to the ocean world as a child growing up on the beaches of Hawaii. His life, as first a free diving big game spearfisherman and now as an underwater photographer, has covered much of this planet's oceans and seas—a lifetime journey, which has also paralleled the decline of the ocean's great wealth. He has written eight books and countless articles about his ocean experiences. His underwater photographs are found in major books and publications worldwide. He recently returned to Hawaii to live and teach free diving.